Using Numbers in Arabic

Jamal Ali

GEORGETOWN UNIVERSITY PRESS | WASHINGTON, DC

Library of Congress Cataloging-in-Publication Data
Ali, Jamal, 1966–
Using numbers in Arabic/Jamal Ali.
pages cm
Includes bibliographical references.
ISBN 978-1-62616-005-7 (pbk.: alk. paper)
1. Arabic language—Numerals.
I. Title.
PJ6143.A55 2013
492.7'55—dc23 2013000033

∞ This book is printed on acid-free paper meeting the requirements of the American National Standard for Permanence in Paper for Printed Library Materials.

15 14 13 9 8 7 6 5 4 3 2 First printing

Printed in the United States of America

CONTENTS

TABLES

INTRODUCTION

This book is intended to serve as a reference for the English-speaking learner of Arabic on the correct use of numbers in Standard Arabic (*fuṣḥa*). It can be of benefit to any student who has reached the late-intermediate to advanced level of study. Though a relatively strong knowledge of Arabic is assumed, including knowledge of the system of case endings, students still at an intermediate stage of progress can benefit greatly as well.

The proper rendering of numbers seems to be the bane of many Arabic students because the topic provides a special set of complications. General grammars and textbooks invariably fail to deal with some of the more intricate issues involving numbers. For example, how does one say 1,001st? How does one say 20 millionth? What should one do with the *yāʾ* on *thamāniya*? When should it be kept and when should it be removed? How should a decimal number be read? How does one express one two-hundredth? Perhaps a reader comes across a strange number-related construction in a classical text and needs help comprehending it.

This book aims to address these types of more obscure questions regarding numbers. It is my hope that it will be the go-to reference work for advanced and high-intermediate students looking to find any number-related information. The reader is encouraged to become familiar with the table of contents in order to have an idea of what is available so that it can be remembered when needed. The glossary at the end explains grammatical and other terms that are used in the book and with which the reader may be unfamiliar.

The information presented in this book is rooted purely in the actual, real-world practice of those whose business it is to communicate in *fuṣḥa* Arabic: novelists, journalists, and other types of writers and speakers who produce Standard Arabic. There is no expectation that the reader should trust any edict given in this book without proof. For this reason, every principle laid down in these pages is supported with real-life evidence in the form of citations taken from all types of *fuṣḥa* writing and oral production: novels, newspapers, news broadcasts, legal documents, works of nonfiction, and websites. Both print and online versions of newspapers have been consulted. When citing web pages, I have, in most cases, given only the domain name of the website, since the location of a page within a site can sometimes change. Citations span all eras of Arabic literature, from the Qurʾan to a recent issue of *al-Quds*. Since the rules used with regard to numbers have remained relatively constant throughout the centuries, examples from classical texts are interwoven with examples from modern ones. However, in areas where practice in the classical period differs from current practice, these differences are pointed out and suitable examples are given from each era.

When I cite passages, I have stayed as true to the original text as possible, duplicating punctuation and even keeping the dotless *yāʾ* found in Egyptian printed works. I have not altered or edited any citations except to correct a handful of obvious typos, all instances of which are noted. More importantly, I have not placed any vowel markings on letters if they did not already exist in the original text. It should be noted that many classical texts in the editions available to us are partially and occasionally fully vowelled. This voweling originates from the modern editor of the text and not from the text itself. Thus, when voweling is provided in a classical text, one should assume that it represents the thinking of a modern editor and not the original author of the text.

As for the number of citations provided, I have erred on the side of abundance in order to account for the many possibilities that exist for each construction. Each citation is followed by a translation. In the translations, elegance has sometimes been sacrificed for precision, especially in the part of the quote where the number appears. The source of the citation is given immediately thereafter. This is intended to help the reader see, at a glance, the range of text types in which a particular construction can be found.

This book makes no claim to be a book of history, historical linguistics, or comparative Semitics. Therefore, no attempt has been made to explain how number rules became what they are today. Also, this book deals solely with Standard, *fuṣḥa* Arabic and does not attempt to treat numbers as they are used in any of the various spoken dialects of colloquial (*ʿāmmiyya*) Arabic. However, some standard structures do have informal variants that no doubt exist due to the influence of *ʿāmmiyya*. These are often pointed out.

Furthermore, there is no attempt to attribute practices described herein to one Arab country or another. To do so would be far beyond the scope of this book. Rather, the goal is to describe the wide range of practices that exist. For example, in the Arab world, both what I call the Hindi numerals (٠١٢٣٤٥٦٧٨٩) and the confusingly named Arabic numerals (0123456789) are used. Yet I have not endeavored to give a detailed breakdown of which set of digits is used in which countries. For our purposes, it will suffice to say that both are used in the Arab world. Citations will consequently include both types.

There is also no attempt to give statistical breakdowns of which constructions are more common than others. To successfully provide such information would require a completely new and different research project, one which is not necessary for the purposes of this work. Therefore, claims that are made regarding which structures are more common than others are based on general impression and not on a rigorous statistic sampling.

Also not present in this book is anything that will not have value to the learner who is trying to write good *fuṣḥa*. Therefore, number-related concepts that issue from the mind of a mathematician but have no practical value in real life, such as gogolplex, infinity, and duodecillion, are not dealt with here. It should be noted that the rules given in this book and their supporting citations reflect what I have found to be the most common practices. Exceptions can always be found. There are many possible number-related constructions that are sometimes used that are not found in this book. But the writer or learner cannot go wrong if he or she sticks with the styles and conventions described herein.

My thanks go to Stephen Cardoos for showing me ways to find many of the sources that were used to put this book together. Thanks also to Kamal Al Ekhnawy for helping me with some of the Arabic. Discussions with Michael Cooperson helped me to see the correct way to understand certain date-related material in classical texts, and Adam McCollum and Miguel Manzano contributed by making me aware of a couple of important references regarding the spelling of مائة.

ARABIC NUMBERS QUICK REFERENCE TABLE

Table 0.0 Arabic Numbers Quick Reference Table

Number	Counted noun, sing./pl.	Case/grammar of counted noun
3–10	plural	مجرور (genitive) مضاف إليه (second term of *iḍāfa*)
11–99	singular	منصوب (accusative) تمييز (*tamyīz*)
100 and multiples of 100, thousands, millions, etc.	singular	مجرور (genitive) مضاف إليه (second term of *iḍāfa*)
Compound numbers greater than 20	Follows the last element in the compound, that closest to the counted noun	

TRANSLITERATION TABLE

Table 0.1 Transliteration Table

ا = ā	س = s	ل = l
ب = b	ش = sh	م = m
ت = t	ص = ṣ	ن = n
ث = th	ض = ḍ	هـ = h
ج = j	ط = ṭ	و = w, ū
ح = ḥ	ظ = ẓ	ي = y, ī
خ = kh	ع = ʿ	ـَ = a
د = d	غ = gh	ـُ = u
ذ = dh	ف = f	ـِ = i
ر = r	ق = q	ء = ʾ
ز = z	ك = k	

Short vowels are not distinct from long vowels at the ends of words except in certain contexts, so vowel length is rarely indicated in the word's final position. Common names and proper nouns that have common spellings in English have been left untransliterated in favor of the well-known spelling.

PART I

Cardinal and Ordinal Numbers

One

Cardinal

To describe a single item, the noun in the singular indefinite form may be used.

كتاب "a book"

EXAMPLES

١ . . . أعلن أنّ جنديًا من مشاة البحرية الأمريكية . . .

1 ". . . announced that an American Marine . . ."
(*al-Ḥayāt*, Jan. 9, 2006, p. 2)

٢ . . . فيتلو فيه سورة من القرآن

2 ". . . where he could recite a chapter from the Qur'an."
(Taha Hussein, *al-Ayyām*, 1/63)

٣ والتقت عيناهما مرة

3 "Their eyes met once."
(Naguib Mahfouz, *al-Ṭarīq*, p. 33)

٤ . . . لمهمة تستغرق ليلة أو أسبوعا أو شهرا . . .

4 ". . . for a mission that takes a night, or a week, or a month . . ."
(Naguib Mahfouz, *al-Ṭarīq*, p. 40)

Using *wāḥid* for Emphasis

To emphasize that only one unit of the item in question is being referred to and no more, the word واحِد may be used as an adjective. It functions as any adjective: It comes after the noun described and agrees with it in case and gender.

معي دولار واحد. "I have (exactly) one dollar."

EXAMPLES

١ لكن اسمحى لى بدقيقة . . . دقيقة واحدة لا غير

1 "But give me a minute . . . one minute no more."
(Tawfiq al-Hakim, *Maṣīr Ṣurṣār*, p. 116)

٢ فكان الطالب يسكن بقرش واحد في الشهر

2 "The student was living on one piastre a month."
(Taha Hussein, *al-Ayyām*, 2/73)

٣ ولم ير في السماء نجما واحدا

3 "He did not see one single star in the sky."
(Naguib Mahfouz, *al-Ṭarīq*, p. 137)

٤ وَإِنَّ هَٰذِهِ أُمَّتُكُمْ أُمَّةً واحِدَةً

4 "This is your community, one community."
(Qur'an, 23:52)

٥ لم يسع إلى رؤيتها مرة واحدة

5 "He did not once try to see her."
(Naguib Mahfouz, *al-Ṭarīq*, p. 91)

Ordinal[1]

"First" is أَوَّل in the masculine and أُولى in the feminine.

As Adjective

أول and أولى can function as adjectives. In this case, like any adjective, they follow the noun described and agree with it in gender, number, and definiteness.

البناية الأولى في الشارع الأول
"The first building on the first street"

The dual form of أولى is أُولَيانِ/أُولَيَيْنِ.

The plural of أول is أولون/أولين or أَوائِل.

The plural of أولى is أُولَيات.

EXAMPLES

١ الموعد الأول

1 "The First Meeting"
(Title of poem by Mahmoud Darwish)

1. Also see "More on Ordinal Numbers," p. 110.

٢ ولأهل المدينة عددان: عدد أول . . . وعدد آخر

2 "The people of Medina have two numbers: a first number . . . and another number."[2]
(Suyūṭi, *al-Itqān fi 'Ulūm al-Qur'ān*, p. 157, *naw'* 19)

٣ . . . ورأى داخلها رجلا جذب انتباهه من النظرة الاولى

3 ". . . and inside he saw a man who attracted his attention from the first glance."
(Naguib Mahfouz, *al-Ṭarīq*, p. 137)

٤ . . . وفي الأيام الأولى التي أعقبت فرار حميدة . . .

4 ". . . and in the first days following Hameeda's flight . . ."
(Naguib Mahfouz, *Zuqāq al-Midaqq*, p. 242)

٥ سوف يتطلب منا الاتصال بجميع سفاراتنا في الخارج كخطوة اولى

5 "It will require us to contact all of our foreign embassies as a first step."
(Naguib Mahfouz, *al-Ṭarīq*, p. 222)

٦ حصل الفائزان الأولان على صيانة مقدمة من تويوتا لمدى الحياة

6 "The first two winners received free lifetime maintenance from Toyota."
(*al-Yawm*, Dec. 27, 2010)

٧ وقد أثار التقريران الأولان ضجة كبرى

7 "The first two reports provoked a great uproar."
(*al-Sharq al-Awsaṭ*, Feb. 6, 2010)

٨ قرأ عليه عشرين بيتًا من المائتين الأوليين

8 "He would read to him twenty of the first two hundred lines."
(Taha Hussein, *al-Ayyām*, 1/76)

٩ هم المتخرجون الأوائل الذين نالوا شهادة جديدة "برنامج دبلوم المنسقين ورؤساء الاقسام"

9 "They were the first graduates to receive a new diploma, the 'Diploma for Coordinators and Division Heads.'"
(*al-Mustaqbal*, June 28, 2011)

١٠ . . . جزاء ذنب اقترفه هو أو أحد آبائه الأولين

10 ". . . a punishment for a sin that he or one of his forefathers committed."
(Naguib Mahfouz, *Zuqāq al-Midaqq*, p. 272)

---

2. "Number" here refers to the number of *āyas* they believe the Qur'an to be made up of.

١١ نطق النهر..فقدسه السكان الأولون

11 "The river spoke. It was held by the first inhabitants to be holy."
(*al-Inshā'*, July 24, 2009)

١٢ المستوطنون الأوائل لأمريكا..يابانيون!

12 "The first settlers in America . . . were Japanese!"
(*al-Ahrām*, July 31, 2001)

١٣ سوريا..والغزاة الأوائل!

13 "Syria . . . and the First Invaders!"
(aleqt.com, Aug. 9, 2011)

١٤ لولا جهود النساء الأوليات لما وصلت الكويت الى ما هي عليه الآن

14 "If not for the efforts of the first women, Kuwait would not be where it is now."
(*al-Waṭan* [Kuwait], Oct. 31, 2011)

As Superlative

أول can also function as a superlative.

Superlative: Before Indefinite

أول can function grammatically as a superlative. In this case, if the noun being described is indefinite, أول will appear before the noun, always in the masculine singular form regardless of the gender or number of the noun described. It occurs in an إضافة construction with the noun described. The construct is translated as "the first":

أول مرّة "the first time"

EXAMPLES

١ ونازعته نفسه إلى العودة في أول قطار

1 "He felt an urge to go back on the first train."
(Naguib Mahfouz, *al-Ṭarīq*, p. 28)

٢ فرأى زوجة عم خليل بمجلسها الذي رآها به أول مرة

2 "He saw Uncle Khalil's wife at her seat where he saw her the first time."
(Naguib Mahfouz, *al-Ṭarīq*, p. 56)

٣ أول انتخابات برلمانية في كوسوفو

3 "The First Parliamentary Elections in Kosovo"
(aljazeera.net, Dec. 12, 2010)

٤ استفتاء مصر أول خطوة ديمقراطية

4 "Egypt's referendum is the first democratic step."
(aljazeera.net, Mar. 19, 2011)

Superlative: Before Definite

An alternative construction is for the word following أول or أولى to be definite and plural or a pronoun referring to a plural. In this case the meaning would be "the first of the . . ." أول is used when the noun it refers to is masculine. If the noun is feminine, then أولى is used. In either case, they form an إضافة construction with the following word:

أول الضيوف "the first of the guests"

The plural أوائل may also be used in this construction (see examples 3 and 4) and is sometimes used to refer to non-humans as well as humans (see examples 5 and 6).

EXAMPLES

١ وشرح رضوان أن هناك ٣ عناصر لخطط مصر الاقتصادية، أولها: ((حلول سريعة)) لدفع الاقتصاد

1 "Ridwan explained that there are three elements to Egypt's economic plans, the first of which is (to find) quick solutions to get the economy moving."
(*al-Sharq al-Awsaṭ*, Apr. 16, 2011)

٢ انطلقت أول من أمس، أولى الدورات التدريبية التي تنظمها أمانة المنطقة الشرقية

2 "The day before yesterday, the first of the training sessions organized by the Eastern Region municipality was launched."
(*al-Ḥayāt*, Apr. 18, 2011)

Note: In the first example above, أول is masculine because it refers to one عنصر. In the second, the feminine أولى is used in agreement with the singular دورة.

٣ كانت من أوائل الذين عملوا بإذاعة (صوت العرب) بالقاهرة

3 "She was one of the first to work (among the first of those who worked) at *Ṣawṭ al-ʿArab* in Cairo."
(*al-Sharq*, June 27, 2012)

٤ أنا من أوائل الممثلين المؤيدين لثورة ٢٥ يناير

4 "I was one of the first actors (among the first of the actors) who supported the January 25 revolution."
(*al-Anbāʾ*, Mar. 25, 2012)

٥ ((إيفا)) من أوائل الشركات في الكويت التي جدولت ديونها

5 "IFA is one of the first companies (among the first of the companies) in Kuwait to reschedule its debts."
(*al-Anbāʾ*, June 23, 2012)

٦ المغرب من أوائل البلدان التي استفادت من برامج تحدي الألفية

6 "Morocco is one of the first countries to benefit (among the first of the countries that have benefited) from the programs of Millenium Challenge."
(*al-Maghribiyya*, June 12, 2012)

Two

Cardinal

"Two" is expressed by attaching the dual ending to nouns: ـانِ in the مرفوع case, and ـَيْنِ in the منصوب and مجرور cases. The *kasra* on the final *nūn* is invariable. It remains there in all three cases. It is never nunated. It remains a single *kasra* regardless of whether the noun is definite or indefinite.

حضر طالبانِ. "Two students attended."

ذهبتُ مع صديقينِ. "I went with two friends."

If the word to which the ـان ending is being added ends in a *tāʾ marbūṭa*, then the *tāʾ marbūṭa* changes to a *tāʾ* before the ending is added:

شَجَرَتان "two trees"

EXAMPLES

١ قتل شرطيان باكستانيان

1 "Two Pakistani policemen were killed."
(*al-Ḥayāt*, Jan. 14, 2011)

٢ فأدار رأسه نحو الجهة التي اختفى فيها الذاهبان

2 "He turned his head in the direction into which disappeared the two people who had left."
(Naguib Mahfouz, *Zuqāq al-Midaqq*, p. 12)

٣ رأيت حمامتين وحشيتين بفم الغار

3 "I saw two wild pigeons at the mouth of the cave."
(Tawfiq al-Hakim, *Muḥammad*, p. 115)

٤ . . . والتي تكثفت في العامين الأخيرين

4 ". . . and which have become more frequent in the last two years."
(*al-Ḥayāt*, Jan. 14, 2011)

٥ أما نداء العينين اللوزيتين المضيئتين . . .

5 "As for the call of the two luminescent, almond eyes . . ."
(Naguib Mahfouz, *al-Ṭarīq*, p. 36)

Dropped *nūn* in *iḍāfa*

The *nūn* is dropped if the dual word is a مضاف. This is true whether the مضاف إليه is a separate noun or an attached pronoun.

يحبّ والدَيْهِ. "He loves his parents."

والدا محمد طيبان. "Muhammad's parents are nice."

EXAMPLES

١ وهما عاملا مطعم أحدهما عراقي

1 "They were restaurant workers, one of whom was Iraqi."
(aljazeera.net, Feb. 28, 2002)

٢ هما زوجتا زعيمين في انصار السنة

2 "They are wives of two leaders in Ansar al-Sunna."
(*al-Riyāḍ*, Oct. 30, 2010)

٣ ونظرا لأن إدارتي بوش وأوباما قد فشلتا في استكمال تلك الجهود الأولية . . .

3 "Given that the administrations of Bush and Obama have failed to follow through on that early effort . . ."
(*al-Sharq al-Awsaṭ*, Apr. 9, 2011)

٤ الإفراج عن عاملي إغاثة بنغلاديشيين خطفا في أفغانستان

4 "The Release of Two Bangladeshi Aid Workers Who Were Kidnapped in Afghanistan"
(*al-Riyāḍ*, Nov. 3, 2008)

٥ اغرورقت عيناه

5 "His eyes welled up with tears."
(first sentence of Naguib Mahfouz, *al-Ṭarīq*)

٦ وعيناك اليوم التقت بعينيها

6 "Your eyes met her eyes today."
(Naguib Mahfouz, *al-Ṭarīq*, p. 36)

٧ تاجر يقتل زوجته وابنيه وينتحر بإطلاق الرصاص على نفسه

7 "A Merchant Kills His Wife and Two Sons Then Commits Suicide by Shooting Himself"
(*al-Ahrām*, Aug. 14, 2009)

Dual Ending Plus First-Person Possessive yā'

When the مضاف إليه is the first-person singular pronoun suffix, it is attached to the dual *alif* or *yā'* as follows: ايَ when the dual is مرفوع, and ـيَّ when it is منصوب or مجرور.

كتاباىَ

كتابَيَّ

"my two books"

EXAMPLES

١ ابناي لا يحبان المدرسة . . . كيف أحببها لهما؟

1 "My two kids don't like school. How do I get them to like it?"
(*al-Ḥayāt*, Mar. 28, 2011)

٢ وفجأة وجدت نفسي اضع عيني الاثنتين على عجوز شمطاء

2 "And suddenly I found myself placing my two eyes on a grey-haired old lady."
(*al-Anwār*, Aug. 1, 2010)

Using *ithnān* for Emphasis

Just as a singular noun may be followed by واحد for emphasis, a dual noun may be followed by اِثنانِ to emphasize the fact that it is two of something, no more and no less, that is being referred to. In this case, اثنان functions as an adjective and is therefore in agreement with the dual noun as shown in table 1.1.

Table 1.1 Two

	Masculine	Feminine
مرفوع	اِثْنانِ	اِثْنَتانِ
منصوب/مجرور	اِثْنَينِ	اِثْنَتَيْنِ

The initial *hamza* on all four forms is a *hamzat waṣl*. As with the dual suffix added to nouns (ـانِ), the *kasra* at the end of all four of these forms is invariable and never nunated.

معي دولارانِ اثنانِ فحسب. "I have only two dollars on me."

EXAMPLES

١ . . . ومن بين القتلى شرطيان اثنان قتلا مساء الجمعة

1 ". . . and among the killed were two police officers who were killed Friday night."
(aljazeera.net, Dec. 18, 2001)

٢ هناك دولتان اثنتان فقط في منطقة الشرق الأوسط تلمستا طريقهما الى الديمقراطية

2 "There are only two countries in the Middle East that have fumbled their way to democracy."
(*Akhbār al-Khalīj*, Apr. 1, 2011)

٣ كانت هذه الأسرة تتألف من عضوين اثنين

3 "This family consisted of two members."
(Taha Hussein, *al-Ayyām*, 2/82)

٤ والنبي ما وجد المشط إلا قملتين اثنتين!

4 "I swear the comb did not find but two lice!"
(Naguib Mahfouz, *Zuqāq al-Midaqq*, p. 25)

Ordinal[3]

"Second" is rendered ثانٍ.

It is a member of the category of nouns known as منقوص. Therefore, when definite or مضاف, it is ثاني in the مرفوع and مجرور cases, and ثانيَ in the منصوب. The feminine is not affected, so it is ثانِية in all cases.

When indefinite and not مضاف, the masculine is ثانٍ in the مرفوع and مجرور cases, and ثانياً in the منصوب case. When indefinite and feminine, it is ثانية and takes regular case endings.

As Adjective

ثانٍ is an adjective and, as such, functions grammatically as any adjective: It follows the noun it describes, and agrees with it in case, gender, and definiteness.

فهمتُ الدرسَ الثانيَ. "I understood the second lesson."

دخلتُ من الباب الثاني. "I entered via the second door."

EXAMPLES

١ الملك الحسن الثاني

1 "King Hasan the 2nd"

٢ . . . النصف الثاني من الليل.

2 ". . . the second half of the night."
(Naguib Mahfouz, *al-Ṭarīq*, p. 92)

٣ ثم رأيناها تخرج وتختفى في الحجرة الثانية

3 "Then we saw her leave and disappear into the second room."
(Yūsuf Idrīs, *al-'Askari al-Aswad*, p. 64)

3. Also see "More on Ordinal Numbers," p. 110.

٤ العودة إلى الحج مرة ثانية

4 "The return to the Hajj a second time . . ."
(Naguib Mahfouz, *Zuqāq al-Midaqq*, p. 270)

٥ ثم فُتح ضده ملف ثان وثالث ورابع

5 "Then a second, third, and fourth file were opened against him."
(*al-Sharq al-Awsaṭ*, Apr. 15, 2011)

٦ . . . فيما يخضع مسؤول ثان إلى التحقيق في القضية ذاتها.

6 ". . . while a second official undergoes investigation in the same case . . ."
(*al-Sharq al-Awsaṭ*, Sept. 22, 2010)

٧ رفضت محكمة اول من أمس طعنا ثانيا ضد احتجاز الضباط

7 "A court rejected the day before yesterday a second challenge to the detention of the officers."
(*al-Ḥayāt*, Apr. 7, 2011)

Before Indefinite Noun

As with أول, ثاني can occur before a noun. The following noun may be indefinite and singular, in which case ثاني means "the second." It occurs in an *iḍāfa* construction with the following noun. ثاني will not take a *tā' marbūta* in this instance, regardless of the gender of the following noun.

ثاني مرة "the second time"

EXAMPLES

١ كيف لم تقابلني وهذا ثاني يوم لك في المدق!

1 "How have you not met me even though this is the second day for you in the alley?"
(Naguib Mahfouz, *Zuqāq al-Midaqq*, p. 244)

٢ وذاك أنها ثاني مدينة بُنيت في الأرض بعد الطوفان

2 "That is because it was the second city built on earth after the Flood."
(Yāqūt, *Mu'jam al-Buldān*, 4/264, #9018 on Fāmiya)

٣ بكين ثاني قوة اقتصادية قريبا

3 "Beijing is soon to be the second economic power."
(aljazeera.net, June 19, 2009)

Before Definite Noun

Alternatively, ثاني may be followed by a definite plural noun, in which case it means "the second of . . ." In such a construction it is almost never seen in the feminine.

ثاني الحلقات "the second of the episodes"

EXAMPLES

١ هو ثاني الأسماء الكبرى

1 "It is the second of the big names."
(*al-'Arabi*, June 1993)

٢ يلتقي منتخبا تركيا وكرواتيا في ثاني مباريات الدور ربع النهائي لكأس أمم أوروبا

2 "The representative teams of Turkey and Croatia meet in the second of the quarter-final matches of the European Nations Cup."
(aljazeera.net, June 20, 2008)

Three Through Ten

Cardinal

The numbers 3–10 are written as shown in table 1.2.

Table 1.2 Three through Ten, Cardinal

	Masculine (used with feminine nouns)	Feminine (used with masculine nouns)
3	ثَلاث	ثَلاثة
4	أَرْبَع	أَرْبَعة
5	خَمْس	خَمْسة
6	سِتّ	سِتّة
7	سَبْع	سَبْعة
8	ثَمانٍ	ثَمانية
9	تِسْع	تِسْعة
10	عَشْر	عَشَرة

The word for "three" is sometimes spelled without the *alif*: ثَلث and ثَلثة. When spelled in this way, it should still be pronounced as if the missing *alif* were present.

The number ثمانية is in the category of nouns called منقوص. Therefore, the masculine form ثمانٍ becomes ثماني when it is a مُضاف or when the definite article الـ is added to it. When this happens, it is ثماني (with no ending vowel) in the مرفوع and مجرور cases, and ثمانيَ in the منصوب case.

دخلت ثماني بنات. "Eight girls entered."

رأيت ثمانيَ طالبات. "I saw eight (female) students."

Note that the internal vowels in عشرة and عشر vary from the feminine to masculine. The feminine عَشَرة has a *fatḥa* on the *shīn*, whereas the *shīn* of the masculine عَشْر has a *sukūn*. This is in contrast to the numbers 3–9, which have the same internal vowels on both forms. It is also in contrast to the forms of عشرة and عشر used to form the teens 11–19, in which the opposite occurs (see p. 20).

The number precedes its counted noun and is in an إضافة relationship with it. The number, therefore, takes no *tanwīn*, and its case ending varies depending on its function in the sentence. The counted noun is plural and is a مضاف إليه to the number word; it is therefore in the مجرور case.

Furthermore, these numbers are subject to polar agreement; that is, the gender of the number word is the opposite of the gender of the counted noun. Thus, when the singular of the counted noun is masculine, the feminine form of the number word (i.e., the form which has a *tā' marbūta* attached) is used. When the singular of the counted noun is feminine, the masculine form of the number word (i.e., the form without *tā' marbūta*) is used.

ثلاث مرات "three times"

ثلاث بنات "three girls"

Here the masculine ثلاث with no *tā' marbūṭa* is used, since the singulars of مرات (مرة) and بنات (بنت) are feminine.

ثلاثة رجال "three men"

ثلاثة كتب "three books"

Here the feminine form ثلاثة (with a *tā' marbūṭa*) is used because the singulars of رجال (رجل) and of كتب (كتاب) are masculine.

EXAMPLES

١ - متى توظفت؟
- منذ ثلاثة أعوام

1 "When were you hired?" "Three years ago."
(Naguib Mahfouz, *al-Ṭarīq*, p. 89)

٢ مقتل خمسة جنود أمريكيين في ثلاث هجمات متفرقة

2 "The Killing of Five American Soldiers in Three Unrelated Attacks . . ."
(*al-Ḥayāt*, Jan. 9, 2006)

(the singular of هجمات is هجمة; the singular of جنود is جندي)

٣ رأى الموت أربع مرات بعينيه ولم يتعلم

3 "He saw death four times with his own eyes but has not learned."
(Naguib Mahfouz, *al-Ṭarīq*, p. 131)

٤ كانت صورة يرجع تاريخها إلى ما قبل ستة أعوام

4 "It was a picture the history of which went back more than six years."
(Naguib Mahfouz, *Zuqāq al-Midaqq*, p. 119)

٥ . . . نشر ست قصائد لم تنشر سابقاً . . .

5 ". . . the publication of six poems which had not been published before . . ."
(*al-Ḥayāt*, Apr. 20, 2011)

٦ كَمَثَلِ حَبَّةٍ أَنبَتَتْ سَبْعَ سَنابِلَ

6 "Like a seed that has sprouted seven ears . . ."
(Qur'an 2:261)

(the singular of سنابل is سنبلة "an ear of grain")

٧ تم الاتفاق على ثمانية جنيهات

7 "Eight pounds was agreed to."
(Naguib Mahfouz, *Zuqāq al-Midaqq*, p. 168)

(the singular of جنيهات is جنيه)

٨ . . . ليرتفع عدد الشركات التي تعمل في القطاع إلى ثماني شركات . . .

8 ". . . which raises the number of companies that operate in the sector to eight . . ."
(*al-Ḥayāt*, Apr. 16, 2011)

٩ . . . ما أسفر عن مقتل تسعة أشخاص . . .

9 ". . . which led to the death of nine persons . . ."
(*al-Ḥayāt*, Jan. 9, 2006)

١٠ . . . وأن يسوق إليها مائة من الإبل وعشرة أعبُد وعشر وصائف وثلاثة أفراس

10 ". . . and to have delivered to her 100 camels, ten slaves, ten servant girls, and three horses."
(*Qiṣaṣ al-ʿArab*, 1/239)

(أعبد is a plural of عبد. The singular of وصائف is وصيفة, and the singular of أفراس is فرس)

١١ احشدوا إذن عشرة صراصير!

11 "Mobilize, then, ten cockroaches!"
(Tawfiq al-Hakim, *Maṣīr Ṣurṣār*, p. 29)

After Counted Noun

An alternative way of expessing a number of objects is to place the number after the counted noun. This style is less common and is seen as more flowery.

In this construction, the counted noun is plural, and the following number will be an adjective that agrees with the counted noun in case. The rules of polar agreement still apply.

أعرف وزراءَ ثلاثةً "I know three ministers."

EXAMPLES

١ زلزلت الحارة بالخبر، كما زلزلت به أسرات أربع

1 "The neighborhood was shocked by the news, just as four families were shocked by it."
(Naguib Mahfouz, *al-Ḥarāfīsh*, p. 368)

٢ إلا أني قد رأيت رجالا ثلاثة قد أناخوا إلى هذا التل

2 "Except that I saw three men resting their camels over towards this hill."
(Tawfiq al-Hakim, *Muḥammad*, p. 152)

٣ توالت على العرب سنون تسع في الجاهلية حطّمت كل شيء

3 "Nine (difficult) years befell the pre-Islamic Arabs, one after the other, which destroyed everything."
(*Qiṣaṣ al-'Arab*, 1/22)

٤ وَالفَجْرِ وَلَيالٍ عَشْرٍ

4 "By the dawn and ten nights . . ."
(Qur'an, 89:1–2)

Ordinal[4]

The ordinal numbers 3–10, shown in table 1.3, are formed by placing the root letters of the number word in the pattern فاعِل. The only exception to this is "sixth," which is rendered سادِس.

Table 1.3 Three through Ten, Ordinal

	Masculine	Feminine
3rd	ثالِث	ثالِثة
4th	رابِع	رابِعة
5th	خامِس	خامِسة
6th	سادِس	سادِسة
7th	سابِع	سابِعة
8th	ثامِن	ثامِنة
9th	تاسِع	تاسِعة
10th	عاشِر	عاشِرة

The ordinal numbers function as adjectives: They follow the noun they describe and agree with it in gender, case, and definiteness. The ordinals are NOT subject to polar agreement.

البناية الثالثة "the third building"

الشارع الرابع "the fourth street"

4. Also see "More on Ordinal Numbers," p. 110.

EXAMPLES

١ فأما فى طوره الثالث هذا فقد كان يجد راحة وأمناً وطمأنينة واستقراراً

1 "In this third stage of his, he found comfort, security, peace of mind, and stability."
(Taha Hussein, *al-Ayyām*, 2/16)

٢ وللمرة الثالثة قالت: اتفضلوا

2 "For the third time she said, 'Come on in.'"
(Yūsuf Idrīs, *al-'Askari al-Aswad*, p. 64)

٣ ومن ثم يترك مساحة أخرى للقارئ حتى يبني تصوراً ثالثاً.

3 "Thus he leaves space for the reader to construct a third conception."
(*al-Ḥayāt*, Jan. 14, 2011)

٤ وأكد ناشط حقوقي ثالث أن ((المروحيات تقصف المدينة)).

4 "A third rights activist confirmed that 'helicopters are shelling the city.'"
(*al-Sharq al-Awsaṭ*, June 11, 2011)

٥ واسقطت العام ٢٠٠٨ قضية رابعة

5 "In 2008 a fourth case was dropped."
(*al-Ḥayāt*, Sept. 26, 2009)

٦ ثم يختار الأعضاء الأربعة شخصاً خامساً ليرأس مجلس التحكيم

6 "Then the four members choose a fifth person to head the arbitration committee."
(*al-Ḥayāt*, June 23, 2008)

٧ . . . في اليوم السادس للثورة ٣٠ يناير . . .

7 ". . . on the sixth day of the revolution, January 30 . . ."
(digital.ahram.org.eg, Apr. 5, 2011)

٨ ونزل من الدرجة السادسة إلى الثامنة

8 "He was demoted from the sixth rank to the eighth."
(Naguib Mahfouz, *Zuqāq al-Midaqq*, p. 15)

٩ ولو كان في أقل من الدرجة التاسعة ما وقع اختياري عليه

9 "If he was any lower than the ninth rank, I would not have chosen him."
(Naguib Mahfouz, *Zuqāq al-Midaqq*, p. 117)

Before Indefinite Noun

Alternatively, as with أول and ثاني (see pp. 5 and 12), the ordinal number can occur before an indefinite singular noun. In this case, it is in an إضافة construction with that noun, and is invariable with regard to gender. That is, it remains masculine whether the noun described is feminine or masculine. The translation of this construction is "the third. . . . / the fourth . . ." etc.:

ثالث ساعة "the third hour"

EXAMPLES

١ بل ذكرت أن هذه ثاني أو ثالث مرة تزورها فى غير أول الشهر

1 "She remembered in fact that this was the second or third time she's visited her at a time other than the beginning of the month."
(Naguib Mahfouz, *Zuqāq al-Midaqq*, p. 19)

٢ هو ثامن لاعب مصرى يدخل نادى المائة فى المشاركات الدولية مع المنتخب

2 "He is the eighth Egyptian player to join the club of those who have participated internationally with the team 100 times."
(*al-Ahrām*, Jan. 9, 2011)

Before Definite Noun

As with أول and ثاني (see pp. 6 and 13), the ordinal number can also occur in an *iḍāfa* construction with a definite plural noun, which will most commonly be a pronoun:

سادسهم "the sixth one of them"

EXAMPLES

١ وكانوا ثلاثة حينًا وأربعة حينًا، وربما بلغوا خمسة فى بعض الأيام، ولكن لخامسهم هذا شأنًا آخر، فالخير ألا يذكر الآن

1 "They were three in number sometimes, four other times, and some days they might get up to five. But this fifth one of them had a different situation. It would be best not to discuss it now."
(Taha Hussein, *al-Ayyām*, 2/23)

٢ وجعل يعد الأسوار حتى بلغ خامسها

2 "He started counting the fences until he got to the fifth one (of them)."
(Naguib Mahfouz, *Zuqāq al-Midaqq*, p. 225)

٣ سَيَقولونَ ثَلاثَةٌ رابِعُهُمْ كَلْبُهُمْ وَيَقولونَ خَمْسَةٌ سادِسُهُمْ كَلْبُهُمْ رَجْما بِالغَيبِ وَيَقولونَ سَبْعَةٌ وَثامِنُهُمْ كَلْبُهُمْ

3 "They will say (there were) three (of them), and the fourth (of them) was their dog. And some say, guessing wildly, five, and the sixth (of them) was their dog. And some say seven, and the eighth (of them) was their dog."
(Qur'an, 18:22)

٤ أما خامس الأجانب فهو الجزائري عبد الملك زياية بسبعة أهداف

4 "As for the fifth of the foreigners, he is the Algerian Abd-al-Malik Ziyaya, with seven goals."
(alarabiya.net, Apr. 13, 2011)

٥ مواهب عربية في عاشرِ حلقات ((الفرصة))

5 "Arab Talents in the Tenth Episode (tenth of the episodes) of *al-Furṣa*"
(*al-Hayāt*, Jan. 14, 2011)

Eleven Through Nineteen: General Principles

The numbers from 11 to 19 are called عدد مُرَكَّب (compound numbers). They consist of a first element plus عَشَرَ or عَشْرَةَ.

عشر is used with a masculine noun and عشرة with a feminine.

The first element is subject to polar agreement if it is 3–9 (see p. 14).

Note that the vowels on the *shīn* of عشر and عشرة here differ from those used when they are not used in compounds (see p. 14). In these compound numbers, the *shīn* of عَشَرَ takes a *fatḥa*, and the *shīn* of عَشْرَةَ takes a *sukūn*. On the other hand, when عشر and عشرة are used alone, not in a compound, to express "ten," عَشْر takes *sukūn* on its *shīn*, and عَشَرة takes *fatḥa*. ʿAbbās Ḥasan expressed the rule thus: If the counted item is masculine, the word for "ten" has a *fatḥa* on its *shīn*. If feminine, it has a *sukūn*.[5]

The vowel endings on both elements of each of the compound numbers from 11 to 19 are invariable. That is, both elements always take a *fatḥa* regardless of case (except for إحدى, which ends in *alif*, and all four variations of اثنا).

The counted noun following is a تمييز and is therefore singular and in the منصوب case.

For the ordinals, polar agreement does not apply, just as it does not apply to the ordinals 3–10.

The ordinals are also invariable with regard to vowel endings: Both elements always take a *fatḥa* regardless of case.

Eleven

Cardinal

The masculine of "eleven," used when the counted noun is masculine, is:

أَحَدَ عَشَرَ

As is the case with all the teens (see above), the vowels at the end of each of the two elements are invariable. That is, there is a *fatḥa* at the end of أحد and at the end of عشر in all instances, regardless of the grammatical case. Note also that عَشَرَ here, as is the case with all of the teens, has a *fatḥa* on the *shīn*, in contrast to عَشْر "ten," which has *sukūn* on its *shīn*.

The feminine of "eleven," used when the counted noun is feminine, is

إِحْدى عَشْرَةَ

5. Ḥasan, *al-Naḥw al-Wāfī*, 4/522.

The *fatḥa* at the end of عشرة is invariable. It remains *fatḥa* regardless of grammatical case. Also note that عَشْرَةَ here has a *sukūn* on its *shīn*, in contrast to عَشَرَة "ten," which has a *fatḥa* on its *shīn*.

The counted noun follows the number and is singular. It is in the منصوب case, as it is a تمييز.

إحدى عَشْرَةَ سنةً "eleven years"

أَحَدَ عَشَرَ يوماً "eleven days"

EXAMPLES

١ . . . والحق المسلوب منهم منذ أكثر من أحد عشر عاما

1 ". . . and the right that has been denied them for more than eleven years . . ."
(*al-Ahrām*, Apr. 5, 2011)

٢ يٰأَبَتِ إِني رأَيْتُ أَحَدَ عَشَرَ كَوْكَبًا وَالشَّمْسَ وَالْقَمَرَ رَأَيْتُهُمْ لي ساجِدينَ

2 "Father, I have seen 11 planets and the sun and the moon. I saw them prostrating themselves to me."
(Qur'an, 12:4)

٣ وَبَيْنَ الْكَدِيدِ وَبَيْنَ مَكَّةَ أَحَدَ عَشَرَ فَرْسَخًا

3 "Between Kadīd and Mecca is 11 parasangs."
(Fayyūmi, *al-Miṣbāḥ al-Munīr*, p. 527, '*al-Kadīd*')

٤ تم تقسيمهم إلى احدى عشرة مجموعة[6]

4 "They have been divided into eleven groups."
(*al-Ahrām*, Mar. 28, 2011)

٥ وجزائر برطانية إحدى عشرة جزيرة

5 "The islands of Britain are eleven (islands)."
(Abu-l-Fidā', *Taqwīm al-Buldān*, p. 187)

٦ ما كان رسول الله صلى الله عليه وسلم يزيد . . . على إحدى عشرةَ ركعةً

6 "The Prophet (peace be upon him) never . . . did more than 11 *rak'as*."
(*Sunan Abi Dāwūd*, 2/500, #1341)

6. Typo corrected: احدى for احدي.

Ordinal

The ordinal of eleven in the masculine, used with masculine nouns, is

حادِيَ عَشَرَ

The feminine is

حادِيَةَ عَشْرَةَ

As is the case with all of the teens, the masculine form عَشَرَ has *fatḥa* on the *shīn*, and the feminine form عَشْرَةَ has *sukūn* on the *shīn*.

As is also the case with all of the teens (see p. 21), the *fatḥa* at the end of both parts of both the feminine and masculine is invariable. That is, it remains *fatḥa* regardless of case.

These both function as adjectives: They follow the noun they describe and agree with it in gender and definiteness. When ال is added, it is added to the first element only, never the second:

الحاديةَ عَشْرَةَ and الحاديَ عَشَرَ

EXAMPLES

١ يأتي الزبون الحادي عشر ليسأله إن كان لديه أعلام أخرى.

1 "The eleventh customer comes in to ask him if he has any other flags."
(*al-Akhbār*, Feb. 2, 2011)

٢ اما شخص حادي عشر فأوقف في قبرص

2 "An eleventh person was stopped in Cypress."
(*al-Akhbār* [Egypt], July 8, 2010)

٣ والصنف الحادي عشر من الرافضة، وهي ((البيانية))، أصحاب ((بيان بن سمعان التميمي))

3 "The eleventh category of the Rafidites, the Bayāniyya, are the followers of Bayān ibn Samʿān al-Tamīmi."
(Ashʿari, *Maqālāt al-Islāmiyyīn*, 1/38)

٤ مات . . . في حادِيَ عَشَرَ جمادى الآخرة

4 "He died . . . on the 11th of Jumādā II"
(Yāqūt, *Muʿjam al-Udabāʾ*, 4/464-5, #684 on ʿUmar ibn al-Ḥusayn al-Khaṭṭāṭ)

٥ رداً علي ما نشر في الصفحة الحادية عشرة بالعدد رقم 7512 ليوم الجمعة . . .

5 "In response to what was published on the 11th page of issue 7512 from Friday . . ."
(*al-Wafd*, Apr. 8, 2011)

٦ وفي السَّنةِ الحاديةَ عشْرَةَ، في شهرِ بول . . .

6 "In the eleventh year, in the month of Bul . . ."
(*al-Kitāb al-Muqaddas*, al-Mulūk al-Awwal [1 Kings] 6:38)

Twelve

Cardinal

The word for "twelve" varies with case and gender and is rendered as in table 1.4.

Table 1.4 Twelve

	Masculine	Feminine
مرفوع	اِثنا عَشَرَ	اِثْنَتا عَشْرَةَ
منصوب/مجرور	اِثْني عَشَرَ	اِثْنَتَيْ عَشْرَةَ

The initial *hamza* on all four of the forms is a *hamzat waṣl.*

Note also that, as is the case with all of the teens, عَشَرَ in the masculine forms has *fatḥa* on the *shīn*, and عَشْرَةَ in the feminine forms has *sukūn* on the *shīn*.

As is the case with all of the teens, the *fatḥa* on عشر or عشرة at the end of all four forms is invariable. That is, it remains *fatḥa* at all times regardless of case.

The counted noun follows the number and is singular. It is in the منصوب case, as it is a تمييز.

اِثْنَتا عَشْرَةَ سنةً "twelve years"

اِثنا عَشَرَ يوماً "twelve days"

EXAMPLES

١ وكان اثنا عشر إندونيسيا بين نشطاء كانوا على متن السفينة «مافي مرمرة»

1 "Twelve Indonesians were among the activists who were aboard the ship *Mavi Marmara.*"
(*al-Bayān*, June 4, 2010)

٢ . . . ولم يبق إلا اثنا عشر رجلا . . .

2 ". . . and only twelve men stayed . . ."
(al-Fakhr al-Rāzi, *Mafātīḥ al-Ghayb*, 30/10 on Qur'an 62:11)

٣ وولد لإسماعيل اثنا عشر ذكرا

3 "Twelve boys were born to Ishmael."
(*Masʿūdi, Murūj al-Dhahab*, 1/62)

٤ كتاب المعجم . . . ٱثْنَا عَشَرَ جزءًا

4 "*Kitāb al-Muʿjam* . . . is 12 parts."
(Yāqūt, *Muʿjam al-Udabā'*, 4/42, #565 on Ibn ʿAsākir)

٥ أخرجوا إليّ منكم اثنى عشر نقيبًا[7]

5 "Send me from amongst you twelve chiefs."
(Tawfiq al-Hakim, *Muḥammad*, p. 109)

٦ سهلت وساطة القادة القبليين عملية تسليم اكثر من اثني عشر مقاتل من ((القاعدة)) لأجهزة الأمن اليمنية

6 "The intervention of tribal leaders facilitated the handing over of more than twelve al-Qaeda fighters to Yemeni security forces."
(*al-Ḥayāt*, Aug. 25, 2011)

٧ مات وخلّف عندها اثْنَيْ عَشَرَ عِدلا محزوماً من الكتب

7 "He died, leaving her with 12 bound sacks of books."
(Yāqūt, *Muʿjam al-Udabā'*, 1/501, #119 on Aḥmad ibn ʿAli ibn Thābit ibn Aḥmad ibn Mahdi)

٨ اختلفت المرجئة في الإيمان ما هو وهم اثنتا عشرة فرقة

8 "The Murji'a differed regarding what faith is. They are (divided into) twelve sects."
(Ashʿari, *Maqālāt al-Islāmiyyīn*, p. 114)

---

7. Note that the book cited is typeset in the Egyptian style in which the *yā'* has no dots, and is therefore not distinguishable from the *alif maqṣūra*. So the word for "twelve" in this particular passage should be read *ithnay ʿashar*.

٩ فَانْفَجَرَتْ مِنْهُ ٱثْنَتَا عَشْرَةَ عَيْنًا

9 ". . . and twelve springs gushed forth from it . . ."
(Qur'an, 2:60)

١٠ كان يستطيع أن يتقدم بعد اثنتى عشرة سنة[8]

10 "He was able to advance after twelve years."
(Taha Hussein, *al-Ayyām*, 2/54)

١١ وقد جاء انخفاض المؤشر العام محصلة لانخفاض أسعار أسهم 28 شركة وارتفاع أسعار أسهم اثنتي عشرة شركة

11 "The fall in the general index is the result of a fall in the prices of the shares of 28 companies and a rise in the price of the shares of 12 companies."
(*al-Sharq*, July 26, 2011)

١٢ فإذا قام بها في اثْنَتَىْ عَشْرَةَ رَكْعَةً . . .

12 "If he completed it in 12 *rak'as* . . ."
(Mālik ibn Anas, *al-Muwaṭṭa'*, p. 115)

Thintā 'ashra

In classical texts, ثِنْتا عشرة in the مرفوع case and ثِنْتَي عشرة in the منصوب and مجرور cases are sometimes used when the counted noun is feminine, in place of اثنتا عشرة/اثنتي عشرة.

EXAMPLES

١ فهذه ثِنْتَا عَشْرَةَ مَسألةً

1 "That makes 12 questions."
(Ḥarīri, *Maqāmāt*, p. 241, 'al-Qaṭī'iyya')

٢ سألت عائشة رضي الله عنها عن صداق النبي صلى الله عليه وسلم، قالت: ثنتا عشرةَ أوقيةً ونشّ.

2 "I asked 'Ā'isha about the Prophet's (peace be upon him) dowry. She said, '(It was) 12 ounces and a *nashsh*.'"[9]
(*Sunan Abi Dāwūd*, 3/444, #2105)

8. See n. 7.

9. An ounce *ūqiyya* is forty dirhams, and a *nashsh* is half that. See n. 1 on the page referenced; also Fīrūzābādi, *al-Qāmūs al-Muḥīṭ*, وقي and نشش.

٣ ما أصدق رسول الله صلى الله عليه وسلم امرأة من نسائه ولا أُصدِقَت امرأةٌ من بناته أكثر من ثنتي عشرة أوقيةً

3 "The Prophet (peace be upon him) never gave any of his wives, nor were any of his daughters given as dowries, more than 12 ounces."[10]
(*Sunan Abi Dāwūd*, 3/444, #2106)

Ordinal[11]

The ordinal in the masculine is ثانِيَ عَشَرَ, and in the feminine is ثانِيَةَ عَشْرَةَ.

Note that, as is the case with all of the teens, the masculine form عَشَرَ has *fatḥa* on the *shīn*, and the feminine form عَشْرَةَ has *sukūn* on the *shīn* (see p. 20).

Also, as with all the teens, the *fatḥa* at the end of both parts of each is invariable. That is, it remains *fatḥa* regardless of case.

This ordinal functions as an adjective: It follows its noun, and agrees with it in gender and definiteness. The definite article is added only to the first word in the compound:

الثاني عشر and الثانية عشرة.

EXAMPLES

١ وهذا ما اعترف به عبد العزيز نفسه في المؤتمر الثاني عشر للجبهة

1 "This is what Abdelaziz himself admitted in the Front's twelfth conference."
(*al-Tajdīd*, Oct. 19, 2010)

٢ والصنف الثاني عشر من أصناف الغالية يزعمون أن عليًا هو الله

2 "The twelfth category of extremists claims that Ali is God."
(Ash'ari, *Maqālat al-Islāmiyyīn*, p. 31)

٣ وكان دخولُهما المدينةَ فى اليومِ الثانىَ عَشَرَ من ربيع الأول

3 "Their entry into Medina was on the 12th day of Rabīʿ I."
(Ibn Kathīr, *al-Bidāya wa-l-Nihāya*, 15/482–3)

10. See n. 9.
11. Also see "More on Ordinal Numbers," p. 110.

٤ يدفع ارتفاع سعر النفط العالمي الكويت باتجاه تسجيل فائض سنوي ضخم آخر، للسنة الثانية عشرة على التوالي

4 "The rise in worldwide oil prices is pushing Kuwait towards another huge yearly surplus for the twelfth year in a row."
(*al-Ḥayāt*, Apr. 3, 2011)

٥ والفرقة الثانية عشرة من المرجئة ((الكرامية)) أصحاب ((محمد بن كرام)) يزعمون أن الإيمان هو الإقرار والتصديق باللسان دون القلب

5 "The twelfth sect of Murji'a, the Karrāmiyya, the followers of Muḥmmad ibn Karrām, claims that faith is declaration and acknowledgment by the tongue only, and not in the heart."
(Ash'ari, *Maqālāt al-Islāmiyyīn*, p. 120)

٦ وقد أبقَوا لهم مع ذلك أربعَ عشرَةَ كنيسةً . . . الثانيةَ عشْرةَ: كنيسة اليهود التي بأيديهم اليوم في حارتهم

6 "Additionally, they allowed them to keep 14 churches . . . the twelfth is the Jewish temple which remains in their possession today in their quarter of the city."
(Ibn Kathīr, *al-Bidāya wa-l-Nihāya*, 9/582)

Thirteen Through Nineteen

Cardinal

The cardinal numbers 13–19 are as shown in table 1.5.

Table 1.5 Thirteen through Nineteen, Cardinal

	Masculine (used with masculine nouns)	Feminine (used with feminine nouns)
13	ثَلاثَةَ عَشَرَ	ثَلاثَ عَشْرَةَ
14	أَرْبَعَةَ عَشَرَ	أَرْبَعَ عَشْرَةَ
15	خَمْسَةَ عَشَرَ	خَمْسَ عَشْرَةَ
16	سِتَّةَ عَشَرَ	سِتَّ عَشْرَةَ

Table 1.5 (*continued*)

	Masculine (used with masculine nouns)	Feminine (used with feminine nouns)
17	سَبْعَةَ عَشَرَ	سَبْعَ عَشْرَةَ
18	ثَمانِيَةَ عَشَرَ	ثَمانِيَ عَشْرَةَ
19	تِسْعَةَ عَشَرَ	تِسْعَ عَشْرَةَ

These contain two elements: a number from three through ten plus عشرة or عشر.

The first element, due to the fact that it represents a number from 3–10, is subject to polar agreement (see p. 14). The عشر and عشرة are not subject to polar agreement.

As is the case with all of the teens, the masculine form عشر has *fatḥa* on the *shīn* and the feminine form عشرة has *sukūn* on the *shīn* (see p. 20).

As is also the case with all of the teens, the *fatḥa* at the end of both elements is invariable. That is, it remains *fatḥa* at all times regardless of case and is never nunated.

The counted noun follows the number and is singular. It is in the منصوب case, as it is a تمييز.

ثلاثةَ عَشَرَ جندياً "thirteen soldiers"

أربعَ عَشْرَةَ نافذةً "fourteen windows"

EXAMPLES

١ مقتل ثلاثة عشر جنديا إسرائيليا في معارك بنت جبيل

1 "The killing of thirteen Israeli soldiers in the battles of Bint Jbeil . . ."
(aljazeera.net, July 26, 2006)

٢ وقدم له خمسة عشر جنيها مقدم أتعاب

2 "He presented him with fifteen pounds as an advance on his fees."
(Naguib Mahfouz, *Zuqāq al-Midaqq*, p. 147)

٣ واليوم خمسَ عشرة ليلة قد أصبحنا منها ولا يخبرنا بشيء

3 "It has been fifteen days (literally: fifteen nights we've entered the morning from), and he still tells us nothing."
(Tawfiq al-Hakim, *Muḥammad*, p. 53)

٤ وبقي حذاؤه—كما قال المترجمون عنه—سبع عشرة سنة يرقّعها ويخيطها

4 "His shoes—according to his biographers—lasted seventeen years with him patching and sewing them up." ('Ā'iḍ al-Qarni, *Lā Taḥzan*, p. 332)

٥ . . . وذلك على ثمانية عشر ميلا من بيت المقدس

5 ". . . and that is 18 miles from Jerusalem." (*Mas'ūdi, Murūj al-Dhahab*, p. 1/47)

٦ بلغ فلان أشده إذا بلغ ثماني عشرة سنة

6 "A person has reached full maturity if he reaches 18 years." (Anbāri, *Kitāb al-Aḍdād*, p. 222)

٧ وابتدأتُ بالنظر في حدود الفراء وسني ثَمانِيَ عَشْرَةَ سَنَةً

7 "I began looking at *al-Ḥudūd* by Farrā' when I was 18 years old." (Yāqūt, *Mu'jam al-Udabā'*, p. 2/64, #206 on Tha'lab)

٨ تسع عشرة أسيرة ينطلقن نحو الحرية

8 "Nineteen female captives head off towards freedom." (*al-Ayyām*, Oct. 3, 2009)

٩ تسعة عشر حادثاً بسبب أمطار الأحساء

9 "Nineteen Accidents Due to the Rains in El-Hasa" (*al-Riyāḍ*, Jan. 20, 2011)

Ordinal[12]

The ordinal numbers 13th–19th are as shown in table 1.6.

Table 1.6 Thirteen through Nineteen, Ordinal

	Masculine (used with masculine nouns)	Feminine (used with feminine nouns)
13th	ثالِثَ عَشَرَ	ثالِثَةَ عَشْرَةَ
14th	رابِعَ عَشَرَ	رابِعَةَ عَشْرَةَ
15th	خامِسَ عَشَرَ	خامِسَةَ عَشْرَةَ
16th	سادِسَ عَشَرَ	سادِسَةَ عَشْرَةَ

12. Also see "More on Ordinal Numbers," p. 110.

Table 1.6 (*continued*)

	Masculine (used with masculine nouns)	Feminine (used with feminine nouns)
17th	سابِعَ عَشَرَ	سابِعَةَ عَشْرَةَ
18th	ثامِنَ عَشَرَ	ثامِنَةَ عَشْرَةَ
19th	تاسِعَ عَشَرَ	تاسِعَةَ عَشْرَةَ

As is the case with all of the teens, the masculine form عشر has *fatḥa* on the *shīn*, and the feminine form عشرة has *sukūn* on the *shīn* (see p. 20).

As is also the case with all of the teens, the *fatḥa* at the end of both elements is invariable. That is, it remains *fatḥa* at all times regardless of case and is never nunated.

These ordinals agree with the following noun in gender and definiteness. As is the case with the ordinals 3–10, these ordinals are not subject to polar agreement (see p. 14) in either of the two elements.

The definite article الـ is added to the first element only, never the second:

الثالث عشر and الرابعة عشرة and so forth.

EXAMPLES

١ . . . وفي المقال الأخير—الثالث عشر—يخص سعد زغلول بالتحية والتهنئة

1 ". . . and in the last article, the thirteenth, he singles out Sa'd Zaghloul for salutes and congratulations."
('Ali Shalash, introduction to Manfalūṭi, *Silsilat al-A'māl al-Kāmila*, p. 42)

٢ . . . تمويل المرحلة الرابعة عشرة من مشروع تحويل السيارات للعمل بالوقود المزدوج . . .

2 ". . . the financing of the fourteenth stage of the project to convert cars to bio-fuel . . ."
(*al-Ahrām*, Nov. 2, 2010)

٣ وسجلت وفاة شخص رابع عشر في مدينة هيو.

3 "The death of a fourteenth person was recorded in the city of Hue."
(*al-Ba'th*, Oct. 18, 2010)

٤ عُرض يومَ أحدٍ في أولِ الرابعةَ عشْرَةَ، ويوم الأحزابِ في أواخرِ الخامسةَ عشْرَةَ

4 "He was presented on the day of Uḥud at the beginning of his fourteenth (year), and on the day of (the Battle of) the Confederates at the end of his fifteenth (year)."
(Ibn Kathīr, *al-Bidāya wa-l-Nihāya*, 6/11)

٥ قلت في قصيدة بعنوان: أبو ذرٍّ في القرن الخامس عشر . . .

5 "In a poem entitled 'Abu Dharr in the fifteenth century,' I said . . ."
('Ā'iḍ al-Qarni, *Lā Taḥzan*, p. 333)

٦ وهو اليومُ السَّادِسَ عَشَرَ من مَهْرَماه

6 "It is the 16th day of the month of Mehr."
(Fayyūmi, *al-Miṣbāḥ al-Munīr*, p. 583, 'Mihrajān')

٧ تلتئم القمة السادسة عشرة للاتحاد الإفريقي في العاصمة الإثيوبية غداً

7 "The sixteenth summit of the African Union meets tomorrow in the Ethiopian capital."
(*al-Waṭan* [Syria], Jan. 30, 2011)

٨ . . . كما اعتقل شخص سادس عشر يشتبه بأنه من عناصر الحركة في روالبندي بضاحية إسلام أباد.

8 "Additionally, a sixteenth person, who is suspected of being a member of the Movement, was arrested in Rawalpindi, just outside of Islamabad."
(*al-Ba'th*, Dec. 9, 2008)

٩ قال فيدرر الساعي الى اللقب السابع عشر في البطولات الكبرى . . .

9 "Federer, who is seeking his seventeenth Grand Slam title, said . . ."
(*al-Ahrām*, Jan. 23, 2011)

١٠ في نهاية القرن الثامن عشر . . .

10 "At the end of the eighteenth century . . ."
(*al-'Arabi*, June 1993)

١١ ورجح . . . مذهب الكوفيين في سبع مسائل هي العاشرة والثامنة عشرة . . .

11 "He preferred the views of the Kufans with regard to seven issues: the tenth, the eighteenth, . . ."
(Shawqi Ḍayf, *al-Madāris al-Naḥwiyya*, p. 278)

١٢ . . . ان المصريين القدماء استخرجوا الذهب في زمن الاسرة التاسعة عشرة من اعماق كبيرة . . .

12 ". . . that the ancient Egyptians in the time of the nineteenth dynasty extracted gold from great depths . . ." (digital.ahram.org.eg, Sept. 10, 2010)

The Tens

Cardinal

The tens, shown in table 1.7, are called عُقود (singular عِقْد/عَقْد).

They vary with regard to case but are invariable with regard to gender.

Table 1.7 Tens

	مرفوع	منصوب\مجرور
20	عِشْرونَ	عِشْرينَ
30	ثَلاثونَ	ثَلاثينَ
40	أَرْبَعونَ	أَرْبَعينَ
50	خَمْسونَ	خَمْسينَ
60	سِتّونَ	سِتّينَ
70	سَبْعونَ	سَبْعينَ
80	ثَمانونَ	ثَمانينَ
90	تِسْعونَ	تِسْعينَ

These are in a category of words called مُلحَق بجمع المذكر السالم, that is, they are inflected in the same way as a masculine sound plural (جمع مذكر سالم) but do not actually refer to a plurality of humans. Thus, they end in ـونَ when in the مرفوع case and ـينَ when in the منصوب or مجرور cases. The *fatḥa* on the *nūn* at the end is invariable: It remains *fatḥa* regardless of case and is never nunated regardless of whether the word is definite or indefinite.

The tens do not vary with regard to gender.

The counted noun follows them and is singular and in the منصوب case, as it is a تمييز.

ثلاثون and ثلاثين are sometimes spelled ثلثون and ثلثين. In this case they should still be pronounced as though the missing *alif* were present.

EXAMPLES

١ . . . حتى لقد كان يسكن غرفة من هذه الغرفات عشرون طالبًا . . .

1 ". . . to the point that twenty students were living in one of these rooms . . ."
(Taha Hussein, *al-Ayyām*, 2/73)

٢ ان عشرين صرصارًا مجتمعة تستطيع دهس وتحطيم طابور طويل من النمل

2 "Twenty cockroaches united together could trample and destroy a long column of ants."
(Tawfiq al-Hakim, *Maṣīr Ṣurṣār*, p. 25)

٣ وبلغت يوميته بها ثلاثين قرشا

3 "His daily wage there reached thirty piastres."
(Naguib Mahfouz, *Zuqāq al-Midaqq*, p. 34)

٤ فسجل لها فيه من المفاخر في ثلاثة أعوام ما لم يسجل لها منذ ثلاثين قرنا

4 "In three years, they recorded great feats therein which they had not recorded for thirty centuries."
(Manfalūṭi, *Silsliat al-A'māl al-Majhūla*, p. 101)

٥ وقد مات الأب منذ أربعين عاما

5 "The father died forty years ago."
(Naguib Mahfouz, *al-Ṭarīq*, pp. 215–216)

٦ وحجّ معها من القيان مُشَيِّعاتٍ لها ومعظِّماتٍ لقَدرها ولِحَقِّها خمسون قينة

6 "Fifty singers accompanied her on the pilgrimage, praising and glorifying her."
(*Qiṣaṣ al-'Arab*, 1/23)

٧ ويعيدك من الشيخوخة إلى الصبا في خمسين دقيقة

7 "It will take you back from old age to youth in fifty minutes."
(Naguib Mahfouz, *Zuqāq al-Midaqq*, p. 151)

٨ الزمن ثابت لا يتغير فالدقيقة ستون ثانية والساعة ستون دقيقة

8 "Time is fixed and doesn't change: A minute is sixty seconds, and an hour is sixty minutes."
(*al-Sharq*, Nov. 24, 2010)

٩ فقتل منهم سبعون رجلا غير من جرح

9 "Seventy men from amongst them were killed in addition to those who were wounded."
(al-*Mas'ūdi*, *Murūj al-Dhahab*, 2/367)

١٠ وكان الاستطلاع قد نظّم بمناسبة مرور ثمانين سنة على تأسيس الجمهورية الإسبانية الثانية

10 "The survey was conducted to mark the passage of eighty years since the foundation of the Second Spanish Republic."
(*al-Sharq al-Awsaṭ*, Apr. 16, 2011)

١١ وقد مرت تسعون عاما منذ آخر عاصفة عملاقة

11 "Ninety years have passed since the last huge storm."
(*al-Sharq al-Awsaṭ*, Aug. 21, 2010)

Ordinal[13]

The ordinals of the tens, 20–90, take exactly the same form as the cardinals (see p. 33). Grammatically, they function as adjectives. They follow the noun described and agree with it in definiteness and case. As with the cardinals, the ـونَ ending is used on the مرفوع, and the ـينَ ending is used on the مجرور and منصوب. Also, as with the cardinals, they do not vary with regard to gender.

EXAMPLES

١ والصنف العشرون من الرافضة: يسوقون الإمامة من علي

1 "The twentieth category of Rafidites traces the imamate from Ali."
(Ash'ari, *Maqālat al-Islāmiyyīn*, p. 41)

13. Also see "More on Ordinal Numbers," p. 110.

٢ القول الثلاثون ما يحكى عن أمه أنها قالت حين جاءها نعيه . . .

2 "The thirtieth thing said was what has been related about his mother, that she said, when the person announcing his death came . . ."
(*Masʿūdi, Murūj al-Dhahab*, 1/291)

٣ وبعد المرة الاربعين يصبح الامر مملا وتشعر كما لو أنك اصبحت جدك.

3 "After the fortieth time, the thing becomes boring, and you feel as if you've become your grandfather."
(alarab.net, Nov. 25, 2010)

٤ السفير الهيفي يحتفل بالعيد الوطني الخمسين وذكرى تحرير الكويت

4 "Ambassador al-Haifi celebrates the fiftieth National Day and the anniversary of Kuwait's liberation."
(*al-Sharq*, Feb. 22, 2011)

٥ لإعلان نتائج المسابقة المدرسية الخمسين . . . وكانت المسابقة المدرسية الخمسون في حفظ القرآن الكريم . . . قد شهدت مشاركة أكثر من 19 ألف طالب وطالبة

5 ". . . for the announcement of the results of the fiftieth school competition. . . . The fiftieth school competition in recitation of the Noble Qurʾan . . . saw the participation of more than 19,000 students."
(*al-Sharq*, Apr. 2, 2011)

٦ فلا يكفي أن نقول وصلنا للمهرجان السبعين أو المؤتمر الثمانين بقدر ما يهم أن نعرف ماذا استفاد الوطن والمواطن من تنظيم هذا الحدث

6 "It is not enough to say 'We have reached the seventieth festival' or 'the eightieth conference' so much as it is important to know how the country and the citizen will benefit from our organizing this event."
(*al-Sharq*, Apr. 19, 2011)

٧ رجح . . . مذهب الكوفيين في سبع مسائل هي العاشرة . . . والسبعون . . .

7 "He preferred the view of the Kufans on seven issues. They are the tenth . . . the seventieth . . ."
(Shawqi Ḍayf, *al-Madāris al-Naḥwiyya*, p. 278)

Tens Plus One Through Nine (21, 32, 44, etc.): General Rules

A number between 21 and 99, inclusive (not counting the عقود), is called عدد معطوف.

It is read with the smaller number first, followed by the conjunction وَ, then the عقد:

خمسة وأربعين "forty-five" (literally, five and forty)

Gender agreement for the first element (1–9) is the same as it is for 1–9 when standing alone. That is, if the first element is one or two, it agrees in gender with the counted noun. If it is 3–9, it is subject to polar agreement (see p. 14): Its gender is opposite that of the counted noun.

The case of each of the two elements is the same and is determined by its position in the sentence.

As with the teens and tens, the counted noun following the number is singular and a تمييز and therefore in the منصوب case.

Tens Plus One (21, 31, 41, 51, 61, 71, 81, 91)

Cardinal

The masculine of (عقد) plus one is (where any of the عقود can be used in place of عشرون):

واحِد وعِشرونَ

The feminine is:

إحْدى وعِشرونَ

Less common, but also sometimes seen, are أَحَد وعشرون in the masculine and واحدة وعشرون in the feminine.

As with any of the tens, عشرون and its fellow عقود do not vary with regard to gender, but take the ـون ending in the مرفوع case and the ـين ending in the منصوب and مجرور cases.

واحد will vary according to case: واحدٌ in the مرفوع, واحدًا in the منصوب, and واحدٍ in the مجرور.

إحدى carries no vowel endings in any of the three cases.

The counted noun following these is a تمييز and is therefore singular and منصوب:

واحدٌ وعشرونَ يوماً	"twenty-one days"
إحدى وعشرونَ ساعةً	"twenty-one hours"

EXAMPLES

١ . . . أن يخلو إلى نفسه فيتلو هذه السورة إحدى وأربعين مرة

1 ". . . to be alone then to read this *sūra* forty-one times."
(Taha Hussein, *al-Ayyām*, 1/106)

٢ وهددت أكثر من إحدى وخمسين عشيرة عربية وكردية بالسيطرة على المدينة بقوة السلاح

2 "More than 51 Arab and Kurdish clans threatened to take over the city by force of arms."
(*al-Ḥayāt*, Oct. 31, 2005)

٣ ومات هيغل بمرض الكوليرا عام 1831، وعمره واحد وستون عاماً فقط.

3 "Hegel died of cholera in 1831 at only 61 years old."
(*al-Sharq al-Awsaṭ*, Aug. 1, 2010)

٤ عندما توفي ج.ر.ر. تولكين في ١٩٧٣ عن إحدى وثمانين سنة . . .

4 "When J.R.R. Tolkein died in 1973 at 81 years of age . . ."
(*al-Ḥayāt*, May 18, 2007)

٥ . . . القائمة العراقية التي يرأسها رئيس الوزراء السابق إياد علاوي والتي فازت بالانتخابات الماضية بعد أن جمعت واحدا وتسعين مقعدا . . .

5 ". . . the Iraqi National List, which is headed by former Prime Minister Iyad Allawi and which won the last election after gaining 91 seats . . ."
(*al-Sharq al-Awsaṭ*, Apr. 16, 2010)

٦ ومعه من النقباء قحطبة بن شبيب والقاسم بن مُجاشع وطلحة بن رزيق؛ و من الشيعة واحد وأربعون رجلا . . . وحمل أثقاله على واحد وعشرين بغلا

6 "With him from among the Abbasid agents were Qaḥṭaba ibn Shabīb, Qāsim ibn Mujāshiʿ, and Ṭalḥa ibn Zurayq and forty-one men from the Shi'a . . . and he loaded his baggage onto twenty-one mules."
(Ṭabari, *Tārikh*, 7/362)

٧ وَاختُلِفَ في اسمِهِ على أَحَدٍ وَعِشْرِينَ قَولاً

7 "Twenty-one different opinions regarding his name were disputed."
(Yāqūt, *Muʿjam al-Udabāʾ*, 3/346, #427 on Zabbān ibn al-ʿAlāʾ)

٨ ومنهم من يجعله بعد ذلك باحدى وعشرين سنة

8 "There are those who say it is twenty-one years after that."
(Bīrūni, *al-Qānun al-Masʿūdi*, 1/171)

٩ لم تكن المأساة واحدة واربعين دقيقة، بل كانت واحدا واربعين عاما

9 The tragedy was not forty-one minutes, it was forty-one years.
(libyaalmostakbal.net, Sept. 1, 2010)

Ordinal[14]

The ordinal "twenty-first" (or "thirty-first," "forty-first," etc.) is rendered as shown in table 1.8 (where any of the عقود may be used in place of عشرين/عشرون).

Table 1.8 Tens Plus One

	Masculine	Feminine
مرفوع	الحادي والعشرونَ	الحادِيَةُ والعِشرونَ
منصوب	الحادِيَ والعِشرينَ	الحادِيَةَ والعِشرينَ
مجرور	الحادي والعِشرينَ	الحادِيَةِ والعِشرينَ

These consist of two elements, the عقد and the "first."

The "first," when feminine, takes a *tāʾ marbuta* and receives all three vowel endings.

14. Also see "More on Ordinal Numbers," p. 110.

As with all of the tens, there is no difference in form between the cardinal and the ordinal of the عقد.

The عقد varies with regard to case, but not gender. The *fatḥa* on the *nūn* at the end is invariable.

These function as adjectives: They follow the nouns they describe and agree with them in case, gender, and definiteness.

The حادي in the masculine is in the category of the منقوص. Therefore, when it is definite, it takes a *fatḥa* when in the منصوب case and no vowel ending in the مرفوع or مجرور cases.

Note that the models given in the table above are all definite. In the event that these are used to describe an indefinite noun, the definite article would be removed from both elements. The "one" in the masculine would follow the rules of the منقوص and become حادِيًا وعشرين in the منصوب case, حادٍ وعشرون in the مرفوع, and حادٍ وعشرين in the مجرور.

Less commonly, واحد and واحدة may be used in place of حادٍ and حادية:

الواحد والعشرون

الواحدة والعشرون

EXAMPLES

١ وفي القرن الحادي والعشرين صار النشر كتابة وصورا وصوتا وفيديو

1 "In the twenty-first century, publishing has turned into (the publishing of) writing, pictures, audio, and video."
(*al-Sharq al-Awsaṭ*, Apr. 24, 2011)

٢ ماتَ بخوارزم يومَ الثلاثاءِ الحادِيَ والعِشرينَ من جمادى الأُولى

2 "He died in Khwarizm on Tuesday, the 21st of Jumāda I."
(Yāqūt, *Muʿjam al-Udabāʾ*, 5/546, #977 on Nāṣir ibn ʿAbd al-Sayyid ibn ʿAli)

٣ جاءت قمة مجلس التعاون الخليجي الحادية والثلاثون التي عقدت في أبو ظبي في الأسبوع الماضي بعد مرور ما يقرب من ثلاثة عقود على مجلس التعاون الخليجي

3 "The thirty-first Gulf Cooperation Council summit, held in Abu Dhabi last week, came after the passage of almost thirty years since (the founding of) the GCC."
(*al-Waṭan* [Kuwait], Apr. 21, 2011)

٤ المصري أسامة عثمان يفوز بسيارة مرسيدس في السحب الحادي والثلاثين لحملة اشتراكات «جريدة الاتحاد»

4 "Egyptian Osama Osman wins a Mercedes in the 31st drawing of *al-Ittiḥād* newspaper's subscription drive."
(*al-Ittiḥād* [UAE], Jan. 25, 2010)

٥ ومات في السنةِ الحاديةِ والأربعينَ من ملكه

5 "He died in the forty-first year of his reign."
(*al-Kitāb al-Muqaddas*, Akhbār al-Ayyām al-Thāni [2 Chronicles] 16:13)

٦ . . . في مطلع القرن الواحد والعشرين . . .

6 ". . . at the dawn of the twenty-first century . . ."
(*al-Ḥawādith*, Nov. 23–29, 2001)

٧ الدورة الواحدة والستون من مهرجان برلين السينمائي تجمع بين الفن والسياسة

7 "The sixty-first edition of the Berlin International Film Festival brings together art and politics."
(*al-Sharq al-Awsaṭ*, Feb. 10, 2011)

Tens Plus Two (22, 32, 42, 52, 62, 72, 82, 92)

Cardinal

Tens plus two is as shown in table 1.9 (where any عقد may substitute for عشرين/عشرون).

Table 1.9 Tens Plus Two, Cardinal

	Masculine	Feminine
مرفوع	اِثْنانِ وَعِشْرونَ	اِثْنَتانِ وَعِشْرونَ
منصوب\مجرور	اِثْنَينِ وَعِشْرينَ	اِثْنَتَينِ وَعِشْرينَ

Note: As with any of the tens, عشرون and its fellow عقود do not vary with regard to gender, but take the ـونَ ending in the مرفوع case and the ـينَ ending in the منصوب and مجرور cases.

The vowel on the *nūn* at the end of the عقد is invariable: It remains *fatḥa* at all times regardless of case and is never nunated. The vowel on the *nūn* at the end of the first element "two" is also invariable: It remains *kasra* regardless of case and is never nunated. The initial *hamza* of the "two" is a *hamzat waṣl*.

The counted noun following these is a تمييز and is therefore singular and منصوب.

EXAMPLES

١ خاض أهله نحو اثنتين وعشرين معركة ضد الحملة الفرنسية

1 "Its people plunged into something like 22 battles against the French campaign."
(*al-Ḥayāt*, Feb. 16, 2011)

٢ اقل من اثنين وعشرين يوما

2 ". . . less than twenty-two days . . ."
(Bīrūni, *al-Qānūn al-Mas'ūdi*, 1/248)

٣ وطولها اثنتان وثلاثون درجة وثلثان

3 "Its longitude is thirty-two and two-thirds degrees."
(Yāqūt, *Mu'jam al-Buldān*, 3/293, #6631 on Sumaysāṭ)

٤ يكفي يا سيدي اثنان وثلاثون عاما وأنت تحكم اليمن

4 "Thirty-two years, sir, of your ruling Yemen is plenty."
(*al-Sharq*, Feb. 22, 2011)

٥ وبعد اثنين وخمسين عاما، رفض عرفات عرضا مماثلا

5 "After fifty-two years, Arafat rejected a similar offer."
(*al-Ṭalī'a*, Apr. 13–19, 2002)

٦ . . . وقد بلغ من السن اثْنَتَيْنِ وَسَبْعِينَ سنةً وستة أشهر وعشرة أيام

6 ". . . having reached the age of 72 years, 6 months, and 10 days."
(Yāqūt, *Mu'jam al-Udabā'*, 4/41, #565 on Ibn 'Asākir)

٧ فقد مضى على ظهور الدعوة—دعوة الشيخ محمد بن عبد الوهاب اثنتان وتسعون سنة

7 "Ninety-two years have passed since the beginning of the missionary activity, the missionary activity of Sheikh Muhammad Abd al-Wahhab."
(*al-Riyāḍ*, Sept. 1, 2006, citing Munīr al-'Ajlāni's *al-Imām Turki ibn 'Abd Allāh*, p. 44, quoting a letter from Ibrahim Pasha to his son Muhammad Ali Pasha)

Thintān + Tens

In classical texts, ثِنتانِ in the مرفوع case and ثِنْتَينِ in the منصوب and مجرور cases are sometimes used with the tens instead of اثنتان/اثنتين when the counted noun is feminine.

١) فهي ثنتان وعشرون فرقة، ثنتان منها ليستا من فرق الإسلام

1 "That makes twenty-two sects, two of which are not sects of Islam."
(Baghdādī, *al-Farq Bayn al-Firaq*, p. 38)

٢) وكان عمره يوم مات النبي صلى الله عليه وسلم ثِنْتَين وعشرين سنة

2 "His age the day the Prophet (peace be upon him) died was 22 years."
(Ibn Kathīr, *al-Bidāya wa-l-Nihāya*, 12/234)

٣) اختلف من كان قبلنا على ثنتين وسبعين فرقة

3 "Those who came before us divided into 72 sects."
(Zamakhshari, *al-Fāʾiq*, 1/40)

Ordinal[15]

The ordinal of tens plus two is as shown in table 1.10 (where any عقد may be used in place of عشرون/عشرين).

Table 1.10 Tens Plus Two, Ordinal

	Masculine	Feminine
مرفوع	الثاني والعِشرونِ	الثانِيَةُ والعِشرونَ
منصوب	الثانيَ والعِشرينَ	الثانِيَةَ والعِشرينَ
مجرور	الثاني والعِشرينَ	الثانِيةِ والعِشرينَ

Note: As with all معطوف numbers, these consist of two elements: the "ten" (عقد) and the "second."

The "second," when feminine, takes a *tāʾ marbuta* and receives all three vowel endings.

---

15. Also see the section "More on Ordinal Numbers," p. 110.

As with all of the tens, there is no difference in shape between the cardinal and the ordinal of the عقد.

The عقد varies with regard to case, but not gender. The *fatḥa* on the *nūn* at the end is invariable. That is, it remains *fatḥa* regardless of case and is never nunated.

These ordinals, as any, function as adjectives: They follow the nouns they describe and agree with them in case, gender, and definiteness.

The ثاني in the masculine is in the category of the منقوص and, as such, takes a *fatḥa* in the منصوب case and no vowel ending in the مرفوع or مجرور.

Note that the items given in the table above are all definite. In the event that these are used to describe an indefinite noun, then the definite article would be removed from both elements. Also, the "second" when masculine follows the rules of the منقوص, and becomes ثانيًا وعشرين in the منصوب case, ثانٍ وعشرون in the مرفوع, and ثانٍ وعشرين in the مجرور.

EXAMPLES

١ وكنتُ في السنةِ الثانيةِ والثلاثينَ من عمري

1 "And I was 32 (in the 32nd year of my life)."
(Yāqūt, *Mu'jam al-Udabā'*, 4/256, #633 on 'Ali ibn Muḥammad al-Tanūkhi)

٢ الفوز الثاني والأربعون لبوسطن

2 "Boston's 42nd victory . . ."
(*al-Jarīda*, Feb. 28, 2011)

٣ شمبانزي يحتفل بعيد ميلاده الثاني والخمسين

3 "A Chimpanzee Celebrates His 52nd Birthday"
(*al-Riyāḍ*, Jan. 26, 2011)

٤ ومهرجان ((كان)) لمن لا يعرف انطلقت دورته الثانية والستون في ١٣ من الشهر الماضي

4 "The sixty-second edition of the Cannes (Film) Festival, for those who don't know, began on the 13th of last month."
(*al-Ḥayāt*, June 14, 2009)

٥ قائمة الترشيحات لجوائز الأوسكار الثانية والثمانين

5 "List of Nominations for the 82nd Oscars"
(*al-Sharq al-Awsaṭ*, Mar. 2, 2010)

Tens Plus Three Through Nine

Cardinal

The numbers 23–99 (not counting tens or tens plus one or two) are formed with the units first, followed by وَ (and), and then the tens (العقد).

ثلاثة وعشرين "23"

The units (3–9) in this construction are indefinite and therefore take *tanwīn*. This differs from their use in counting 3–9, where they are مضاف and therefore take no *tanwīn*.

The rules of polar agreement apply to this element (the units 3–9) of the number (see p. 14).

Note that ثمانٍ is in the category of nouns known as منقوص. Therefore, when describing a feminine counted noun, it is ثمانٍ in the مرفوع and مجرور cases and ثمانيًا in the منصوب.

في الشارع ثمانٍ وعشرون بناية.

"There are 28 buildings on the street."

قرأتُ ثمانياً وعشرين مقالة. "I read 28 articles."

The عقد has the same case as 3–9 and carries the ـونَ ending in the مرفوع and the ـينَ ending in the منصوب and مجرور. The *nūn* at the end of the عقد has an invariable *fatḥa*, which remains a single *fatḥa* regardless of definiteness. It is never nunated.

The counted noun following the number is a تمييز, so it is singular and in the منصوب case.

EXAMPLES

١ وسأشتغل بادئ الأمر بيومية مقدارها خمسة وعشرون قرشا

1 "I'll work at the beginning for a daily pay of 25 piastres."
(Naguib Mahfuz, *Zuqāq al-Midaqq*, p. 84)

٢ فقد ذكرت في النص القرآني ثمانيا وثلاثين مرة

2 "It is mentioned in the text of the Qur'an 38 times."
('Ushayri, *al-Taṣawwur al-Lughawi 'ind al-Ismā'īliyya*, p. 302)

٣ وقد روى عنه أربعًا وأربعين رواية

3 "He transmitted information from him 44 times."
(Shawqi Ḍayf, *al-Madāris al-Naḥwiyya*, p. 81)

٤ كتاب الإشراف على معرفة الأطراف ثَمانِيَةٌ وَأَرْبَعونَ جزءًا

4 "The book *al-Ishrāf ʿala Maʿrifat al-Aṭrāf* is 48 volumes."
(Yāqūt, *Muʿjam al-Udabāʾ*, 4/42, #565 on Ibn ʿAsākir)

٥ وطول سميساط أربع وخمسون درجة وثلثان وعرضها ست وثلاثون درجة وثلث

5 "The longitude of Sumaysāṭ is 54 degrees and one-third, and the latitude is 36 degrees and one-third."
(Yāqūt, *Muʿjam al-Buldān*, 3/293, #6631 on Sumaysāṭ)

٦ . . . لأن الفراء عاش ثلاثا وستين سنة

6 ". . . because Farraʾ lived 63 years."
(Farrāʾ, *Maʿāni al-Qurʾān*, p. 7, introduction by Najjār, M. and Najāti, A.)

٧ طفولته التي رافقته ثمانيا وستين سنة . . .

7 "His childhood, which stayed with him for sixty-eight years . . ."
(*al-Ḥayāt*, Oct. 3, 2003)

٨ . . . وتفترق أمتي على ثلاث وسبعين فرقةً

8 ". . . and my community will divide into seventy-three sects."
(*Sunan Abi Dāwūd*, 7/5, #4596)

٩ . . . وتغل عليه آخر الشهر خمسة وسبعين قرشًا

9 ". . . and which yields him at the end of the month 75 piastres."
(Taha Hussein, *al-Ayyām*, 2/55)

١٠ طولها ثمان وسبعون درجة ونصف، وعرضها تسع وعشرون درجة ونصف

10 "Its longitude is 78 degrees and a half, and its latitude is 29 degrees and a half."
(Yāqūt, *Muʿjam al-Buldān*, 3/431, #7386 on Shīrāz)

١١ ماتَ . . . ودُفِنَ في داره وعمره تِسعٌ وثَمانونَ سنةً ونصفٌ

11 "He died . . . and was buried in his house at the age of 89 years and a half."
(Yāqūt, *Muʿjam al-Udabāʾ*, 4/188, #615 on ʿAli ibn ʿĪsa ibn Dāwūd ibn al-Jarrāḥ)

١٢ تم احتلال سبع وثمانين قرية أخرى

12 "87 other villages were occupied."
(*al-Ḥayāt*, Apr. 26, 2007)

١٣ وجاء قرار الجمعية للأمم المتحدة بتأييد ثمان وتسعين دولة

13 "The resolution of the U.N. (General) Assembly came with the support of 98 countries."
(*al-Riyāḍ*, Feb. 27, 2010)

Using "Minus"

A number just under one hundred might occasionally be expressed using 100 followed by a particle meaning "minus" or "but," such as إلا or غير, and then followed by the difference between the desired number and 100.

EXAMPLE

١ وكان داود عليه السلام تزوج مائة امرأة غير امرأة

1 "David had married 99 women (100 women save one)."
(Rāzi, *Kitāb al-Zīna*, 263v)

Note on *thamāniya*:

The pattern of the word ثماني is of the same shape as words of the plural pattern known as صيغة منتهى الجموع. Therefore, it might occasionally be treated as a ممنوع من الصرف and, when part of a معطوف, take no *tanwīn* in the منصوب case.[16]

Contrast this with the treatment of ثمانٍ seen above, where it is not treated as ممنوع من الصرف.

EXAMPLES

١ فبلغت جميع مدن لاوي في وسط أرض بني إسرائيل ثَمَانِيَ وأربعين مدينةً بمراعيها

1 "The total number of Levite cities within the land of the Israelites was 48 cities along with their pasture lands."
(*al-Kitāb al-Muqaddas*, Yashūʿ [Joshua] 21:41)

---

16. According to ʿAbbās Ḥasan, ثماني can be treated as a ممنوع من الصرف, as it is on the same pattern as other words in this category. In this case, the indefinite منصوب would receive a single *fatḥa* but no *tanwīn* on the *yāʾ*, (ثَمَانِيَ). Alternately, it can be treated as a منقوص that is not ممنوع من الصرف, in which case the منصوب would take a *tanwīn fatḥ*. In both cases, whether treated as ممنوع من الصرف or not, the مرفوع and the مجرور would be ثمانٍ. See Ḥasan, *al-Naḥw al-Wāfī*, 4/537, n. 2.

٢ وكان هناك رجل مريض من ثمانٍ وثلاثينَ سنةً

2 "There was a man there who had been sick for 38 years."
(*al-Kitāb al-Muqaddas*, Yūḥanna [John] 5:5)

٣ وكانت أيّام ملكه بالسامرة ثَمانِيَ وعشرينَ سنةً

3 "The time of his rule in Samarria was 28 years."
(*al-Kitāb al-Muqaddas*, al-Mulūk al-Thāni [2 Kings] 10:36)

Thamānī: Same form regardless of case

Sometimes writers simply use ثماني in all معطوف numbers, regardless of the grammatical case.

EXAMPLES

١ يأخذك في رحلة تمتد ثماني وخمسين دقيقة إلى الكثير من الأماكن

1 "In a 58-minute journey, it takes you to many places."
(*al-Sharq al-Awsaṭ*, Jan. 11, 2010)

٢ أبو علي يطا يتنسم الحرية بعد ثماني وعشرين عاما خلف القضبان

2 "Abu ʿAli Yatta breathes in freedom after 28 years behind bars."
(*al-Quds*, Aug. 26, 2008)

٣ ثماني وعشرون ضحية حتى الآن فقدوا حياتهم ينتظرون على الجانب المصري من المعبر

3 "Twenty-eight victims now have lost their lives waiting on the Egyptian side of the crossing."
(*al-Ayyām*, July 9, 2007)

Ordinal[17]

The ordinals for these consist of the ordinal version of the unit, followed by وَ (and), and then followed by the ordinal of the ten, which is the same as the ten itself.

الخامس والسبعون "the 75th"

The compound ordinal number follows the word it describes and agrees with it in definiteness. When definite, both parts

17. Also see the section "More on Ordinal Numbers," p. 110.

of the compound take the definite article الـ. If it were to describe an indefinite noun, both would be without الـ.

The 3–9 element, being an ordinal, is not subject to polar agreement (see p. 14), so it follows the described noun in gender as well as in case and definiteness.

The عقد, as all ordinal عقود, does not change with gender. It takes the same grammatical case as the unit, and takes the ـونَ ending when مرفوع and the ـينَ ending when منصوب or مجرور. The *fatḥa* on the *nūn* is invariable: It is always *fatḥa* regardless of case and is never nunated:

هذه هي الصفحةُ السابعةُ والعشرون "This is the 27th page."

قرأتُ الصفحةَ السابعةَ والعشرين "I read the 27th page."

وراء الباب السابعِ والعشرينَ "behind the 27th door"

EXAMPLES

١ وأول يوم من السنة عند القبط هو اليوم التاسع والعشرون من شهر آب

1 "The first day of the year for the Copts is the 29th day of the month of August."
(*Mas'ūdi, Murūj al-Dhahab*, 2/195)

٢ احتفلت جامعة البصرة الاربعاء الاول من نيسان الجاري بالذكرى الخامسة والاربعين لتأسيسها

2 "Basra University, on Wednesday the first of this April, celebrated the 45th anniversary of its founding."
(aljadidah.com, Apr. 5, 2009)

٣ في ختام اجتماعه السابع والستين . . .

3 "At the end of its 67th meeting . . ."
(*al-Wasaṭ* [Bahrain], Feb. 25, 2011)

٤ في دورتها الرابعة والخمسين بالمغرب . . .

4 "In its 54th session in Morocco . . ."
(aljazeera.net, Jan. 9, 2011)

٥ بعد الاطلاع على المادة الثامنة والخمسين من النظام الأساسي . . . أمرنا بما هو آت . . .

5 "After reviewing the 58th article of the Basic Law . . . we hereby order the following:"
(*al-Ḥayāt*, Apr. 25, 2011)

٦ والصنف الثالث والعشرون من الرافضة: يسوقون الإمامة من علي إلى ((موسى بن جعفر))

6 "The twenty-third category of Rafidites traces the imamate from ʿAli to Mūsa ibn Jaʿfar."
(Ashʿari, *Maqālat al-Islāmiyyin*, p. 42)

٧ مات في اليومِ الثامنِ والعشرينَ من ربيعٍ الأولِ

7 "He died on the 28th day of Rabīʿ I."
(Yāqūt, *Muʿjam al-Udabāʾ*, 5/590, #1011 on Hibat Allāh ibn Ṣāʿid)

٨ ورجح . . . مذهب الكوفيين في سبع مسائل هي العاشرة . . . والسادسة والعشرون . . . والسابعة والتسعون . . .

8 "He preferred the views of the Kufans regarding seven issues. They are the tenth, . . . the 26th, the 97th . . ."
(Shawqi Ḍayf, *al-Madāris al-Naḥwiyya*, p. 278)

One Hundred

Cardinal

"One hundred" is مِائَة.

Note that it contains a silent *alif*, which is generally not pronounced. The pronunciation is *miʾa*. Nonetheless, some, under the influence of the orthography, pronounce مائة as *māʾa*.[18]

---

18. Many classical scholars expressed the opinion that مائة is written with a silent *alif* to distinguish it from منه, since in the days before dots and vowel markings the two would have had an identical shape: مىه. Ibn Qutayba implies that the two are more likely than other pairs to appear in the same contexts, as he says that the *alif* would be needed to distinguish أخذت منه from أخذت مئة. See Ibn Qutayba, *Adab al-Kātib*, p. 177, and Ulrich Haarmann, "An eleventh century précis of Arabic orthography" in Wadad Al-Qadi (ed.), *Studia arabica & islamica: Festschrift für Ihsan Abbas on his sixtieth birthday*. Beirut: American University of Beirut, 1981, 165–182.

Some orientalists believed the alif in مائة was nothing more than the result of sloppiness on the part of Qurʾanic scribes. See, for example, Wright, *Grammar*, 1/258, and Nöldeke, *Beitrage*, p. 153.

Though the inclusion of the silent *alif* is a constant in classical texts, in modern times it is also frequently written without the silent *alif*: مِئة. This spelling has been approved by the Cairo Arabic Language Academy.[19]

مائة is invariable with regard to gender. It remains مائة regardless of whether the counted noun is feminine or masculine.

The counted noun is singular and indefinite, follows مائة, and is in an إضافة relationship with it. Thus, the case of مائة is determined by its position in the sentence and, being a مضاف, it takes no *tanwīn*. The following counted noun will be indefinite and in the مجرور case.

أعرف مائةَ وزيرٍ. "I know 100 ministers."

فيها مائةُ صفحةٍ. "It has 100 pages."

EXAMPLES

١ فإن صلى وعليه صوم؟ قال: يعيد، ولو صلى مائةَ يَوْمٍ

1 "'And if he prays while he has ostrich droppings on him?' He said, 'Then he must repeat the prayer, even if he prayed for 100 days.'"
(Ḥarīri, *Maqāmāt*, p. 334, 'Al-Ṭayyibiyya')

٢ . . . وأنا اليوم لا أقوم على حفظِ مِائَةِ حديثٍ

2 ". . . and today I can't even remember 100 Hadiths."
(Yāqūt, *Mu'jam al-Udabā'*, 3/538, #534 on 'Ali ibn Ibrāhīm al-Qaṭṭān al-Qazwīni)

٣ . . . كيف تحتفظ بشبابك مائة عام

3 ". . . how to preserve your youth for 100 years."
(Naguib Mahfouz, *al-Ṭarīq*, p. 219)

٤ أمريكي يقفز بالمظلة احتفالاً ببلوغه مائة سنة

4 "An American skydives to celebrate reaching 100 years (of age)."
(*al-Waṭan* [Bahrain], Mar. 22, 2011)

٥ من بين مائة طبيب أو يزيد يصبح هو، الزعيم، أحقرهم

5 "Out of a hundred doctors or more, he, the head, becomes the most despised."
(Yūsuf Idrīs, *al-'Askari al-Aswad*, p. 23)

19. See Ḥasan, *al-Naḥw al-Wāfi*, 4/518, n. 3.

٦ إعلان قائمة أكثر مئة جامعة مرموقة على مستوى العالم

6 "The Announcement of the 100 Most Prestigious Universities Worldwide"
(*al-Quds*, Mar. 10, 2011)

Ordinal[20]

The ordinal for one hundred takes the same exact form as the cardinal.

It functions as an adjective to the noun described and, as such, follows it and agrees with it in case and definiteness.

It does not vary according to gender.

هذه هي المرةُ المائةُ. "This is the 100th time."

كنتُ الخريجَ المائةَ. "I was the 100th graduate."

EXAMPLES

١ أول أيامه في السنة المائة من عمره المديد . . .

1 "The first days of the hundredth year of his long life . . ."
(*al-Maṣri al-Yawm*, Jan. 10, 2011)

٢ بلغ اضرابه عن الطعام يومه المئة

2 "His hunger strike has reached its hundredth day."
(*al-Riyāḍ*, Apr. 18, 2007)

٣ هذه فهرست الأنواع بعد المقدمة: . . . المائة: المبهمات

3 "This is a list of the chapters after the introduction: . . . The hundredth is (on) those mentioned in the Qurʾan whose names are not given."
(Suyūṭi, *al-Itqān fī ʿUlūm al-Qurʾān*, pp. 20–23, introduction)

20. Also see "More on Ordinal Numbers," p. 110.

Two Hundred

Cardinal

Two hundred is مِائَتانِ in the مرفوع case and مِائَتَينِ in the منصوب and مجرور cases.

However, as with any dual, the final *nūn* is dropped when it occurs as a مضاف. All hundreds occur as مضاف with their counted nouns, therefore مائتان and مائتين lose their *nūns* when followed by a counted noun.

The counted noun, as with all hundreds, is singular and indefinite. It is in the مجرور case, as it is a مضاف إليه.

فيها مائتا صفحةٍ. "It has 200 pages."

قرأتُ مائتَيْ صفحةٍ. "I read 200 pages."

When مائتانِ and مائتَيْنِ are written alone, with no counted noun, the *nūn* is retained, and, as with all duals, has a *kasra* regardless of grammatical case. The *kasra* is never nunated, regardless of the definiteness or indefiniteness of the word.

As with one hundred, the *alif* in مائتان and مائتين is silent (see p. 50). Both can be written without the silent *alif*, whether the *nūn* is dropped or not.

مئتان/مئتين

EXAMPLES

١ كيلو قمح أم مائتا جالون ماء!؟

1 "A kilo of wheat or 200 gallons of water?!"
(*al-Riyāḍ*, Aug. 25, 2007)

٢ رحت أقلب صفحات الدوسيه الكثيرة أكثر من مائتى صفحة

2 "I started flipping through the many pages of the dossier—more than 200 pages."
(Yūsuf Idrīs, *al-ʿAskari al-Aswad*, p. 32)

٣ ولم يبق من أيام العز كلها سوى مائتى جنيه في صندوق التوفير بالبريد

3 "Nothing remained from the glory days except for two hundred pounds in the safe deposit box at the post office."
(Yūsuf Idrīs, *al-ʿAskari al-Aswad*, p. 71)

٤ وقد نقل عنه أكثر من مائتى مرة

4 "He transmitted information from him more than 200 times."
(Shawqi Ḍayf, *al-Madāris al-Naḥwiyya*, p. 81)

٥ وقد تكرر في سورة يونس من الكلم الواقع فيها الراء مائتا كلمة، أو أكثر

5 "The number of words containing the letter *rā'* which occur in *sūrat Yūnus* is 200 words or more."
(Suyūṭi, *al-Itqān fī 'Ulūm al-Qur'ān*, p. 733, *naw'* 62)

٦ مئتا قتيل على الأقل في انفجار صهريج الوقود في الكونغو الديمقراطية . . .

6 "At least 200 killed in a fuel tanker explosion in the Democratic Republic of Congo . . ."
(*al-Quds*, July 3, 2010)

٧ ولو تمّ كان مقدارُهُ مِائَتَيْ جُزْءٍ أو أكثر

7 "If it had been completed it would have been 200 volumes or more."
(Yāqūt, *Mu'jam al-Udabā'*, 4/44, #565 on Ibn 'Asākir)

Ordinal[21]

The ordinal of 200, as is the case for all hundreds as well as a thousand, takes the same exact form as the cardinal. "200th" is مائتان in the مرفوع case and مائتين in the منصوب and مجرور cases. Since they are no longer in an إضافة relationship with a counted noun, the *nūn* is retained. As does the *nūn* on all duals, it takes an invariable, single *kasra*.

It functions as an adjective to the noun described and, as such, follows it and agrees with it in case and definiteness.

It does not vary according to gender.

وصلت إلى الصفحةِ المائتين. "I got to the 200th page."

دخل الزبون المائتان. "The 200th customer entered."

21. Also see "More on Ordinal Numbers," p. 110.

EXAMPLES

١ المادة المئتان

1 "Article 200" (lit., "the 200th article")
(from the Saudi labor statute, issued by royal decree m/51)

٢ الاحتفال بالذكرى المائتين للثورة الأرجنتينية

2 "Celebration of the 200th Anniversary of the Argentine Revolution"
(*al-Maṣri al-Yawm*, May 27, 2010)

Three Hundred Through Nine Hundred

Cardinal

The numbers from 300 to 900 are as shown in table 1.11.

Table 1.11 Hundreds

	المرفوع	المنصوب	المجرور
300	ثَلاثُمِائة	ثَلاثَمِائة	ثَلاثِمِائة
400	أَرْبَعُمِائة	أَرْبَعَمِائة	أَرْبَعِمِائة
500	خَمْسُمِائة	خَمْسَمِائة	خَمْسِمِائة
600	سِتُّمِائة	سِتَّمِائة	سِتِّمِائة
700	سَبْعُمِائة	سَبْعَمِائة	سَبْعِمِائة
800[a]	ثَمانُمِائة	ثَمانَمِائة	ثَمانِمِائة
900	تِسْعُمِائة	تِسْعَمِائة	تِسْعِمِائة

a. See also "Special note on 800," p. 57.

Notes: Note that the number consists of two elements: the number 3–9, followed by مائة.

They are written as one word, but are also sometimes written as two separate words:

ثلاث مائة

أربع مائة

خمس مائة

ثمان مائة, etc.

As with all the hundreds, the *alif* in مائة is silent (see p. 50), and the مائة can be written without the *alif*, whether separated from the 3–9 or not: أربع مئة, خمسمئة, ثمانمئة, سبع مئة, etc.

ثلاثمائة, whether separated or not, is sometimes written without the *alif*: ثلثمائة or ثلث مائة. When this is the case, it should still be pronounced as if the *alif* were present.

Whether separated or not, the 3–9 element takes the appropriate case ending determined by the word's position in the sentence. As it is in an إضافة relationship with the following مائة, it takes a single *ḍamma*, *fatḥa*, or *kasra*; that is, it is never nunated. The attached مائة is always مجرور since it is a مضاف إليه.

مائة in turn is in an إضافة relationship with the counted noun. The مائة therefore has only a single *kasra*, and the following counted noun is singular, indefinite, and in the مجرور case.

قرأت ثلاثمائةِ كتابٍ. "I read 300 books."

EXAMPLES

١ فبلغت أقلَّ من ثلاثمِائةِ دينارٍ

1 "It reached less than 300 dinars."
(Yāqūt, *Mu'jam al-Udabā'*, 2/68, #206 Tha'lab)

٢ ثلاثمائة رجل، يزيدون قليلا أو ينقصون

2 "300 men, give or take . . ."
(Tawfiq al-Hakim, *Muḥammad*, p. 155)

٣ . . . فوجد ذلك أكثر من أربعِمائة عنزٍ

3 ". . . and he found it to be more than 400 goats."
(Ibn Muqaffa', *Kalīla wa Dimna*, pp. 288–289)

٤ وذهب خَمْسُ مئَةِ رجلٍ من بني شِمعون شرقًا إلى جبل سعير وعلى رأسهم بنو يشعي

4 "Five hundred men from among the Simeonites went east to the mountain of Seir with the sons of Ishi at their head."
(*al-Kitāb al-Muqaddas*, Akhbār al-Ayyām al-Awwal [1 Chronicles] 4:42)

٥ . . . أن يهلك الرجل ويترك ابنين له، ويترك سِتَّمِائَةِ دينارٍ فيأخذ كل واحد منهما ثَلاثَمِائَةِ دينارٍ

5 ". . . for a man to die and leave two sons, and leave 600 dinars. Each one one of them will take 300 dinars."
(Mālik ibn Anas, *al-Muwaṭṭa'*, 741)

٦ إن ما بين شحمة أذُنِه إلى عاتِقِه مسيرةُ سبع مئةِ عام

6 "The distance between his earlobe and shoulder is a 700-year walk."
(*Sunan Abi Dāwūd*, p. 109, #4727)

٧ . . . فأخبرني أن عنده أسرتين، وأكثر من عشرة أبناء، ودخله في الشهر ثمانمائة ريال فحسب

7 ". . . and he told me that he has two families, and more than ten children, and that his monthly income is only 800 riyals."
('Ā'iḍ al-Qarni, *Lā Taḥzan*, p. 274)

٨ نقل تسعمئة سجين أردني لسجن جديد لتخفيف الاكتظاظ

8 "The transfer of 900 Jordanian prisoners to a new prison to ease overcrowding."
(aljazeera.net, May 30, 2007)

Special Note on Eight Hundred

ثمانمائة, as any other hundred, receives its case ending at the end of the first of the two elements, that is, on the *nūn* of ثمان.

ثمانُمائة

ثمانَمائة

ثمانِمائة

EXAMPLES

١ وقيل إنه ثمانُمائةِ كُرّاسةٍ

1 "And it has been said that it is (made up of) 800 fascicles."
(Yāqūt, *Mu'jam al-Udabā'*, 1/426, #100 on Abu-l-'Alā' al-Ma'arri)

٢ والنسخة الجديدة ثَمَانُمِائَةِ جزءٍ

2 "The new version is (made up of) 800 sections."
(Yāqūt, *Mu'jam al-Udabā'*, 4/42, #565 on Ibn 'Asākir)

٣ وبلغت على عهد رسول الله صلى الله عليه وسلم ما بين أربع مئةِ دينارٍ إلى ثمانِ مئةِ دينارٍ.

3 "And in the time of the Prophet (peace be upon him), it reached between 400 and 800 dinars."
(*Sunan Abi Dāwūd*, 6/620, #4564)

٤ قلت: كم كنتم يومئذ؟ قال: سبعَ مئة أو ثمانَ مئة

4 "I said, 'How many were you that day?' He said, '700 or 800.'"
(*Sunan Abi Dāwūd*, 7/124, #4746)

٥ أعطه ثَمانَمِائةِ دِرهمٍ

5 "Give him 800 dirhams."
(Mālik ibn Anas, *al-Muwaṭṭa'*, p. 748)

٦ كان طول عوج ثمانَمائة ذراع

6 "Og's height was 800 cubits."
(Ṭabari, *Tārīkh*, 1/431)

٧ وقتل فيها ثمانُمائة شخص حسبما أعلن الصليب الأحمر الدولي

7 "Eight-hundred people were killed in it, according to the International Red Cross."
(broadcast on Euronews Arabic, Apr. 6, 2011)

٨ بعد أن استمر ثمانَمائةٍ واثنينِ وسبعينَ يومًا . . .

8 "After it had continued for 872 days . . ."
(broadcast on RT Arabic, Jan. 27, 2010)

Eight Hundred: Fixed kasra

William Wright, author of *A Grammar of the Arabic Language*, appears to believe that the vowel on ثمان should be a fixed *kasra* regardless of case.

ثمانِمائة (*kasra* on the *nūn* regardless of case)

He does not explicitly say this but, in his listing of the hundreds, he gives a *ḍamma* to the 3–9 element in 300–700 and in 900, but ثمان in ثمانِ مائة receives a *kasra*. This is due to the fact that ثمان مائة is a contraction of ثماني مائة.[22] News broadcasters and others can sometimes be heard taking this approach, putting a *kasra* on ثمان regardless of case.

22. Wright, *A Grammar of the Arabic Language*, 1/258.

EXAMPLES

١ من المؤكد أنه يتجاوز ثمانمائة مترٍ.

1 "It is confirmed that it tops 800 meters."
(broadcast on al-Jazeera, Jan. 4, 2010)

٢ . . . الذي يقوم بحمايته ثمانمائة جندي.

2 ". . . which is being protected by 800 soldiers."
(broadcast on Euronews Arabic, Dec. 31, 2010)

Eight Hundred: With fully realized yā'

Wright also states that the correct form for 800 is in fact ثماني مائة. This form is also sometimes seen. In this case, ثماني may be treated as a منقوص: with a *fatḥa* in the منصوب case and no ending on the *yā'* in the مرفوع or مجرور cases.

EXAMPLES

١ وعاش آدم بعدما ولد شيتًا ثمانيَ مئةِ سنةٍ

1 "Adam lived 800 years after begetting Seth."
(*al-Kitāb al-Muqaddas*, al-Takwīn [Genesis] 5:4)

٢ هزّ الرمح على ثماني مئةٍ فقتلهم بمرة واحدة

2 "He wielded his spear against 800 (men) and killed them all at once."
(*al-Kitāb al-Muqaddas*, Ṣamū'īl al-Thānī [2 Samuel] 23:8)

٣ ومن بني أفرايم: عشرون ألفًا وثماني مئةِ جبّارٍ من الجبابرة

3 "From the Ephraimites: twenty-thousand eight-hundred valiant warriors . . ."
(*al-Kitāb al-Muqaddas*, Akhbār al-Ayyām al-Awwal [1 Chronicles] 12:31)

٤ ومضى بعد نوح ثماني مائة سنة

4 "Eight-hundred years passed after Noah."
(*al-Ittiḥād* [UAE], July 23, 2012)

Ordinal[23]

The ordinals for the hundreds take the same exact form as the cardinals.

---

23. Also see "More on Ordinal Numbers," p. 110.

They function as adjectives to the noun described, and, as such, follow it and agree with it in case and definiteness.

They do not vary according to gender.

All of the spelling variations that may apply to the hundreds may also apply when they are being used as ordinals: The *alif* in مائة may be dropped, the two elements of 300–900 may be separated, and ثلاث in ثلاثمائة may be spelled ثلث, in which case it is still pronounced as if the *alif* were present (see p. 56).

The 3–9 element is in an إضافة relationship with the مائة. Therefore, it takes the case ending required by its position in the sentence (it is in agreement with the word described), and never a *tanwīn*.

The مائة is in the مجرور case as it is a مضاف إليه. Since it is not in an إضافة relationship with a following counted noun as it is when used as a cardinal number, it is indefinite. Thus, it takes a *tanwīn kasra*.

قرأت الصفحةَ الستَّمائةٍ. "I read the 600th page."

EXAMPLES

١ الذكرى الأربعمئة لولادة رامبرندت

1 "The 400th Anniversary of the Birth of Rembrandt"
(*al-Riyāḍ*, June 5, 2006)

٢ في السنةِ السِّتِّ مِئَةٍ من عمر نوحٍ . . .

2 "In the 600th year of Noah's life . . ."
(*al-Kitāb al-Muqaddas*, al-Takwīn [Genesis] 7:11)

٣ الذكرى السبعمائة لميلاد ابن بطوطة

3 "The 700th anniversary of the birth of Ibn Battutah"
(from a Moroccan postage stamp, 2004)[24]

24. Retrieved from http://hiwayatcom.canalblog.com

Hundreds Plus One (101, 201, etc.)

Cardinal

To express a multiple of 100 plus one (101, 201, etc.), 100 (or its multiple) units of the counted noun is stated, then the counted noun is repeated in the singular following the conjunction وَ: "one-hundred (noun) and a (noun)."

مائة رجل ورجل "101 men"

The second instance of the counted noun is in the same grammatical case as the مائة or its multiple.

EXAMPLES

١ . . . كما أن تلك الرسوم استقت أفلامها الطويلة الأولى من حكايات الأطفال (مثل . . . «مئة كلب وكلب دلميشن» . . .)

1 ". . . just as those full-length animated films drew inspiration from children's stories, such as . . . *101 Dalamations*."
(*al-Bayān*, Dec. 16, 2008)

٢ . . . أنّ الخليطين يكون لكل واحد منهما مِائَةُ شاةٍ وَشاةٌ . . .

2 ". . . that each of the two associates has 101 sheep . . ."
(Mālik ibn Anas, *al-Muwaṭṭa'*, p. 264)

٣ . . . على بعد أمتار معدودة من موقع الجريمة الإرهابية التي أودت بحياة الرئيس الشهيد رفيق الحريري ورفاقه الأبرار قبل مائة يوم ويوم

3 ". . . just a few meters from the site of the terrorist crime which took the life of the martyred president Rafiq al-Hariri and his innocent companions 101 days ago."
(*al-Sharq al-Awsaṭ*, May 27, 2005)

٤ . . . وحين اجتمع مائة نائب ونائب مجددا من أصل 128 نائبا . . .

4 ". . . and when 101 representatives out of 128 original representatives met anew . . ."
(omandaily.om, Mar. 1, 2010)

٥ الخطوة التالية كانت دفع رسوم التسجيل للمواد, وكلفتها هي مئتا ليرة وليرة واحدة للمادة

5 "The next step was to pay the registration fees for my classes. The cost was 201 liras per class."
(aljaml.com, Aug. 26, 2006)

٦ فكان يأخذ عطاء هشام مائتى دينار ودينارًا

6 "He used to take Hisham's stipend, 201 dinars."
(Ṭabari, *Tārīkh*, 7/202)

٧ وأضاف المسؤولون ان الحزب حصل على مائتين وأربعة عشر مقعدا من إجمالي ثلاثمائة مقعد ومقعد واحد

7 "The official added that the party gained 214 seats out of a total of 301 seats."
(BBC Arabic, bbc.co.uk, May 1, 2003)

٨ فذلك سبعمائة سنة وسنة وأشهر

8 "That is a total of 701 years and some months."
(Ṭabari, *Tārīkh*, 1/292)

Informal

More informally, مائة وواحد is sometimes also used, with the following counted noun in the singular. واحد here does not vary with respect to gender.

EXAMPLE

١ . . . بزاوية داخلية مقدارها (١٠١\٣٠\٥٤) مائة وواحد درجة وثلاثون دقيق واربعة وخمسون ثانية . . .

1 ". . . at an interior angle which measures 101 degrees, 30 minutes, and 54 seconds . . ."
(public announcements section, *al-Yawm*, Apr. 26, 2011)

Ordinal[25]

101st in the masculine is (where any multiple of 100 can be used in place of مائة):

الواحد بعد المائة or الأول بعد المائة

The feminine is:

الواحدة بعد المائة or الأولى بعد المائة

25. Also see the section "More on Ordinal Numbers," p. 110.

EXAMPLES

١ وهذه فهرست الأنواع بعد المقدمة . . . الأول بعد المائة: أسماء من نزل فيهم القرآن

1 "Here is an index of the chapters after the introduction: . . . The 101st is on the names of those about whom the Qur'an was revealed."
(Suyūṭi, *al-Itqān fī 'Ulūm al-Qur'ān*, pp. 20–23, introduction)

٢ المادة الأولى بعد المائة

2 "Article 101 (the 101st article)"
(Law of Procedure before Shari'ah Courts, Saudi Arabia, Royal Decree #M/21, Aug. 19, 2000)

٣ وقال هاتوياما للصحافيين أمس وهو اليوم الاول بعد المائة من بدء ادارته . . .

3 "Hatoyama told reporters yesterday, the 101st day since the beginning of his administration . . ."
(*al-Khalīj*, Dec. 26, 2009)

٤ ورجح . . . مذهب الكوفيين في سبع مسائل هي العاشرة . . . والواحدة والسادسة بعد المائة

4 "He agreed with the Kufans on seven issues: the tenth . . . the 101st and the 106th."
(Shawqi Ḍayf, *al-Madāris al-Nahwiyya*, p. 278)

٥ كاد كلود ليفي شتراوس يكمل العام الواحد بعد المائة

5 "Claude Levi-Strauss almost completed his 101st year."
(*al-Sharq al-Awsaṭ*, Nov. 19, 2009)

٦ المسألة الواحدة بعد المائة

6 "The 101st Issue"
(chapter heading from table of contents of Anbāri, *al-Inṣāf fī Masā'il al-Khilāf*, 2/469)

٧ انتظرت عامها الواحد بعد المائة لتنتحر . . . السيدة كانت هادئة وتتمتع بصحة معقولة رغم إحتفالها بعيد ميلادها الاول بعد المائة منذ شهر

7 "She waited until her 101st year to kill herself. . . . The lady was calm and in decent health despite having just celebrated her 101st birthday a month before."
(sonara.net, Aug. 29, 2010)

Hundreds Plus Two (102, 202, 302, etc.)

Cardinal

To express a multiple of 100 plus 2 (102, 202, etc.), one begins with 100 (or its multiple) units of the counted noun, then the counted noun is repeated in the dual following the conjunction وَ: "one-hundred (noun) and (two nouns)."

مائة امرأة وامرأتان "102 women"

The counted noun in the dual is in the same grammatical case as the مائة or its multiple.

EXAMPLES

١ وقال جايا كومار . . . إن "مائة شخص وشخصين قتلوا"

1 "Jayakumar . . . said that 102 people were killed."
(*al-Sharq*, Jan. 16, 2011)

٢ يلتزم المحامي بدفع رسم سنوي للخزانة يحدد مقداره على النحو التالي: . . . مائة دينار وديناران ممن تجاوز الستين سنة من عمره

2 "Attorneys are obligated to pay a yearly fee to the treasury, the amount of which is set as follows: . . . 102 dinars from those over 60 years of age."
(Amendment 58 [2000] to subarticle 49, article 3 of Jordanian statute 501 [1970] regarding the retirement and social security of attorneys)

٣ وعرضه أربعمائة ميل وميلان

3 "Its width is 402 miles."
(Yāqūt, *Mu'jam al-Buldān*, 1/46, chap. 2 of introduction)

Informal

Less formally, مائة واثنان or مائة واثنين are sometimes used, and اثنان and اثنين are usually invariable with regard to gender.

EXAMPLES

١ إن عدد الدول التي مايكروسوفت فاتحة فيها أفرع, أو تنزل منتجها حوالي مائة واثنين دولة

1 "The number of countries in which Microsoft has opened branches, or sells its products is about 102 countries."
(idaleel.tv, Jan. 20, 2010)

٢ وقد صدر عن مطبعة "اقرأ" بالناظور سنة 2006م في مائة واثنين صفحة (102)

2 "It was published by Iqra press in Nador in 2006, and was 102 pages."
(diwanalarab.com, June 8, 2007)

Ordinal[26]

102nd (where any multiple of 100 may be used in place of مائة), in the masculine is:

الثاني بعد المائة

and in the feminine is:

الثانية بعد المائة

EXAMPLES

١ وهذه فهرست الأنواع بعد المقدمة . . . الثاني بعد المائة التاريخ

1 "Here is an index of the chapters after the introduction: . . . the 102nd is about history."
(Suyūṭi, *al-Itqān fī 'Ulūm al-Qur'ān*, pp. 20–23, introduction)

٢ المادة الثانية بعد المائة

2 "Article 102 (the 102nd article)"
(Law of Procedure before Shari'ah Courts, Saudi Arabia, Royal Decree #M/21, Aug. 19, 2000)

٣ المسألة الثانية بعد المائة

3 "The 102nd issue"
(chapter heading from table of contents of Anbāri, *al-Inṣāf fī Masā'il al-Khilāf*, 2/470)

26. Also see "More on Ordinal Numbers," p. 110.

Multiples of One Hundred in Compounds (103–999)

Cardinal

To state a multiple of 100 in a compound, state the multiple of 100 first, and then the smaller element. They are separated by وَ.

Multiple of One Hundred

The multiple of 100 is indefinite, and its case will be determined by its position in the sentence. Hence, the 3–10 element of 300–900 will take whatever grammatical case is required by its position in the sentence and not be nunated since it is a مضاف for مائة. The following مائة will be indefinite and thus take a *tanwīn kasr*, since it is not in an إضافة relationship with a following counted noun. For the same reason, مائتين or مائتان will keep their *nūns*.

Second Element (3–99)

The case of the second element in the compound (3–99) is also determined by its position in the sentence and will be the same as that of the multiple of 100.

The grammatical status of the counted noun, that is, its case and number, is determined by the element of the compound number closest to it.

Polar agreement (see p. 14) applies to any element in the compound that is 3–10.

Second Element Is 3–10: 103–110

If the number needed is a multiple of 100 plus 3–10 (e.g., 104, 207, 609, etc.), polar agreement applies to the 3–10, and the counted noun is plural and in the مجرور case. This is because the number closest to the counted noun is a number 3–10. Therefore, rules that apply to counted nouns for those numbers apply here to the counted noun.

مائة وثلاثة رجال "103 men"

مائة وأربع نساء "104 women"

Second Element Is 11–19 or Multiple of 10: 111–120, 130, 140, etc.

If the number following the multiple of 100 is a teen (11–19) or a multiple of 10 (120, 240, 360, etc.), then the counted noun is singular and in the منصوب case. This is because the number closest to the counted noun is a teen or a multiple of ten. Therefore, rules that apply to these numbers apply here also to the counted noun.

مائة وخمسة عشر شخصا "115 persons"

مائة وسبعين كتابا "170 books"

Second Element Is Compound Number

If the number following the multiple of 100 is a multiple of 10 plus 1–9 (i.e., 121, 332, 644, 256, etc.), then the number is read: (multiple of 100) *wa* (number 1–9) *wa* (multiple of ten). In other words, the number is not read largest to smallest (100's then 10's then 1's), but 100's then 1's then 10's.

مائة وسبعة وستون "167" (one-hundred and seven and sixty)

The counted noun is singular and in the منصوب case since the element of the compound closest to it is the multiple of ten.

Rules which apply to multiples of 10 in compounds (see p. 45) apply here also. Polar agreement (see p. 11) will apply to the smaller element (the 1's) of such a compound if that element is 3–10.

مائة وخمسة وسبعون طالبا "175 students"

ثلاثمائة وست وأربعين سيارة "346 cars"

Here طالبا is singular and in the منصوب case because the element closest to it is سبعون, the counted noun of which is singular and منصوب.

خمسة is feminine (has a *tāʾ marbūṭa*) because the counted noun طالب is masculine.

Similarly, سيارة is singular and in the منصوب case because the number element closest to it is أربعين, the counted noun of which is singular and منصوب. ست is masculine (has no *tāʾ marbūṭa*) because سيارة is feminine.

EXAMPLES

١ وفي مصحف ابن مسعود مائة واثنتا عشرة سورة

1 "In the codex of Ibn Mas'ud are 112 *sūras*."
(Suyūṭi, *al-Itqān fī 'Ulūm al-Qur'ān*, p. 153, *naw'* 19)

٢ وكان ملكه مائة واثنتى عشرة سنة

2 "(The period of) his rule was 112 years."
(Ṭabari, *Tārīkh*, 1/569)

٣ من ترك بسم الله الرحمن الرحيم فقد ترك مائة وثلاث عشرة آية

3 "He who omits *bismillah al-raḥmān al-raḥīm* (from his reading of the Qur'an, it is as if he) has omitted 113 verses."
(Rāzi, *Mafātīḥ al-Ghayb*, 1/213)

٤ أما سوره فمائة وأربع عشرة سورة بإجماع من يعتد به

4 "As for its *sūras*, they number 114 *sūras*, according to the consensus of those who can be relied upon."
(Suyūṭi, *al-Itqān fī 'Ulūm al-Qur'ān*, 153, *naw'* 19)

٥ وارتفعت حصيلة قتلى المظاهرات التي شهدتها بعض المدن
السورية الجمعة والسبت إلى أكثر من مائةٍ وعشرينَ قتيلاً

5 "The total number of those killed in the demonstrations seen in some Syrian cities on Friday and Saturday has gone up to more than 120 (people) killed."
(broadcast on Euronews Arabic, Apr. 25, 2011)

٦ وكان ملكه مائةً وإحدى وعشرين سنة

6 "(The period of) his rule was 121 years."
(Ṭabari, *Tārīkh*, 2/98)

٧ . . . ليحرز هدفه السادس والعشرين في المنافسة التي لعب فيها
مائةً وخمسًا وعشرينَ مباراةً . . .

7 ". . . to score his 26th goal in the competition, in which he has played 125 games . . ."
(broadcast on Euronews Arabic, Apr. 27, 2011)

٨ فلم يزل كذلك حتّى مات لبيد وهو ابن مائة وثمان وثلاثين سنة

8 "And he remained that way until Labid died at the age of 138 years."
(Anbāri, *Sharḥ al-Qaṣāi'd al-Sab'*, p. 514)

٩ وقال بعضهم: عاش لبيد مائة وأربعين سنة

9 "Some say that Labid lived for 140 years."
(Anbāri, *Sharḥ al-Qaṣāi'd al-Sab'*, 512)

١٠ الرجل الذي خلّف وراءه مائةً وسبعةً وأربعينَ عامًا . . .

10 "The man who has left behind him 147 years . . ."
(broadcast on aljazeera, Aug. 2009)

١١ فهو يحكي بالتفصيل عن وقائعَ مضت على بعضها مائةٌ وخمسةٌ وعشرونَ عامًا

11 "He speaks in detail about events, some of which happened 125 years ago."
(broadcast on aljazeera, Aug. 2009)

١٢ مقتل مائة واثنين وخمسين شخصا في تحطم طائرة ركاب باكستانية

12 "The Killing of 152 People in a Crash of a Pakistani Passenger Plane"
(arabic.euronews.net, July 29, 2010)

١٣ مائة واثنان وخمسون شخصاً لقوا حتفهم نتيجة تحطم طائرة ركاب باكستانية

13 "152 people were killed in the crash of a Pakistani passenger plane . . ."
(arabic.euronews.net, July 29, 2010)

١٤ حادث تصادم مروع بين أكثر من مائةٍ وسبعينَ مركبة . . .

14 ". . . a terrible collision among more than 170 vehicles . . ."
(newscast from Reuters, Mar. 12, 2010)[27]

١٥ أعضاء الأمم المتحدة مائة واثنتان وتسعون دولة

15 "The members of the United Nations are 192 countries."
(*al-Khalīj*, Feb. 7, 2010)

١٦ بينها وبين نيسابور مائتان وعشرون فرسخًا

16 "(The distance) between it and Nishapur is 220 parasangs."
(Yāqūt, *Muʿjam al-Buldān*, 3/431, #7386 on Shīrāz)

١٧ ووكّل سليمانُ مئتينِ وخمسينَ رجلاً

17 "Solomon appointed 250 men."
(*al-Kitāb al-Muqaddas*, Akhbār al-Ayyām al-Thani [2 Chronicles], 8:10)

١٨ ومن زرادشت إلى الأسكندر مائتان وثمان وخمسون سنة

18 "And from Zoroaster to Alexander is 258 years."
(*Masʿūdi, Murūj al-Dhahab*, 1/282)

27. Posted on masrawy.com

١٩ وكان عمر ناحور كله مائتين وثمانيا وأربعين سنة

19 "The total lifespan of Nahor was 248 years."
(Ṭabari, *Tārīkh*, 1/211)

٢٠ وعددهم مائتان وستون شخصًا

20 "Their number is 260 (people)."
(heard on Kuwait Radio news, Nov. 13, 2001)

٢١ وزعمت المجوس أن من وقت زرادشت بن أسبيمان نبيهم إلى الأسكندر مائتين وثمانين سنة

21 "The Magi (Zoroastrians) claim that from the time of Zoroaster, son of Spitama, their prophet, to Alexander was 280 years."
(*Mas'ūdi, Murūj al-Dhahab*, 2/267)

٢٢ مائة واثنتان وتسعون دولة تجتمع في كوبنهاغن لبحث ما جنته يد البشر

22 "292 countries meet in Copenhagen to discuss what (crimes) human hands have committed."
(*al-Waqt*, Dec. 9, 2009)

٢٣ لم لم يقل ثلثمائة وتسع سنين

23 "Why did he not simply say '309 years'?"
(Rāzi, *Mafātīḥ al-Ghayb*, 21/113, on Qur'an 18:25)

٢٤ وكنا يومئذ ثلثمائة وثلاثة عشر رجلا

24 "On that day we were 313 men."
(Rāzi, *Mafātīḥ al-Ghayb*, 6/197, on Qur'an 2:249)

٢٥ لأن المسلمين كانوا يوم بدر ثلثمائة وأربعة عشر رجلا، وكان المشركون تسعمائة وخمسين رجلا

25 ". . . because the Muslims on the Day of Badr were 314 men, and the polytheists were 950 men."
(Anbāri, *Kitāb al-Aḍdād*, p. 132)

٢٦ . . . حيث أدت موجة الاحتجاجات الى مقتل حوالي ثلاثِمائةٍ وخمسينَ شخصًا

26 ". . . where the wave of protests has led to the killing of around 350 people."
(broadcast on Euronews Arabic, Apr. 24, 2011)

٢٧ . . . وكتاب بدان في علامات أربعمائة وأربعة أدواء ومعرفتها بغير علاج

27 ". . . and the book of Bedan on the symptoms of 404 diseases and ways to recognize them, but no treatments (are given)."
(Ibn Abi Uṣaybi'a, *'Ṭabaqāt al-Aṭibbā'*, p. 474)

٢٨ وكان ملك الإسكندر وملك سائر ملوك الطوائف في النواحي خمسمائة وثلاثًا وعشرين سنة

28 "The (period of) rule of Alexander and of all of the local kings in the various areas was 523 years."
(Ṭabari, *Tārīkh*, 1/584)

٢٩ المساحة الإجمالية للوحدات السكنية تبلغ ٦٤٦ ستمائة وستة وأربعين هكتارًا

29 "The total area of the residential units is 646 hectares."
(*al-Fajr al-Jadīd*, Feb. 23, 2010)

٣٠ فذلك سبعمائة وأربع سنين

30 "That is (a total of) 704 years."
(Suyūṭi, *al-Itqān fī 'Ulūm al-Qur'ān*, 511, *naw'* 43)

٣١ . . . فذبح منهم نبوزراذان على ذلك الدم سبعمائة وسبعين روحًا من رءوسه

31 ". . . so Nabuzaradhan slaughtered, over that blood, 770 souls from among their leaders."
(Ṭabari, *Tārīkh*, 1/591)

٣٢ . . . أن أخطاء فنية صاحبت توزيع بطاقات الاقتراع في ستة وعشرين (٢٦) من جملة ثمانمئة وواحد وعشرين (٨٢١) مركزاً انتخابياً في ولاية الخرطوم

32 ". . . that technical errors accompanied the distribution of ballots in 26 out of a total of 821 voting centers in the State of Khartoum."
(*al-Ḥayāt*, Apr. 13, 2010)

٣٣ وكان عمر يارد تسعمائة واثنتين وستين سنة

33 "Jared's age was 962 years."
(Ṭabari, *Tārīkh*, 1/170)

Multiples of One Hundred in Compounds: The Old Style of Reading Numbers

An alternative to the way of reading numbers described above (hundred followed by the unit then by the ten) is to read each element of the compound in order from smallest to largest. This style is frequently used in classical texts or by those imitating the classical style.

As with the modern style, the case and plurality of the counted noun is determined by the element closest to it.

EXAMPLES

١ زعم الأصمعيّ أنّ الحارث قال قصيدته وهو يومئذ ابن خمس وثلاثين ومائة سنة

1 "Al-Aṣmaʿi claimed that on the day Ḥārith recited his poem he was at the age of 135 years."
(Anbāri, *Sharḥ al-Qaṣāi'd al-Sab'*, p. 433)

٢ كان يحفظ عشرين ومائة تفسير من تفاسير القرآن بأسانيدها

2 "He had memorized 120 of the Qur'anic commentaries along with their chains of transmission."
(Anbāri, *al-Zāhir*, p. 17, editor's introductory material)

٣ وذلك أن الرجل إذا هلك وترك عبدًا مُدبَّرًا قيمته خَمسون ومائةُ دينارٍ . . .

3 "That is because if a man dies and leaves a slave who is to be freed upon his death, the value of whom is 150 dinars . . ."
(Mālik ibn Anas, *al-Muwaṭṭa'*, p. 816)

٤ الألف واحدة، واللام ثلاثون؛ والميم أربعون، والصاد ستون، فهذه إحدى وثلاثون ومائة سنة

4 "The *alif* represents one, the *lām* 30, the *mīm* 40, and the *ṣād* 60. This is (a total of) 131 years."
(Suyūṭi, *al-Itqān fī 'Ulūm al-Qur'ān*, p. 511, *naw'* 43)

Using "Minus"

In another style sometimes seen in classical texts, if a number is very close to a larger round number, the round number is stated followed by a particle equivalent to "minus," such as إلا or غير, then the difference between it and the number intended is given.

EXAMPLES

١ آل عمران: مائتان، وقيل: إلا آية

1 "Āl 'Imrān is 200 (verses in length), and some say it is 199 (lit., 'minus a verse')."
(Suyūṭi, *al-Itqān fī 'Ulūm al-Qur'ān*, p. 159, *naw'* 19)

٢ قتلتم ستمائة إلا رجلاً

2 "You killed 599 men (six hundred but one)."
(Ṭabari, *Tārīkh*, 4/488)

٣ فَلَبِثَ فِيهِمْ أَلْفَ سَنَةٍ إِلاّ خَمسِينَ عَامًا

3 "He stayed with them for 950 years (1000 years minus 50 years)."
(Qur'an 29:14)

Repeating the Counted Noun

Another style sometimes seen is to repeat the counted noun, that is, to state it both after the hundred and after the second element. This is often seen in classical texts or in the writings of those aiming to imitate a classical style.

EXAMPLES

١ . . . فلا يكون له أكثر من ذلك. وذلك مائةُ دينارٍ وعَشَرَةُ دنانيرَ

1 ". . . and he does not get more than that amount, the amount being 110 dinars."
(Mālik ibn Anas, *al-Muwaṭṭa'*, 669)

٢ وهو ربع يوم بمائتى سنة وخمسين سنة من أعوام الدنيا

2 "And that is a quarter of a day, equivalent to 250 years on earth."
(*Mas'ūdi, Murūj al-Dhahab*, 1/34)

٣ قصة أصحاب الكهف وبقاؤهم في النوم أحياء سالمين عن الآفات مدة ثلثمائة سنة وتسع سنين . . .

3 "The story of the people of the cave and their remaining asleep and alive, safe from harm for a period of 309 years . . ."
(Rāzi, *Mafātīḥ al-Ghayb*, 21/86, on Qur'an 18:11)

٤ وكان عمر أرفخشد أربعمائة سنة وثمانيا وثلاثين سنة

4 "Arpachshad's age was 438 years."
(Ṭabari, *Tārīkh*, 1/210)

٥ وذرع ما بين الصفا والمروة—وهو المسعى—سبع مائة ذراع وثمانون ذراعا

5 "The distance between Safa and Marwa, the *mas'a*, is 780 cubits."
(alriyadh.com/php/hajj)

Numbers Written in Digits Only

When compound numbers which include multiples of 100 are not written out in words, but digits are used, all of the above rules regarding agreement and the status of the counted noun still apply.

EXAMPLES

١ وسجلت على مدى حياتها الفنية قرابة ٧٠٠ أغنية.

1 "Over the course of her artistic life she recorded nearly 700 songs."
(*al-Ḥayāt*, Jan. 14, 2011)

٢ سرّعت وتيرة برنامجها لخفض الكلفة بمقدار ٣٠٠ دولار لطن ألألومنيوم

2 "It has picked up the pace of its program to reduce costs by 300 dollars per ton of aluminum."
(*al-Ḥayāt*, Jan. 14, 2011)

٣ وقد قمنا بإعادة افتتاح ١٠٠ ناد

3 "We have reopened 100 clubs."
(*al-Ahrām*, Aug. 14, 2009)

٤ . . . مشيرة إلى وصول ٣٥٦ ممرضة إلى جازان من إجمالي ٤٠٤ ممرضات تعاقدت وزارة الصحة معهن . . .

4 ". . . pointing to the arrival of 356 nurses to Jizan out of a total of 404 nurses with whom the Ministry of Health has contracted . . ."
(*al-Ahrām*, Dec. 31, 2009)

٥ وفي لندن تحدد سعر أونصة الذهب في جلسة القطع الصباحية أمس على ٩٤٦ دولارًا ارتفاعًا من ٩٤٥ دولارًا.

5 "In London, the price of an ounce of gold was set in the morning gold fixing at 946 dollars, up from 945 dollars."
(*al-Ḥayāt*, Aug. 12, 2009)

٦ . . . لانتاج خبز مدعم عن طريق ٥٠٨ مخابز بلدية . . .

6 ". . . to produce subsidized bread via 508 municipal bakeries . . ."
(*al-Ahrām*, Aug. 20, 2009)

٧ وانخفض سعر السولار في عقود يونيو (حزيران) 50 سنتا الى 203 دولارات للطن.

7 "The price of diesel fuel has gone down in June contracts by 50 cents to 203 dollars per ton."
(*al-Riyāḍ*, May 25, 2002)

Ordinal[28]

The ordinals of the compound hundreds may be expressed either by:

(a) giving the ordinal of the smaller element (the element of the compound smaller than 100) followed by بعد المائة (where any of the hundreds may be substituted for المائة)

السبعون بعد المائة "the 170th"

or

(b) المائة و followed by the ordinal of the next element of the compound (where any of the hundreds may be substituted for المائة).

المائة والسبعون "the 170th"

Less formally, if the second element is a compound containing a multiple of ten plus one (41, 61, 71, etc.), sometimes الواحد or الواحدة is used here instead of الحادي or الحادية (see p. 40).

28. Also see the section "More on Ordinal Numbers," p. 110.

EXAMPLES

١ قوانين فلسطين الباب المائة والثالث قانون الشركات

1 "Laws of Palestine, Section 103 (103rd section): Corporate Law"
(title of item #42 in the rare book collection of Montesquieu Library, Birzeit University)

٢ المسألة الثالثة بعد المائة . . . المسألة العاشرة بعد المائة . . . المسألة الرابعة عشرة بعد المائة

2 "The 103rd issue . . . the 110th issue . . . the 114th issue . . ."
(chapter headings from table of contents of al-Anbārī, *al-Inṣāf fī Masā'il al-Khilāf*, 2/470–1)

٣ المادة الثالثة بعد المائة . . . المادة الحادية عشرة بعد المائة . . . المادة السابعة عشرة بعد المائة . . . المادة الثلاثون بعد المائة . . . المادة الحادية والخمسون بعد المائة . . . المادة الرابعة والثمانون بعد المائة . . . المادة الثامنة بعد المائتين . . . المادة الثانية عشرة بعد المائتين . . . المادة التاسعة عشرة بعد المائتين . . . المادة العشرون بعد المائتين . . . المادة الثانية والأربعون بعد المائتين . . . المادة الرابعة والخمسون بعد المائتين . . . المادة الحادية والستون بعد المائتين . . .

3 "Article 103 (the 103rd article) . . . Article 111 (the 111th article) . . . Article 117 (the 117th article) . . . Article 130 (the 130th article) . . . Article 151 (the 151st article) . . . Article 184 (the 184th article) . . . Article 208 (the 208th article) . . . Article 212 (the 212th article) . . . Article 219 (the 219th article) . . . Article 220 (the 220th article) . . . Article 242 (the 242nd article) . . . Article 254 (the 254th article) . . . Article 261 (the 261st article) . . ."
(Law of Procedure before Shari'ah Courts, Saudi Arabia, Royal Decree #M/21, Aug. 19, 2000)

٤ تلغى القوانين التالية: . . . الباب المائة والثالث والثلاثون من مجموعة القوانين الفلسطينية

4 "The following laws are repealed: . . . the 133rd section of the Palestinian legal code."
(from Jordan's law #27, 1952, on stamp duties)

٥ من اليوم الحادي والتسعين إلى اليوم المئة والعشرين: ٢٤ أربع وعشرون ليرة لبنانية، من اليوم المئة والواحد والعشرين فما فوق: ٣٢ اثنتان وثلاثون ليرة لبنانية

5 "From the 91st to the 120th day: 24 Lebanese Liras; from the 121st day and above: 32 Lebanese Liras."
(from the Lebanese customs law, section 5, chapter 1, article 323)

٦ نظرية النشوء والتطور في ذكراها الخمسين بعد المائة

6 "The Theory of Evolution on its 150th Anniversary"
(arabic.rt.com, May 13, 2009)

٧ العالم يحتفل بالذكرى المائة والخمسين لتشيكوف

7 "The World Celebrates the 150th Anniversary of Chekhov"
(*al-Ayyām*, Feb. 1, 2010)

٨ وهي تحتفل هذه السنة بالذكرى الثلاثين بعد الخمسمائة بإصدار أول قانون للبراءات في جمهورية البندقية

8 "This year it is celebrating the 530th anniversary of the issuance of the first patent law in the Republic of Venice."
(media alert from the World Intellectual Property Organization [WIPO], May 6, 2004)

٩ في الصفحة المائة والواحدة والأربعين من الكتاب . . .

9 "On the 141st page of the book . . ."
(*al-Riyāḍ*, Sept. 28, 2003)

One Thousand[29]

Cardinal

One thousand is:

أَلْف

Grammatically, it functions the same as مائة: Its case is determined by its position in the sentence, and the following counted noun is singular and in an إضافة relationship with it.

29. Also see the section "Writing Out Large Numbers," p. 79.

Thus, that counted noun is in the مجرور case and indefinite, and ألف takes no *tanwīn*.

مكثت هناك ألفَ يومٍ. "I stayed there for 1000 days."

EXAMPLES

١ قالت منظمات حقوقية سورية أمس، إن أكثر من ألف شخص اعتُقلوا منذ يوم السبت الماضي

1 "Syrian rights organizations said yesterday that more than 1000 persons have been arrested since last Saturday."
(*al-Ḥayāt*, May 4, 2011)

٢ وصير تحت يد كل قائد ألف رجل من أبطال الجند

2 "And he placed 1000 elite men from the elite soldiery under the command of each commander."
(Ṭabari, *Tārīkh*, 1/544)

٣ قلت لك ذلك ألف مرة

3 "I've told you that 1000 times."
(Tawfiq al-Hakim, *Maṣīr Ṣurṣār*, p. 24)

٤ لَيْلَةُ الْقَدْرِ خَيْرٌ مِنْ أَلْفِ شَهْرٍ

4 "The Night of Power is better than a thousand months."
(Qur'an, 97:3)

Ordinal[30]

The ordinal for one thousand, as those for the hundreds, takes the same exact form as the cardinal.

It functions as an adjective to the noun described, and as such follows it and agrees with it in case and definiteness.

It does not vary according to gender.

EXAMPLES

١ اليوم الألف للانتفاضة

1 "The Thousandth Day of the Intifada: . . ."
(*al-Mustaqbal*, June 26, 2003)

30. Also see the section "More on Ordinal Numbers," p. 110.

٢ أغاسي يخوض مباراته الألف في مسيرته بدورة كوينز الإنجليزية غدا

2 “Agassi Plays His 1,000th Match of His Career at the Queen’s Club Tournament Tomorrow”
(*al-Sharq al-Awsaṭ*, June 10, 2003)

٣ ولم تعرف بعد هوية القتيل الثاني الذي قضى قبل بضع دقائق من مهنا ليكون القتيل الالف منذ اندلاع الانتفاضة في 28 ايلول/سبتمبر 2000.

3 “The identity of the second person killed, who died a few minutes before Mihna, making him the thousandth person killed since the eruption of the intifada on September 28, 2000, is still not known.”
(*al-Riyāḍ*, Nov. 30, 2001)

Multiples of One Thousand: Writing Out Large Numbers

When a number 1000 or larger is written out in digits, commas are very rarely used if the number is only four digits in length (see examples 1, 2, 6, 11, 12, 13).

Larger numbers may be written out without a comma (see examples 3, 6, 9, 15), or, as in English, with a comma separating every group of three digits (see examples 5, 7, 8, 10, 14).

Occasionally when “Arabic numerals” are used, a period may be used in place of the comma (see example 4).

EXAMPLES

١ القوات العراقية تتسلم من القوات الأميركية ١٥٠٠ معتقل شهرياً

1 “Iraqi forces receive 1500 detainees from the American forces each month.”
(*al-Ḥayāt*, Jan. 9, 2009)

٢ وسيتم إنشاؤه على مساحة 7500 م2

2 “It will be built over a 7500 m^2 area.”
(*al-Yawm*, Apr. 26, 2011)

٣ استدانت هذه المرأة بدين بلغ 655300 ريال لصالح البنك التجاري

3 "This woman incurred debt of 655,300 riyals to the Commercial Bank."
(*al-Sharq*, Aug. 2, 2011)

٤ يهدف لتغطية نحو 15.000 نسمة بتوفير مياه الشرب النظيفة

4 "It seeks to provide around 15,000 people with clean drinking water."
(*al-Sharq*, Feb. 22, 2011)

٥ تم إيداع 333,705 ملف مشروع خلال السداسي الأول 2011 مقابل 29,499 ملف خلال نفس الفترة من سنة 2010

5 "333,705 project files were submitted in the first semester of 2011, as compared with 29,499 files during the same period in 2010."
(*al-Shurūq*, July 31, 2011)

٦ وصل الدفع إلى (١٣١٥١٩٣ كغ) أي أكثر من (١٣١٥ طن)

6 "The thrust reached 1,315,193 kg, more than 1315 tons."
(Ḥaffār, *Makkūk al-Faḍā'*, p. 23)

٧ يتألف مجتمع النحل، داخل الخلية من 20.000 إلى 50.000 فرد

7 "A bee colony, inside the hive, is comprised of 20,000 to 50,000 individuals."
(*al-Aṭlas al-'Ilmi*, p. 99)

٨ أسعار تبدأ من 95,000 جنية[31]

8 "prices starting at 95,000 pounds"
(*al-Ahrām*, Jan. 21, 2011)

٩ نسبة الحضور بلغت ١٧,٦% بعد ادلاء 46263 ناخبا بأصواتهم من اجمالي 262728 ناخبا مقيدا بجداول الدائرة الانتخابية.

9 "The turnout rate was 17.6%, as 46,263 voters voted out of a total of 262,728 registered voters in the electoral district."
(*al-Ahrām*, Aug. 14, 2009)

١٠ يشاهده أكثر من مليون و٣٠٠,٠٠٠ مشاهد

10 "More than 1,300,000 viewers watch it."
(*al-'Arabi*, Dec. 2004)

31. جنية sic

١١ فجزء صغير للغاية . . . من سرب متوسط الحجم يستطيع أن يأكل كعشرة أفيال أو ٢٥ جملا أو ٢٥٠٠ إنسان

11 "An extremely small part of a medium-sized swarm can eat the same amount as ten elephants, 25 camels, or 2500 humans."
(*al-'Arabi*, Dec. 2004)

١٢ واستفاد منها حوالي 800 أسرة متضررة أي ما يقارب 5600 شخص

12 "Around 800 afflicted families benefited from it, nearly 5600 people."
(*al-Sharq*, July 24, 2011)

١٣ الانتهاء من ٩٤٤٦ وحدة سكنية بالشرقية

13 "The Completion of 9,446 Housing Units in Sharqia"
(*al-Ahrām*, Aug. 20, 2009)

١٤ تبلغ مساحة ايطاليا (٣٠١,٢٦٨) كلم٢ وعدد سكانها (٥٧,٤٤١,٠٠٠) نسمة

14 "The area of Italy is 301,268 km^2, and its population is 57,441,000."
(*Aṭlas al-'Ālam al-Ṣaḥīḥ*, p. 98)

١٥ كان سيحتاج الى زمن قدره: ٠٠٠ ٠٠٠ ٠٠٠ ٠٠٠ ٠٠٠ ٠٠٠ ٠٠٠ ١ ثانية او الى ثلاثين الف بليون سنة!

15 "He would have needed 10^{21} (one sextillion) seconds, or 30 trillion years!"
(Perelman, *al-Fīziyā' al-Musalliya*, p. 42)

Two Thousand[32]

Cardinal

2000 is أَلْفانِ in the مرفوع case and أَلْفَينِ in the منصوب and مجرور cases.

However, as with any dual, the final *nūn* is dropped when it occurs as a مضاف. And as ألف and its multiples occur as مضاف

32. Also see the section "Writing Out Large Numbers," p. 79.

for their counted nouns, these will lose their *nūn* when followed by a counted noun.

The counted noun, as with all thousands, is singular and indefinite. It is in the مجرور case, as it is a مضاف إليه.

قبل ألفَي سنةٍ "2000 years ago"

When ألفان and ألفين are written alone, with no counted noun, the *nūn* is retained, and as with all duals, has a *kasra* regardless of grammatical case. The *kasra* is single, i.e., not nunated, regardless of the definiteness or indefiniteness of the word.

EXAMPLES

١ وبينها وبين القيروان ألفا ميل

1 "Between it and Qairawan is 2000 miles."
(Yāqūt, *Mu'jam al-Buldān*, 4/49, #7979 on Ṭanja)

٢ يُخبز في داري ألفا رغيفٍ في كل يوم

2 "2000 loaves of bread are baked in my house every day."
(Yāqūt, *Mu'jam al-Udabā'*, 4/420, #678 on 'Imāra ibn Ḥamza)

٣ كان علي بن محمد بن علي الصليحي . . . عزم على التوجه إلى مكة في ألفي فارس

3 "'Ali ibn Muḥammad ibn 'Ali al-Ṣulayḥi . . . had decided to head towards Mecca with 2000 cavalry."
(Yāqūt, *Mu'jam al-Buldān*, 2/473, #4531 on Khaymat Umm Ma'bad)

٤ وقرر مجلس الأمن زيادة عددها الى الفي جندي

4 "The Security Council has decided to increase their number to 2000 soldiers."
(*al-Ḥayāt*, Jan. 14, 2011)

٥ ألفا رجل أمن خاص يعملون في العراق

5 "2000 Private Security Men Are Working in Iraq"
(*al-Mustaqbal*, Apr. 24, 2004)

Ordinal[33]

The ordinal of 2000 is exactly the same as the cardinal: ألفان in the مرفوع case and ألفين in the منصوب and مجرور cases.

33. Also see the section "More on Ordinal Numbers," p. 110.

As an adjective, it agrees in case and definiteness with the preceding noun. It does not vary with regard to gender.

EXAMPLES

١ وتعود بحسب الخبراء إلى السنة الألفين قبل الميلاد

1 "According to experts, it goes back to the 2,000th year B.C."
(*al-Ḥayāt*, Feb. 20, 2009)

٢ في مطلع العام الالفين، بوشر بتنفيذ مبنى جديد يتألف من خمسة عشر صفًا

2 "At the beginning of the year 2000 (the 2,000th year), the construction of a new building that consists of 15 classrooms has been undertaken."
(from the description of campus facilities at Bethlehem University, bethlehem .edu)

Multiples of One Thousand (3000–999,000)[34]

Cardinal

To form a multiple of 1000, ألف is treated as any counted noun. It is plural (آلاف) and in an إضافة construction with the number preceding if that number is 3–10 or a multiple of 100 plus 3–10:

خمسة آلافٍ "five thousand"

مائة وخمسة آلافٍ "105,000"

It is singular and منصوب if that number is 11–99 or a multiple of 100 plus 11–99:

سبعون ألفاً "70,000"

سبعمائة وخمسون ألفاً "750,000"

34. Also see the section "Writing Out Large Numbers," p. 79.

It is singular and in an إضافة construction with the preceding number if that number is a multiple of 100:

أربعمائة ألفٍ "400,000"

Then, the counted noun following ألف or آلاف is in an إضافة construction with ألف or آلاف. Thus, ألف or آلاف takes no تنوين, and the following counted noun is singular, مجرور and indefinite.

وصل أربعُمائةِ ألفِ جنديٍّ. "400,000 troops arrived."

وصل سبعةُ آلافِ جنديٍّ. "7000 troops arrived."

EXAMPLES

١ كان له في قصره ثلاثة آلاف امرأة يطؤهنّ . . . وثلاثة آلاف رجل يقومون بخدمته . . . واثنا عشر ألف بغل لثقله

1 "He had in his palace 3000 women to sleep with . . . and 3000 men serving him . . . and 12,000 mules to carry his things."
(Ṭabari, *Tārīkh*, 2/215–6)

٢ لها أبواب على كل باب منها خمسة آلاف ملك يحفظونها

2 "It has gates, at each of which are 5000 angels guarding it."
(Yāqūt, *Mu'jam al-Buldān*, 3/282, #6592 on Samarqand)

٣ خمسة آلاف جنيه مبلغ جميل تقضي بها احتياجات اخوتها

3 "Five thousand pounds is a nice sum that she can take care of her siblings' needs with."
('Alā' al-Aswāni, *'Imārat Ya'qūbiyān*, p. 224)

٤ ثم ذهب فبعث إلى ابن جعفر بعشرة آلاف دينار

4 "Then he left and sent to Ibn Ja'far 10,000 dinars."
(*Qiṣaṣ al-'Arab*, 1/21)

٥ وكان عمر بن جيلانَ يزعم أن الدنيا كلها سبعة وعشرون ألف فرسخ، فبلد السودان اثنا عشر ألف فرسخ، وبلد الروم ثمانية آلاف فرسخ، وبلد فارس ثلاثة آلاف فرسخ، وأرض العرب أربعة آلاف فرسخ

5 "'Umar ibn Jīlān claimed that the entire earth was 27,000 parasangs, as Sudan is 12,000 parasangs, the land of the Romans is 8,000 parasangs, Persia is 3,000 parasangs, and the Arab land is 4,000 parasangs."
(Yāqūt, *Mu'jam al-Buldān*, 1/33-34, chap. 1 of introduction)

٦ فارتفع توزيع الجريدة في عهده إلى ثلاثين ألف نسخة يوميا

6 “The circulation of the newspaper increased during his time to 30,000 copies daily.”
(ʿAlāʾ al-Aswāni, *ʿImārat Yaʿqūbiyān*, p. 251)

٧ فكان مبلغه ثلاثةً وثَلاثينَ أَلْفَ دينارٍ

7 “The amount of it was 33,000 dinars.”
(Yāqūt, *Muʿjam al-Udabāʾ*, 4/379, #674 on ʿAli ibn Yaḥya ibn Abi Manṣūr)

٨ حملتُ المال واشتريتُ كل شيء جاورك بسبعين ألف درهم

8 “I carried the money and I bought everything in your vicinity for 70,000 dirhams.”
(*Qiṣaṣ al-ʿArab*, 1/45)

٩ أنشئت مقبرة الكلاب عام 1896 وباتت تضم بقايا أكثر من سبعة وسبعين ألف كلب

9 “The dog cemetery was built in 1896 and still holds the remains of 77,000 dogs.”
(*al-Qabas*, May 17, 2010)

١٠ أنفقت فى حبك يا ست مائة ألف جنيه

10 “I have spent on your love, madam, 100,000 pounds.”
(Naguib Mahfouz, *Zuqāq al-Midaqq*, p. 55)

١١ . . . منها اتفاقيتان مع ماليزيا واندونيسيا لنقل مئتين وثلاثة آلاف حاج من البلدين

11 “. . . among which are two agreements with Malaysia and Indonesia to transport 203,000 pilgrims from the two countries.”
(*al-Mustaqbal*, Oct. 26, 2004)

١٢ قد أمرت لأبي محمد إسحاق أنا وأخواك بثلاثمائة ألف درهم لمنزلٍ يبتاعه ونفقة ينفقها عليه

12 “I and your two brothers have ordered 300,000 dirhams for Abu Muḥammad Isḥāq for him to buy a house and to cover expenditures for it.”
(*Qiṣaṣ al-ʿArab*, 1/45)

١٣ ويتوزع نحو ستمئة وثمانية عشر الف فلسطيني على دول اجنبية.

13 “Around 618,000 Palestinians are spread out over various foreign countries.”
(*al-Mustaqbal*, Jan. 11, 2010)

١٤ . . . وعقد توريد وتطبيق مشروع خدمات الدعم الفني من شركة ميكرسوفت لمركز تقنية المعلومات بقيمة سبعمائة وواحد وثمانين ألف ريال، وعقد صيانة المعامل وشبكات الحاسب الآلي بكلية

التربية وكليات البنات والكليات الصحية ومركز تقنية المعلومات التابعة للجامعة بقيمة ستمائة وتسعة وتسعين ألف ريال . . . وعقد توريد اثنتي عشرة سيارة بقيمة تسعمائة وتسعة وتسعين ألف ريال، وعقد توريد أجهزة شبكة لربط الكليات بالجامعة والمستشفى بمركز تقنية المعلومات بقيمة ثلاثمائة وخمسة وثمانين ألف ريال

14 ". . . and a contract to create and implement a project in which the Microsoft Corporation will provide technical support services to the IT center, at a value of 781,000 riyals; and a contract to maintain computer labs and networks at the College of Education, the girls' colleges, and the colleges of health, as well as the university's IT center, at a value of 699,000 riyals . . . and a contract to provide 12 cars at a value of 999,000 riyals, and a project to provide network devices to connect the colleges of the university and the hospital with the IT center, with a value of 385,000 riyals."
(*al-Riyāḍ*, May 14, 2011)

١٥ فوجه كل ملك من ملوك الطوائف إلى بلاش من الرجال والسلاح والمال بقدر قوته، حتى اجتمع عنده أربعمائة ألف رجل

15 "Each of the local kings sent to Balash whatever men, soldiers, and money he was able to, until he had gathered 400,000 men."
(Ṭabari, *Tārīkh*, 1/581)

١٦ . . . ومن غلة ضياعه بجندي سابور والسوس والبصرة والسواد في كل سنة . . . ورقا ثماني مائة الف درهم

16 ". . . and from the revenues of his estates in Gundishapur, Sous, Basra, and the Sawad of Iraq each year . . . 800,000 *waraq* dirhams."
(Ibn Abi Uṣaybiʿa, *'Ṭabaqāt al-Aṭibbā'*, p. 200)

Repeating *alf*

In some classical texts, the ألف may be repeated when enumerating large multiples.

EXAMPLES

١ وخرج موسى في ستمائة ألف وعشرين ألف مقاتل

1 "Moses went out with 620,000 fighters."
(Ṭabari, *Tārīkh*, 1/414)

٢ فقتل من أصحابه في ليلة واحدة مائة ألف وخمسة وثمانين ألف رجل

2 ". . . and in one night he killed from among his companions 185,000 men."
(Ṭabari, *Tārīkh*, 1/535)

٣ روي أن ابن الزبير بعث إليها بمائة ألف وثمانين ألف درهم في غرارتين

3 "It has been related that Ibn Zubayr had sent to her 180,000 dirhams in two bags."
(Rāzi, *Mafātīḥ al-Ghayb*, 32/62 on Qur'an 99:7–8)

101,000 and 102,000[35]

Just as 101 and 102 require a repetition of their counted nouns (see pp. 61–64), 101,000 and 102,000 require a repetition of the ألف. In this case, the counted noun is ألف, so ألف or ألفين must be stated after the multiple of 1000.

EXAMPLES

١ وضبطت ايضا (101.000) مئة ألف وألف حبة مخدرة

1 "101,000 narcotic pills were also seized."
(*al-Riyāḍ*, Dec. 5, 2007)

٢ أربعة وأربعون عاماً مضت من عمر الجامعة وأكثر من مائة ألف وألفي خريج

2 "Forty-four years have passed since the foundation of the university, and more than 102,000 graduates (have graduated)."
(*al-Riyāḍ*, June 17, 2001)

Ordinal[36]

The cardinals of the multiples of 1000 may also be used as ordinals. When this occurs, the number functions as an adjective. Thus, it follows the noun it describes and

35. Also see the section "Writing Out Large Numbers," p. 79.
36. Also see the section "More on Ordinal Numbers," p. 110.

agrees with it in definiteness and case. When definite, the definite article الـ is placed only on the first element of the construction.

However, it is much simpler, and probably as common or more common to express the ordinal by simply using رَقَم "number" plus the ordinal.

EXAMPLES

١ ولكن خالف المؤشر تلك التوقعات وواصل تراجعه إلى النقطة الثلاثة آلاف

1 "But the index countered those predictions and continued its decline to the 3,000th point."
(*al-Ahrām al-Masā'i*, May 13, 2009)

٢ قبل اسابيع قليلة رفع الصليب على شاهدة لقبر القتيل رقم ثلاثة آلاف من الجنود الأمريكيين في العراق.

2 "A few weeks ago, a cross was raised over the gravestone of the 3,000th person killed (person killed #3000) from among the American soldiers in Iraq."
(iraqpa.net, Jan. 28, 2007)

٣ جوتي يسجل الهدف رقم 5000 لريال مدريد

3 "Guti Scores his 5,000th Goal (goal #5000) for Real Madrid"
(*al-Ayyām*, Sept. 16, 2008)

٤ المشروع الثاني الأهم في حياتي هو المعجم العربي—العربي الذي بدأناه منذ أكثر من ثلاثين عامًا، وهو في صفحته رقم ثمانية آلاف.

4 "The other, more important project in my life is the Arabic-Arabic dictionary which we began more than 30 years ago. It is now on its 8,000th page (page #8000)."
(interview with Samah Idriss, iwffo.org, June 22, 2010)

٥ الصايرة تحتفي بالعضو رقم عشرة آلاف

5 "Alsayra celebrates its 10,000th member (member #10,000)."
(alsayra.com)

٦ وبمناسبة صدور العدد رقم عشرة آلاف من «الاتحاد» . . .

6 "On the occasion of the issuance of the 10,000th issue (issue #10,000) of *al-Ittiḥād* . . ."
(*al-Wasaṭ* [Bahrain], Jan. 22, 2003)

٧ وذلك في احتفال المؤسسة بصدور العدد العشرة آلاف من جريدة الاتحاد.

7 "That was during the Foundation's celebration of the publication of the 10,000th issue of *al-Ittiḥād*."
(*al-Waṭan* [Oman], Mar. 3, 2004)

٨ وبفضل الله نجحوا في اقتناص المركز رقم ثلاثة وعشرين الف على مستوى العالم

8 "Thanks to God they have succeeded in snagging the 23,000th position (position #23,000) worldwide."
(egycrazy.com)

٩ فقد كان الأول يناقش الثاني—للمرة المائة ألف—في مغزى لقب (أبو تسعة)

9 "The former was discussing with the latter, for the 100,000th time, the significance of the nickname Abu Tisʿa."
(Muḥammad Mustajāb, *Dayrūṭ al-Sharīf wa Nuʿmān ʿAbd al-Ḥāfiẓ*, p. 172)

١٠ احتفالاً بالمسافر رقم مائة ألف..طيران ناس يمنح مواطنًا 100 ألف كيلو متر مجانًا

10 "In celebration of its 100,000th passenger (passenger #100,000), Nasair awards a citizen 100,000 free kilometers."
(*al-Riyāḍ*, May 27, 2007)

١١ و كان الموقع الألكتروني السعودي الصايرة . . . قد سجل رقما قياسيا بتسجيل العضو رقم أربعمائة ألف

11 "The Saudi website alsayra . . . had set a record when it registered its 400,000th member (member #400,000)."
(bishannet.net, June 19, 2008)

١٢ واحتفالا بالمناسبة، منحت الشركة، محمد الجوريشي، العضوية رقم خمسمائة ألف في برنامج ضيف الاتحاد

12 "In celebration of the occasion, the company granted Muhmmad al-Jurishi the 500,000th membership (membership #500,000) in the Etihad Guest program."
(etihadairways.com, Dec. 17, 2008)

Thousands Plus One (1001, 2001, etc.)[37]

Cardinal

As with مائة, to add one to a multiple of 1000, the counted noun must be repeated: the thousand plus the counted noun (see also p. 61).

EXAMPLES

١ وكان الصبي قد سمع اسم الشيخ . . . ألفَ مرة ومرة

1 "The boy had heard the shaykh's name 1,001 times."
(Taha Hussein, *al-Ayyām*, 1/142)

٢ جرت العادة منذ ألفي سنة وسنة

2 "The custom has been followed for 2,001 years."
(Palestine Media Center report, May 5, 2002)

Figurative Use of 1001

Frequently, the number 1001 is used in exaggeration. That is, it is often used to mean simply "a very large number of," akin to how one might use "thousand" or "million" in English, as in, "He has a million different excuses" or "I've told you a thousand times."

EXAMPLES

١ . . . وألف كيف وكيف لا يمكن أن يُجاب عنها في جمل قصيرة . . .

1 ". . . a thousand and one 'how?'s' that cannot be answered in short sentences . . ."
(*al-Ḥayāt*, May 6, 2011)

٢ رأينا أن عينا واحدة لا تكفي لرؤية المدينة . . . أنت في حاجة لألف عين وعين، ألف يد ويد، ألف قدم وقدم، ألف أذن وأذن، ألف لسان ولسان، وألف حياة وحياة.

2 "We saw that one eye is not enough to see the city. . . . You need 1,001 eyes, 1,001 hands, and 1,001 feet, 1,001 ears, 1,001 tongues, and 1,001 lives."
(*al-Riyāḍ*, Nov. 14, 2008)

---

37. Also see the section "Writing Out Large Numbers," p. 79.

٣ وهو ما يبدو ((طبيعيًا)) في مجتمعات مسكونة بهاجس أمني وبالآخر الذي يخترقها بألف لبوس ولبوس.

3 "It appears normal in societies which are haunted by apprehensions over security and by the 'other,' who is infiltrating in 1,001 different disguises."
(*al-Ḥayāt*, Jan. 14, 2011)

1001 Nights

The most famous example of the use of 1001 in Arabic culture is the title of the beloved story collection ألف ليلة وليلة "A Thousand and One Nights." Thus, the number 1001 is frequently used to allude to this collection in some way.

EXAMPLES

١ ألف اختراع واختراع يستقبل زواره في نيويورك

1 "The '1001 Inventions' (exhibition) welcomes visitors in New York."
(*al-Riyāḍ*, Jan. 15, 2011)

Note: The purpose of the exhibition described here is to highlight Arab/Islamic civilization's contributions to science, hence the allusion in its name to *1001 Nights*.

٢ حكايات ألف يوم ويوم

2 "*The Tales of 1001 Days*"
(title of book by Muhammad Rif'at)

Ordinal[38]

1001st in the masculine is

الواحد بعد الألف or الأول بعد الألف

In the feminine it is

الواحدة بعد الألف or الأولى بعد الألف

where the ordinal of any multiple of 1000, which is identical to the cardinal, may be used in place of الألف.

38. Also see the section "More on Ordinal Numbers," p. 110.

EXAMPLES

١ . . . فرضيات لما حدث في الليلة الاولى بعد الالف

1 ". . . Speculation on What Happened on the 1001st Night."
(musaad.com, Nov. 2, 2010)

٢ خلع ملابسه وجلس يكتب الرسالة الواحدة بعد الألف.

2 "He removed his clothes and sat down to write the 1001st letter."
(Manṣūr, Midḥat, "Alf Risālat Ḥubb")[39]

٣ أما اليوم الأول بعد الألف في كتاب «ألف يوم ويوم» فقد كان الزلزال الذي أصاب الصين يوم 12 مايو (أيار) سنة 2009.

3 "The 1001st day in the book *1001 Days* was (the day of) the earthquake which hit China on May 12, 2009."
(*al-Sharq al-Awsaṭ*, Feb. 28, 2011)

٤ التأجيل الواحد بعد الألف

4 "The 1001st Postponement"
(*al-Mustaqbal*, Mar. 11, 2008)

Thousands Plus Two (1002, 2002, etc.)[40]

Cardinal

As with مائة, to add two to a multiple of 1000, the counted noun must be repeated. Here, the repeated noun must be in the dual form (see p. 64).

EXAMPLE

١ وذلك من على ارتفاع شاهق يبلغ تسعة وعشرين ألف قدم وقدمين (29002).

1 "That was from a tremendously high altitude of 29,002 feet."
(alawan.org, Sept. 26, 2010.)

39. Posted on arabicstory.net, Sept. 26, 2010.
40. Also see the section "Writing Out Large Numbers," p. 79.

Ordinal[41]

"1,002nd" in the masculine is

الثاني بعد الألف

and in the feminine is

الثانية بعد الألف

where the ordinal of any multiple of 1000, which is identical to the cardinal, may be used in place of الألف.

EXAMPLES

١ شهرزاد في الليلة الثانية بعد الالف

1 *"Scheherazade on the 1002nd Night"*
(title of book by Dāwūd Sulaymān al-ʿAbīdi)

٢ الليلة الثانية بعد الالف

2 "The 1002nd Night"
(title of a Syrian TV series)

٣ كان لشهيدنا الاستشهادي أبو حمزة شرف الالتحاق بركب الجماعة المسلمة جماعة الإخوان المسلمين في العام الثاني بعد الألفين

3 "Our martyred hero Abu Hamza had the honor of joining the Muslim group the Muslim Brotherhood in the 2002nd year (the year 2002)."
(alqassam.ps, Apr. 19, 2008)

Thousands in Compounds[42]

Cardinal

Multiples of thousands in compounds are created by beginning with the multiple of 1000, followed by the hundreds. Then follow the ones, then the tens, or the teen if the next number is a teen. Each element is connected to the next with وَ "and."

41. Also see the section "More on Ordinal Numbers," p. 110.
42. Also see the section "Writing Out Large Numbers," p. 79.

Polar agreement (see p. 14) applies to any element of the compound that is 3–10.

The number and grammatical case of the following counted noun is determined by the number in the compound which is closest to it.

Thus, if the last number of the compound is 3–10, polar agreement applies to the 3–10, and the counted noun is plural and in the مجرور case.

ثلاثة آلاف وخمسة رجال "3005 men"

If the last number of the compound is a multiple of 10, then the counted noun is singular and in the منصوب case.

أربعة آلاف وخمسمائة وسبعين دولارا "4,570 dollars"

If the last number of the compound is a multiple of 100, then the counted noun will be in an إضافة construction with the 100, and thus will be singular and in the مجرور case.

ألفان وثلاثمائة لاجئٍ "2300 refugees"

EXAMPLES

١ الجدير ذكره أن المبنى يقع على مساحة أربعة آلاف وستمائة وخمسة وعشرين متراً مربعاً تشتمل على مواقف للسيارات ومرافق خدمية أخرى.

1 "It is notable that the building sits on a lot of 4,625 square feet that includes parking spots and other service facilities."
(*al-Jumhūriyya* [Yemen], Nov. 15, 2010)

٢ إن رجال مكافحة المخدرات تمكنوا بفضل الله . . . من ضبط (2.942) ألفين وتسعمائة واثنين وأربعين جرامًا من الهيروين المخدر النقي . . . و (454.507) أربعمائة وأربعة وخمسين ألفًا وخمسمائة وسبع حبات مخدرة.

2 "Anti-drug men were able, thanks to God, to seize 2,942 grams of pure heroin . . . and 454,507 narcotic pills."
(*al-Riyāḍ*, May 15, 2008)

٣ وذلك في حسابات (723.642) سبع مئة وثلاثة وعشرين ألفًا وست مئة واثنتين وأربعين حالة من مستفيدي ومستفيدات الضمان

الاجتماعي . . . مشيرًا إلى أن هناك عددًا من الحالات المسجلة بلغت (5866) خمسة آلاف وثمان مئة وستًا وستين حالة . . .

3 "It (was placed) into the accounts of 723,642 cases of beneficiaries of social security . . . pointing to the fact that the number of recorded cases has reached 5866 (cases) . . ."
(*al-Riyāḍ*, Mar. 10, 2011)

٤ . . . حيث تم تخصيص ما يقارب ثلاثة عشر الفا وخمسمائة موقف في الكليات الجديدة . . .

4 ". . . as nearly 13,500 spaces have been set aside in the new colleges . . ."
(*al-Qabas*, Dec. 22, 2010)

٥ أن عدد القروض التي منحها المصرف . . . بلغ (40,859) أربعين ألفا وثمانمائة وتسعة وخمسين قرضًا. وتتوزع هذه القروض بين (27,008) سبعة وعشرين ألفا وثمانية قروض للرجال و(13,851) ثلاثة عشر ألفا وثمانمائة وواحد وخمسين قرضا للنساء

5 "The number of loans granted by the bank . . . is 40,859 (loans). These loans are split between 27,008 loans to men and 13,851 loans to women."
(*al-Fajr al-Jadīd*, Feb. 16, 2011)

٦ طول قطر الأرض بالفراسخ ألفان ومائة وثلاثة وستون فرسخًا وثلثا فرسخ، ودورها بالفراسخ ستة آلاف وثمانمائة فرسخ

6 "The diameter of the earth, in parasangs, is 2,163 and two-thirds parasangs. Its circumference in parasangs is 6,800 parasangs."
(Yāqūt, *Mu'jam al-Buldān*, 1/33, chap. 1 of introduction)

٧ وَفيهِ مِنْ شَواهِدِ الشِّعْرِ أَلْفٌ وَمِائَتَا بَيتٍ

7 "It contains 1,200 lines of poetry citations."
(Yāqūt, *Mu'jam al-Udabā'*, 4/227, #627 on 'Ali ibn Muḥammad ibn Wahb al-Mis'ari)

٨ يُؤْكَلُ مِنْهَا أَلْفٌ وَتِسْعُمِائَةٍ وتِسْعَةٌ وَتِسْعُونَ رَغِيفًا حَلالاً

8 "Of those, 1,999 loaves are eaten lawfully."
(Yāqūt, *Mu'jam al-Udabā'*, 4/420, #678 on 'Imāra ibn Ḥamza)

٩ وروى صاحب الكشاف أنه كان بين نوح وإبراهيم ألفان وستمائة وأربعون سنة

9 "The author of *al-Kashshāf* related that between Noah and Abraham there were 2,640 years."
(Rāzi, *Mafātīḥ al-Ghayb*, 26/146 on Qur'an 37:83)

١٠ وطوله من المشرق إلى المغرب تسعة آلاف وثلاثمائة واثنا عشر ميلاً

10 "Its length from east to west is 9,312 miles."
(Yāqūt, *Mu'jam al-Buldān*, 1/46, chap. 2 of introduction)

١١ . . . فضلا عن تواجد أكثر من أربعةَ عَشَرَ ألفاً وثلاثِمائةٍ وسبعةٍ وسبعين آخرين في عداد المفقودين . . .

11 ". . . in addition to more than 14,377 others who are considered lost . . ."
(broadcast on CNTV Arabic, Apr. 12, 2011)

Repeating the Counted Noun

In classical texts, the counted noun is sometimes repeated in a long compound.

EXAMPLES

١ وتَفسيرُ ذلك أَنْ تَكونَ قيمَةُ ذلِكَ كُلِّهِ أَلْفَ دِرْهَمٍ وخَمْسَمائَةِ دِرْهَمٍ

1 "The explanation is that the value of that is 1500 dirhams."
(Mālik ibn Anas, *al-Muwaṭṭa'*, p. 679)

٢ وقيل: الميل ألفا خطوة وثلاثمائة وثلاث وثلاثون خطوة

2 "It is said that a mile is 2,333 steps."
(Yāqūt, *Mu'jam al-Buldān*, 1/53, chap. 3 of introduction)

٣ . . . وأن الصحيح من القول في قدر مدة أيام الدنيا . . . خمسة آلاف سنة وتسعمائة سنة واثنتان وتسعون سنة وأشهر

3 ". . . and that the correct view regarding the age of the world . . . is (that it is) 5,992 years and some months."
(Ṭabari, *Tārīkh*, 1/18)

٤ إنّ القرآن ستة آلاف آية، ومائتا آية وكسر

4 "The Qur'an is 6,200-some verses."
(Suyūṭi, *al-Itqān fī 'Ulūm al-Qur'ān*, p. 834, *naw'* 73)

٥ وعد قوم كلمات القرآن سبعة وسبعين ألف كلمة، وتسعمائة وأربعًا وثلاثين كلمة

5 "Some have counted the words in the Qur'an (and found them) to be 77,934 words."
(Suyūṭi, *al-Itqān fī 'Ulūm al-Qur'ān*, p. 163, *naw'* 19)

٦ وجميع حروف القرآن ثلاثمائة ألف حرف وثلاثة وعشرون ألف حرف وستمائة حرف وواحد وسبعون حرفًا

6 "The total number of letters in the Qur'an is 323,671 letters."
(Suyūṭi, *al-Itqān fī 'Ulūm al-Qur'ān*, p. 157, *naw'* 19)

Compounds That Include One or Two Thousand[43]

As mentioned on p. 87, when the compound number includes some multiple of 1000 plus 1 or 2 (e.g., 201,000 or 202,000), the rules for 101 and 102 apply: The counted noun must be repeated in the singular or the dual after the multiple of 100 is stated. In this case, the counted noun is ألف, so ألف or ألفين must be stated after the multiple of 1000.

EXAMPLES

١ أولئِكَ المَعدودونَ مِنْ بَني إسرائيلَ ستُّ مئَةِ ألفٍ وألفٌ وسَبعُ مئةٍ وثَلاثونَ

1 "These are the ones from the children of Israel who had been counted: 601,730."
(*al-Kitāb al-Muqaddas*, al-'Adad [Numbers] 26:51)

٢ تمكن رجال الجمارك بمنفذ حالة عمار من إحباط تهريب مائتي ألف وألف وسبعمائة حبة كبتاجون المحظورة مخبأة بطريقة فنية داخل الإطار الاحتياطي

2 "Border agents at the Halat Ammar border crossing were able to thwart the smuggling of 201,700 banned Captagon tablets cleverly hidden inside a spare tire."
(*al-Riyāḍ*, Mar. 21, 2011)

٣ مائة ألف وألفان وأحد وستون دينارًا

3 "102,061 dinars"
('Ali ibn 'Īsa ibn al-Jarrāḥ, Financial statement, 918–19 A.D., p. 51)

---

43. Also see the section "Writing Out Large Numbers," p. 79.

Ordinal[44]

To form the ordinal of compound numbers in the thousands, بعد may be used between the multiple of 1000 and the element of the compound smaller than 1000. The construction is thus:

(ordinal of the multiple of 100 plus the following numbers) + بعد + (ordinal of the multiple of 1000).

الخمسمائة والسابع بعد الألفين "the 2,507th"

Or, less commonly, the thousands and hundreds may both occur after the بعد.

السابع والخمسون بعد الألف والثلاثمائة "the 1,357th"

The ordinal of the multiples of 1000 are the same as the cardinal, and the definite article الـ is attached only to the first element of it (see p. 87).

رَقَم ("number") plus the cardinal is also often used.

الزبون رقم ألف وخمسمائة

"the 1,500th customer (customer number 1500)"

EXAMPLES

١ المزاد اليومي الثلاثمائة والحادي والخمسون بعد الألف لبيع وشراء العملة الأجنبية

1 "The 1,351st daily auction for the purchase and sale of foreign currency."
(announcement from Iraqi National Media Center, nmc.gov.iq, Feb. 23, 2009)

٢ اغلق البنك المركزي العراقي مزاده اليومي الثلاثمائة والسابع عشر بعد الالف لبيع وشراء العملة الاجنبية

2 "The Central Bank of Iraq closed its 1,317th daily auction for the sale and purchase of foreign currency."
(al-iraqnews.info, Dec. 30, 2008)

٣ تقضي المبادرة بإصدار نسخ إضافية لطابع بريدي فاتيكاني مكرس للذكرى الخمسمائة بعد الألف لمزار مريمي هو مزار "سيدة النعم" المعروف باسم مزار منتوريلا

3 "The initiative provides for the issuance of extra copies of a Vatican postage stamp commemorating the

44. Also see the section "More on Ordinal Numbers," p. 110.

1,500th anniversary of a shrine to the Virgin Mary, the Our Lady of Graces Sanctuary, known as the Shrine of Mentorella."
(al-iklim.com, Jan. 26, 2010)

٤ . . . الاحتفال الباذخ للغاية الذي أقامه زوجها في عام 1971 بالذكرى السنوية الخمسمائة بعد الألفين لقيام الامبراطورية الفارسية

4 ". . . the extremely extravagant celebration put on by her husband in 1971 for the 2,500th yearly commemoration of the rise of the Persian Empire."
(*al-Riyāḍ*, May 4, 2004)

٥ وكأن أغاني السبعينات السورية بقيت (على عكس الكثير من الأشياء) تناسب العام الحادي عشر بعد الألفين

5 "It is as if Syrian songs of the 70s have remained, unlike many things, appropriate to the year 2011 (the 2,011th year)."
(*al-Waṭan* [Syria], Apr. 17, 2011)

٦ محضر حرفي مؤقت للجلسة الرابعة والعشرين بعد الثلاثة آلاف والمائتين

6 "Provisional verbatim record of the 3,224th meeting."
(record of U.N. meeting S/PV 3224, May 27, 1993)[45]

٧ في الأول من يونيه/حزيران ٢٠٠٥، تلقى مركز التحكيم والوساطة القضية رقم سبعة آلاف وخمسمائة

7 "On June 1, 2005, the Arbitration and Mediation Center received its 7,500th case (case #7500)."
(document A/41/3 from the World Intellectual Property Organization [WIPO], "Program Implementation Overview, January 1 to June 30, 2005," Aug. 24, 2005)

٨ المباراة رقم ثلاثة آلاف وخمسمائة للإنتر

8 "The 3,500th Game (game #3500) for Inter Milan."
(intermilan.ae, May 14, 2006)

45. Retrieved from moqatel.com

Millions, Billions, and Beyond

Million[46]

"One million" is مَليون/مِليون. Its plural is مَلايين.

It is usually pronounced *milyōn*/*malyōn*, that is, the و is pronounced with the nonstandard *ō* sound, similar to the vowel in English "boat."

Since it is equivalent to ألف ألف, grammatical rules regarding its counted noun are the same as those for that of ألف.

Rules for placing it in compounds are the same as for ألف and its multiples.

EXAMPLES

١ . . . وبذلك تحصل على مليون دولار

1 ". . . and thus to obtain a million dollars."
(Muṣṭafa Amīn, *al-Mi'atā Fikra*, p. 19)

٢ . . . أدى إلى سرقة البيانات الشخصية وكلمات السر والعناوين الالكترونية لحوالي مليون مستخدمٍ في "سوني بيكتشرز انترتينمت" . . . وأدى إلى سرقة بيانات حوالي سبعةٍ وسبعينَ مليونَ مستخدمٍ

2 ". . . which led to the theft of personal data, passwords and email addresses of around a million users in Sony Pictures Entertainment . . . and led to the theft of data of 77 million users."
(broadcast on Euronews Arabic, June 3, 2011)

٣ أكثر من مليوني حاج في أكبر تظاهرة إسلامية اليوم

3 "More than 2 million pilgrims today in the largest Islamic display . . ."
(*al-Ḥayāt*, Jan. 9, 2006)

٤ وصل إلى أكثر من ثلاثة ملايين ومائتين وخمسين ألف سائح

4 "It has reached more than 3,250,000 tourists . . ."
(*al-'Arabi*, June 1993)

٥ . . . ما يقرب من ٧ ملايين نسمة . . .

5 ". . . nearly 7 million people . . ."
(*al-'Arabi*, June 1993)

46. Also see the section "Writing Out Large Numbers," p. 79.

٦ إن محمد علي كلاي ربح في عام ١٩٧٥ مبلغ ثمانية ملايين ونصف مليون دولار وفي سنة ١٩٧٧ ربح مبلغ ١٤ مليونًا وثمانمائة ألف دولار

6 "In 1975 Muhammad Ali made 8,500,000 dollars, and in 1977 he made 14,800,000 dollars."
(Muṣṭafa Amīn, *al-Mi'atā Fikra*, p. 20)

٧ . . . بقيمة إجمالية بلغت تسعة ملايين وثلاثمائة وواحدا وعشرين ألفا وثمانمائة وواحدا وستين ريالا . . .

7 ". . . with a total value reaching 9,321,861 riyals."
(*al-Sharq al-Awsaṭ*, Jan. 14, 2006)

٨ الحكومةُ باعت ثلاثمئةِ مليونِ سهمٍ مقابل تسعة وعشرين دولارا للسهم الواحد

8 "The government sold 300 million shares at $29 per share."
(broadcast on Euronews Arabic, May 25, 2011)

٩ وصل عدد مستخدمي موقع التواصل الاجتماعي ((فيسبوك)) إلي خمسِمائةِ مليونِ شخص

9 "The number of users of the social networking site Facebook has reached 500 million people."
(broadcast on Al Aan TV, July 22, 2010)[47]

Billion[48]

"One billion" may be rendered بِليون (plural, بَلايين), or مِليار (plural, مِليارات).

بليون is usually pronounced *bilyōn*, that is, the و is pronounced with the nonstandard *ō* sound, similar to the vowel in English "boat."

Since one billion is a multiple of ألف, grammatical rules regarding its counted noun are the same as those for that of ألف.

Rules for placing it in compounds are the same as for ألف and its multiples.

47. Retrieved from www.youtube.com/watch?v=FBVqvpu1D8s
48. Also see the section "Writing Out Large Numbers," p. 79.

EXAMPLES

١ السعوديون ينفقون 1.5 بليون دولار سنويًا على أدوية علاج الضعف الجنسي!

1 "Saudis spend 1.5 billion dollars yearly on medications to treat impotence!"
(*al-Riyāḍ*, Jan. 1, 2011)

٢ مكتبة الإسكندرية ترقمن ٣ بلايين وثيقة

2 "The Alexandria Library is digitizing 3 billion documents."
(*al-Ḥayāt*, Apr. 18, 2011)

٣ . . . أن شركات الطيران الصينية حققت أرباحًا بلغت ٣٥ بليون يوان (٥,٣ بليون دولار) والمطارات ٥ بلايين

3 ". . . that Chinese airline companies made profits of 35 billion yuan (5.3 billion dollars) and airports made 5 billion."
(*al-Ḥayāt*, Jan. 14, 2011)

٤ 77 بليون دولار في العام 2012 للاقتصاد غير النفطي

4 "77 Billion Dollars in 2012 for the Non-Petroleum Economy"
(*al-Ittiḥād* [UAE], Nov. 14, 2010)

٥ انباء عن عرض الملك عبدالله 150 بليون دولار لشراء موقع فيسبوك والسعودية تنفي

5 "Reports that King Abdallah Has Offered 150 Billion Dollars to Buy the Website Facebook, which Saudi Arabia Denies"
(alquds.co.uk, Feb. 27, 2011)

٦ مليار كاتب ينشطون على الشبكة العنكبوتية

6 "A billion writers are active on the World Wide Web."
(*al-Sharq al-Awsaṭ*, Apr. 24, 2011)

٧ . . . إن هناك فرصة لأن يصل عدد مستخدمي الموقع إلى مليارِ مستخدمٍ في غضون خمسةِ أعوام.

7 ". . . that there is a chance that the number of users of the site reaches a billion users within five years."
(broadcast on Al Aan TV, July 22, 2010)[49]

49. Retrieved from www.youtube.com/watch?v=FBVqvpu1D8s

٨ أودعت وزارة الشؤون الاجتماعية . . . مبلغ (1.024.670.083) مليار وأربعة وعشرين مليونًا وست مئة وسبعين ألفًا وثلاثة وثمانين ريالاً

8 "The Ministry of Social Affairs has deposited . . . the amount of 1,024,670,083 riyals."
(*al-Riyāḍ*, Mar. 10, 2011)

٩ صرف ملياري ريال لمستفيدي الضمان الاجتماعي

9 "The Spending of Two Billion Riyals on Beneficiaries of Social Security"
(*al-Riyāḍ*, Feb. 16, 2011)

١٠ تقدر إيرادات الأمانات والبلديات . . . بمبلغ 3.257.320.000 ريال (ثلاثة مليارات ومائتان وسبعة وخمسون مليونا وثلاثمائة وعشرون ألف ريال).

10 "Revenues from the municipalities and districts . . . are estimated to be 3,257,320,000 riyals."
(*al-Sharq al-Awsaṭ*, Dec. 21, 2010)

١١ نجحت اسبانيا في بيعِ سنداتٍ حكوميةٍ بأجَلِ عشرِ سنواتٍ وثلاثَ عشرةَ سنة بقيمةِ ثلاثةِ ملياراتٍ وأربعِمئةِ مليون يورو

11 "Spain has succeeded in selling 10- and 13-year government bonds with a value of 3,400,000,000 Euros."
(broadcast on Euronews Arabic, Apr. 20, 2011)

١٢ . . . بكلفة مالية قدرها مائة وخمسة مليارات ريال يمني . . .

12 ". . . at a cost of 105 billion Yemeni riyals . . ."
(*al-Jumhūriyya* [Yemen], Nov. 16, 2006)

١٣ ويفيد تقرير علمي جديد أن تكلفة معالجة المرضى بألزهايمر في العالم تصل إلى ستمئة مليار دولار

13 "A new scientific report states that expenditures on treatment of Alzheimer's patients worldwide has reached 600 billion dollars."
(arabic.euronews.net, Sept. 22, 2010)

١٤ تقدر إيرادات وتعتمد مصروفات جامعة القصيم بمبلغ 1.707.475.000 ريال (مليار وسبعمائة وسبعة ملايين وأربعمائة وخمسة وسبعون ألف ريال)

14 "The revenues are estimated and expenditures authorized for Qassim University at an amount of 1,707,475,000 riyals."
(*al-Sharq al-Awsaṭ*, Dec. 21, 2010)

Millionaire/Billionaire

A person with a million dollars (a millionaire) is a مليونير.
A billionaire is a بليونير or ملياردير.

In all of these words, the last ي is pronounced with the nonstandard *ē* sound, similar to the vowel in English "safe": *milyōnēr, bilyōnēr, milyārdēr.*

EXAMPLES

١ كان ومازال مليونيرا

1 "He was and still is a millionaire."
(Naguib Mahfouz, *al-Ṭarīq*, p. 214)

٢ سألت مجلة أمريكية قارئتها، هل تريدين أن تصبحي مليونيرة؟؟؟

2 "An American magazine asked its female reader(s), 'Do you want to become a millionaire???'"
(Muṣṭafa Amīn, *al-Mi'atā Fikra*, p. 19)

٣ اصغر بليونير في العالم

3 "The Youngest Billionaire in the World"
(*al-Ahrām*, Nov. 3, 2010)

٤ ملياردير هندي يقيم في لندن يؤسس أكبر شركة للحديد والصلب في العالم

4 "An Indian billionaire residing in London founds the largest iron and steel company in the world."
(*al-Sharq al-Awsaṭ*, Nov. 25, 2004)

Trillion[50]

Trillion may be expressed as تريليون (plural تريليونات).

EXAMPLES

١ «الكويت الوطني» يتوقع ارتفاع إيرادات السعودية من النفط إلى تريليون ريال

1 "The Kuwait National Bank Expects Saudi Arabia's Revenues from Oil to Increase to a Trillion Riyals."
(*al-Ittiḥād* [UAE], June 5, 2011)

50. Also see the section "Writing Out Large Numbers," p. 79.

٢ ١,٦ تريليون دولار قيمة سوق تكنولوجيا المعلومات في العالم نهاية السنة

2 "1.6 trillion dollars will be the value of the information technology market worldwide at the end of the year."
(*al-Ḥayāt*, Aug. 12, 2009)

٣ . . . التي تحقق أرباحا سنوية قدرها 6 تريليونات دولار . . .

3 ". . . which achieves yearly profits of 6 trillion dollars . . ."
(*al-Sharq al-Awsaṭ*, June 11, 2011)

٤ وتقدر «إنبكس» . . . ان هناك أكثر من ١٠ تريليونات قدم مكعبة من الغاز الطبيعي في حقل أبادي

4 "INPEX . . . estimates that there are more than 10 trillion cubic feet of natural gas in the Abadi field."
(*al-Ra'y* [Kuwait], Jan. 9, 2009)

٥ ذوبان جليد القطب الشمالي يكلف العالم 24 تريليون دولار بحلول 2050.

5 "The melting of ice at the North Pole will cost the world 24 trillion dollars by 2050."
(*al-Ittiḥād* [UAE], Feb. 7, 2010)

٦ في جسمك 100 تريليون جرثومة

6 "There are 100 trillion germs in your body."
(*al-Qabas*, Nov. 4, 2010)

Higher than Trillion[51]

"Quadrillion" is expressed as كدريليون or كوادريليون, and quintillion as كوينتيليون.

EXAMPLES

١ وذكرت الدراسة أنه تم تنفيذ أكثر من 4.8 كدريليون (كدريليون = ألف تريليون) عملية مصرفية عبر شبكة الإنترنت.

1 "The study mentioned that more than 4.8 quadrillion (1 quadrillion = 1000 trillion) bank transactions were conducted over the internet."
(*al-Iqtiṣādiyya*, June 3, 2009)

51. Also see the section "Writing Out Large Numbers," p. 79.

٢ . . . أنه مدين للبنك بأكثر من 23 كدريليون دولار أو تحديداً مبلغ
.23148855308184500

2 ". . . that he owed the bank more than 23 quadrillion dollars, specifically, the amount of $23,148,855,308,184,500."
(aljazeera.net, July 16, 2009)

٣ قامت الصين بتطوير أسرع "سوبر كومبيوتر" تنتجه بقدرة اجراء كوادريليون (ألف تريليون) عملية حسابية في الثانية.

3 "China has developed the fastest "supercomputer" it has produced, with the ability to carry out a quadrillion (1000 trillion) calculations per second."
(*al-Iqtiṣādiyya*, May 28, 2010)

٤ . . . إجمالي استخدام الطاقة في العام 2009 يقدر بـ 94.6 كوادريليون وحدة حرارة بريطانية مقارنة بـ 99.2 كوادريليون وحدة حرارة بريطانية (BTU) في العام 2008

4 ". . . the total use of energy in the year 2009 is estimated to be 94.6 quadrillion BTUs, as compared with 99.2 quadrillion BTUs in the year 2008."
(*al-Wasaṭ* [Bahrain], Aug. 28, 2010)

٥ في اللحظة التي أكتب فيها هذا المقال بلغت معدلات التضخم في زيمبابوي مستوى لا يمكن تصوره . . . ما يزيد على خمسمئة كوينتيليون في المئة (الكوينتيليون عدد يتألف من الرقم واحد وأمامه ثمانية عشر صفراً، أي ألف تريليون).

5 "As I write this, the inflation rate in Zimbabwe has reached a level that is unimaginable, . . . more than 500 quintillion percent (a quintillion is a number made up of 1 followed by 18 zeros, that is, 1,000 trillion)."[52]
(*al-Jarīda*, Feb. 5, 2009)

Millions and Higher: Ordinal[53]

Forming the ordinal of numbers one million and higher is done using the same techniques as are used with multiples of 1000.

52. The author errs here, as a quintillion is actually a million trillion.
53. Also see the section "More on Ordinal Numbers," p. 110.

EXAMPLES

١ الزائر رقم مليون للجناح السعودي في (أكسبو شانغهاي) يفوز بقضاء أسبوع في المملكة

1 "The millionth visitor (visitor #1 million) to the Saudi pavilion in Expo Shanghai wins a week in the Kingdom."
(*al-Riyāḍ*, June 19, 2010)

٢ للمرة المليون . . . فككوها!

2 "For the millionth time . . . break it up!"
(*al-Ra'y* [Kuwait], Oct. 22, 2010)

٣ أقولها للمرة المليون

3 "I say it for the millionth time."
(*al-Ittiḥād* [UAE], Apr. 21, 2011)

٤ بلدية الغربية تكرم المراجع رقم مليون في مركز الخدمات الحكومية ((تم))

4 "The Al Gharbia region honors the millionth client (client #1 million) in the Tam Center for Government Services."
(*al-Ittiḥād* [UAE], Mar. 3, 2011)

٥ نصر الله يزرع الشجرة رقم مليون أمام منزله . . . يفيد بان أمينه العام زرع «الشجرة المليون» أمام منزله في حارة حريك

5 "Nasrallah plants the millionth tree (tree #1 million) in front of his home . . . which states that its Secretary General planted 'the millionth tree' in front of his house in Haret Hreik . . ."
(*al-Sharq al-Awsaṭ*, Oct. 9, 2010)

٦ للمرة الألف بعد المليون نكرر نداءنا لشباب اليمن الأحرار . . .

6 "For the 1,001,000th time, we repeat our call to the free youth of Yemen . . ."
(*al-Jumhūriyya* [Yemen], May 12, 2011)

٧ . . . وفي عام 1997م احتفلت الشركة ببيع الجهاز رقم عشرة مليون

7 ". . . and in 1997 the company celebrated the sale of its 10 millionth computer (computer #10 million)."
(*al-Riyāḍ*, July 3, 2009)

٨ لنحتفل بقدوم الأميركي رقم 300 مليون

8 "Let us celebrate the arrival of the 300 millionth American (American #300 million)."
(*al-Ittiḥād* [UAE], Oct. 13, 2006)

٩ احتفل الروائي البرازيلي باولو كيولهو بطبع النسخة رقم مائة مليون من كتبه.

9 "The Brazilian novelist Paulo Coelho celebrated the printing of the 100 millionth copy (copy #100 million) of his books."
(*al-Ahrām*, Feb. 9, 2008)

١٠ احتفلت منظمة الأمم المتحدة العام الماضي بمولد الفرد رقم سبعة بلايين

10 "The United Nations last year celebrated the birth of the seven billionth person."
(*al-Ḥayāt*, Oct. 27, 2012)

Multiples of 1000: Classical Texts

In the classical period, the highest number for which a word existed was 1000. Thus, any number above 999,999 was referred to as 1000 multiplied by 1000 as many times as necessary.

EXAMPLES

١ القرآن ألف ألف حرف، وسبعة وعشرون ألف حرف[54]

1 "The Qur'an is (made up of) 1,027,000 letters."
(Suyūṭi, *al-Itqān fī 'Ulūm al-Qur'ān*, p. 162, *naw'* 19)

٢ وتبعهم فرعون، وعلى مقدمته هامان، في ألف ألف وسبعمائة ألف حصان

2 "They were followed by Pharaoh, with Haman in the forefront with 1,700,000 horses."
(Ṭabari, *Tārīkh*, 1/414)

٣ وقد كان الحجاج قصده وعذّبه، وأغرمه أربعة آلاف ألف درهم ظلماً، ثم طالبه بعدها بثلاثة آلاف ألف درهم

3 "Ḥajjāj had arrested and tortured him, and wrongly fined him 4 million dirhams. Then after that he demanded another 3 million dirhams."
(*Qiṣaṣ al-'Arab*, 1/163)

54. Typo corrected: The phrase "وسبعة وعشرون حرف" is out of place in the printed edition and placed at the beginning of the paragraph. The correct order is as I have it here and is confirmed by other editions of the book such as that printed by Dar al-Kotob al-Ilmiyah.

٤ وعلى هذا تكون مساحة سطحها الخارج . . . أربعة عشر ألف ألف وسبعمائة وأربعة وأربعين ألفًا ومئتين واثنين وأربعين فرسخًا وخمس فرسخ

4 "Given this, the surface area of the earth would be . . . 14,744,242 and one-fifth parasangs."
(Yāqūt, *Mu'jam al-Buldān*, 1/33, chap. 1 of introduction)

٥ ولم تزل قطيعة الري اثني عشر ألف ألف درهم . . . فأسقط عنهم منها ألفي ألف درهم

5 "The tax due from Rayy remained 12 million dirhams . . . so he reduced it by 2 million dirhams."
(Yāqūt, *Mu'jam al-Buldān*, 3/134, #5887 on Rayy)

٦ وكان خراجها ثلاثين ألف ألف درهم

6 "Its land tax was 30 million dirhams."
(Yāqūt, *Mu'jam al-Buldān*, 1/339, #1163 on al-Ahwāz)

٧ . . . يكون ما فيها ألف ألف ألف مثقال وستمائة ألف ألف مثقال

7 ". . . in which were 1,600,000,000 miskals."
(Ṭabari, *Tārīkh*, 2/227)

٨ وأعداد أضعاف الشطرنج ثمانية عشر ألف ألف ألف ألف ألف ألف وأربعمائة ألف وستة وأربعون ألف ألف ألف ألف ألف وسبعمائة وأربعون ألف ألف ألف ألف، وثلاثة وسبعون ألف ألف ألف، وسبعمائة ألف ألف، وسبعة آلاف ألف وخمسمائة ألف وأحد وخمسون ألف وستمائة وخمسة عشر

8 "The number that results from doubling in chess is 18,446,740,073,707,551,615."[55]
(*Mas'ūdi, Murūj al-Dhahab*, 1/81)

---

55. That is, the number that results from starting with one item on the first square of a chessboard, then doubling its amount on the second square, then doubling the resulting amount on the third square, and so on until the final, 64th square has been reached.

The ألف between أربعمائة and وستة وأربعون may be understood as a repetition of the counted noun ألف. So the number given is أربعمائة ألف وستة وأربعون ألف "Four-hundred thousand and 46 thousand" (446,000). In turn, the counted noun for this number is ألف ألف ألف ألف, "a trillion," i.e., 446,000 trillions, which equals 446 quadrillion.

More on Ordinal Numbers

Using *raqam*

Any cardinal number can be made into an ordinal by placing رَقَم "number" before it, just as one can place "number" before a number in English and create an ordinal number (e.g., "attempt number 3").

EXAMPLES

١ وكانت المحاولة رقم سبعة وعشرين هي التي حققت حلمها

1 "It was the 27th try (attempt #27) which led to her realizing her dream."
(*al-Riyāḍ*, Sept. 26, 2003)

٢ . . . الاحتفالات التي تقام بمناسبة الذكرى رقم مئتين لانتخاب المارشال الفرنسي جان بابتيست بيرنادوت وريثا للعرش السويدي.

2 ". . . the celebrations that were held on the occasion of the 200th anniversary (anniversary #200) of the election of Marshal Jean Baptiste Bernadotte as heir to the Swedish throne."
(*al-Riyāḍ*, June 23, 2010)

٣ أمريكا تنفذ الإعدام رقم ألف منذ 1976

3 "America Carries Out Its 1,000th Execution (execution #1000) Since 1976"
(*al-Bayān*, Dec. 3, 2005)

٤ انصب اهتمام الصحافة وأجهزة الإعلام . . . على مصرع الجندي الأميركي رقم ألفين في العراق.

4 "There has been great interest in news and media organizations . . . over the death of the 2000th American soldier (American soldier #2000) in Iraq."
(*al-Ittiḥād* [UAE], Nov. 4, 2005)

Mukammil

Ordinals of large round numbers 100 or greater may be formed by using المُكَمِّل لِـ (المكملة لـ in the feminine), followed by the number, where المكمل functions as an adjective to the noun being described.

EXAMPLES

١ المسألة المكملة للمائة

1 "The hundredth issue"
(chapter heading in table of contents of Anbāri, *al-Inṣāf fi Masā'il al-Khilāf*, 2/469)

٢ وفي اليوم المكمل للسبعمائة بدأت الجارية رباب تحكي حكاية أزمرالدة

2 "On the 700th day, the slave girl Rabab began telling the story of Esmerelda."
(Muhammad Rif'at, *Ḥikāyāt Alf Yawm wa-Yawm*)[56]

٣ ادخر العريس راتبه لمدة سنة لشراء 99.999 من الورود الحمراء لعروسه في يوم زفافهما لتكون هي الورده المكمله للمئة الف

3 "The groom saved up his salary for a year in order to buy 99,999 red roses for his bride on their wedding day, so he could say that she is the 100,000th rose."
(posting by Ṭāriq on forum of alwid.org)

Ordinal with Superlative

"Third largest," "second largest," and so forth are expressed with the ordinal number in the masculine followed by the superlative. Both the ordinal number and the superlative remain masculine regardless of the gender of the noun being described.

ثاني أكبر مدينة "the second largest city"

ثالث أغنى رجل "the third richest man"

Sometimes the order is reversed: The ordinal comes after the superlative instead of before.

EXAMPLES

١ المملكة ثالث أكبر مالك للسندات الأمريكية

1 "The Kingdom Is the Third Largest Owner of American Securities"
(*al-Yawm*, June 15, 2011)

56. Cited in a post on www.uaepulse.net, Mar. 23, 2010.

٢ التشيك تفاجئ كرواتيا في رابع أطول مباراة

2 "The Czech Republic takes Croatia by surprise in the fourth longest game."
(*al-Khalīj*, Sept. 20, 2009)

٣ الإمارات ثاني أكثر الدول إنجازاً للأبراج الشاهقة عام 2010

3 "The Emirates Is the Second Most Prolific Country in Building Tall Buildings (the secondmost of countries in terms of achieving tall buildings) in 2010."
(*al-Ittiḥād* [UAE], Apr. 11, 2011)

٤ فإن دبي تعد ثالث أكثر دولة في العالم يتم استخدام المراكب البحرية للتنقل والسياحة فيها

4 "Dubai is considered the country with the third highest usage of boats in transportation and tourism (lit., the thirdmost country in which boats are used)."
(*al-Sharq al-Awsaṭ*, July 25, 2007)

٥ البورصة تخسر 29 مليار جنيه أمس وتسجل أكبر ثالث هبوط في تاريخها بسبب المظاهرات

5 "The stock market lost 29 billion pounds yesterday, recording the third biggest drop in its history due to demonstrations."
(digital.ahram.org.eg, Jan. 27, 2011)

PART II

Other Number Topics

Biḍ'a and *Nayf*

Biḍ'a

بِضْعة means "some unknown number from one to ten." It is best translated as "a few" or "several."

Its relationship with counted nouns is the same as that of the numbers from 3 to 10. It is subject to polar agreement (see p. 14). That is, when the counted noun is masculine, بضعة retains its *tā' marbūṭa*. When the counted noun is feminine, the *tā' marbūṭa* is dropped (بِضْع).

The following counted noun is plural and in an إضافة relationship with بضعة.

Also like the numbers from 3 to 10, it can be combined with عشر (or عشرة in the feminine), in which case it means "ten-something," that is, some number between ten and twenty.

The rules that apply to combining numbers 3–10 with عشر or عشرة apply to بضعة as well:

Polar agreement continues to apply to بضعة, but not to the عشرة, just as with any teen number.

Also like the teens, the *fatḥa* at the end of بضع and بضعة is invariable when it is placed in combination with عشر or عشرة, as is the *fatḥa* on عشر or عشرة.

The counted noun is singular and منصوب.

بِضْعةَ عَشَرَ	used with masculine nouns
بِضْعَ عَشْرَةَ	used with feminine nouns

بضعة can also combined with one of the tens (10, 20, 30, etc.). The same rules which apply to combining a number from 3 to 10 with one of the tens apply to بضعة (see p. 45): Polar agreement applies to it; it is placed before the larger number and is connected to it with a *wāw*; the following counted noun is singular and in the منصوب case.

EXAMPLES

١ أطقم كامل أم بضع أسنان فقط؟

1 "A whole set or just a few teeth?"
(Naguib Mahfouz, *Zuqāq al-Midaqq*, p. 223)

Note: سِنّ is feminine.

٢ ويأخذ في مقابل هذا بضعة قروش

2 "And in return he gets a few piastres."
(Yūsuf Idrīs, *al-'Askari al-Aswad*, p. 22)

٣ . . . خلافاً لكثير من عمليات الاحتجاج التي تستغرق بضع ساعات . . .

3 ". . . unlike many protests which last a few hours . . ."
(*al-Ḥayāt*, Jan. 14, 2011)

٤ يحتشد الحجاج في «منظر مهيب»، في نطاق ضيق لا يتعدى بضعة كيلومترات

4 "In an awe-inspring sight, pilgrims gather in a confined space of no more than a few kilometers."
(*al-Ḥayāt*, Jan. 9, 2006)

٥ فبَقِيَ في السجن بِضْعَ سنين

5 "He remained in prison for several years."
(Yāqūt, *Mu'jam al-Udabā'*, 1/183, #41 on Ibrāhīm ibn Hilāl ibn Zahrūn)

٦ كانت سريّة غالب بن عبد الله بضعةَ عشرَ رجلاً

6 "Ghālib ibn 'Abd Allāh's party was (made up of) ten-some men."
(Ṭabari, *Tārīkh*, 3/28)

٧ وله بِضْعَةَ عَشَرَ كتاباً في الأوصاف

7 "He has ten-some books on descriptions."
(Yāqūt, *Mu'jam al-Udabā'*, 5/444, #918 on Muḥammad ibn al-Marzubān)

٨ ولَزِمْتُ أبا عبد اللهِ بن الأعرابي، بضعَ عَشْرَةَ سَنَةً

8 "I stayed with Abu 'Abd Allāh ibn al-A'rābi for ten-some years."
(Yāqūt, *Mu'jam al-Udabā'*, 2/59, #206 on Tha'lab)

٩ وكانوا بضعة وثلاثين ألف رجل

9 "They were thirty-some thousand men."
(Ṭabari, *Tārīkh*, 1/413)

١٠ والله لا يخرج من النار أحد حتى يمكث فيها أحقاباً، والحُقُب بضع وثمانون سنة

10 "By God no one leaves hell until he has stayed there for many *ḥuqubs*. A *ḥuqub* is eighty-some years."
(Suyūṭi, *al-Itqān fī 'Ulūm al-Qur'ān*, p. 926, *naw'* 80)

Nayf

نَيْف or نَيِّف was used frequently in classical texts. Like بضعة, it means some number from one to ten.

It is most frequently combined with one of the tens. Its gender does not change. It remains نيف regardless of the gender of the counted noun.

EXAMPLES

١ فمن لدن عُمِر بيت المقدس بعد تخريبه بختنصر إلى الهجرة—على قولهم—ألف سنة ونيف، ومن ملك الإسكندر إليها تسعمائة سنة ونيّف وعشرون سنة

1 "From the building of Jerusalem after Nebuchadnezzar destroyed it to the Hijra, they say, was one-thousand years and some. And from the rule of Alexander to the Hijra was 920-some years."
(Ṭabari, *Tārīkh*, 1/608)

٢ سكن مرو ومات بها في سنة نيف وتسعين ومائتين

2 "He lived in Merv and died there in the year 290-something."
(Yāqūt, *Mu'jam al-Buldān*, 3/136, #5887 on Rayy)

٣ وبين الدينور وهمذان نيف وعشرون فرسخاً[57]

3 "(The distance) between Dīnawar and Hamadhān is twenty-some parasangs."
(Yāqūt, *Mu'jam al-Buldān*, 2/616, #5187 on Dīnawar)

57. Typo corrected: الدينور for الدنيور

Making Numbers Definite

There are several ways to make a number and its counted noun definite, that is, to say something like "*the* seven books," "*the* fourteen members of the committee," "my ten best friends."

Numbers in an *iḍāfa* Construction: 3–10, 100 and Its Multiples, 1000

Iḍāfa Construction; Definite Article on Second Term

Traditional Arabic grammars state that when the relationship between a number and its counted noun is an إضافة, as occurs with 3–10, 100 and its multiples, and 1000 and its multiples, that the construction is rendered definite as any إضافة construction is rendered defininte: by placing the definite article الـ on the مضاف إليه, or by making the مضاف إليه definite in some other way. Thus, "the seven books" would be سبعة الكتب.[58]

In actual practice, however, this structure is not particularly common, though it is sometimes seen.

EXAMPLES

١ قالت شركة زين انها احتفلت مع عملائها والجمهور بفرحة العيد على مدار أربعة الأيام الماضية

1 "The Zain Corporation said that it celebrated Eid with its employees and with the general public over the course of the last four days."
(*al-Qabas*, Sept. 15, 2010)

٢ لا تعد نفسك من الاحياء حتى تطوف بأربعة أركان المعمورة

2 "Do not count yourself among the living until you have traveled the four corners of the world."
(Naguib Mahfouz, *al-Ṭarīq*, p. 220)

---

58. See for example, Jārim and Amīn, *al-Naḥw al-Wāḍiḥ*, 5/205-206; Ni'ma, *Mulakhkhaṣ Qawā'id al-Lugha al-'Arabiyya*, 1/90; Zamakhshari, *al-Mufaṣṣal*, pp. 265–266.

3–10 After Counted Noun

For numbers 3–10, it is far more common to place the number after the counted noun and treat it as an adjective for the counted noun. As such, it will agree with the counted noun in definiteness. Polar agreement (see p. 14), however, still applies: If the counted noun is feminine, the following number has no *tāʾ marbūṭa*, and if it is masculine, the counted noun has *tāʾ marbūṭa*.

الأصدقاء الخمسة "the five friends"

EXAMPLES

١ وقد اعترف المتهمون الثلاثة بعد ضبطهم بجرائمهم

1 "After being caught, the three suspects confessed to their crimes."
(*al-Riyāḍ*, June 2, 2009)

٢ . . . بعد إسقاط مروحية بريطانية ومقتل أفراد طاقمها الأربعة . . .

2 ". . . after the crash of a British helicopter and the deaths of its four crew members . . ."
(*al-Ḥayāt*, May 7, 2006)

٣ فإنه أحد المساجد الأربعة ركعتان فيه تعدلان عشراً فيما سواه من المساجد

3 "It is one of the four mosques in which two *rakʿa*s are equivalent to ten in another mosque."
(Yāqūt, *Muʿjam al-Buldān*, 4/559, #10473, on al-Kūfa)

٤ فمن المؤسف حقا أن أحدا من أبنائه الثلاثة لم يقع له في خاطر أن يتقدم لمعاونة أبيه في عمله

4 "It is truly regrettable that it did not occur to a single one of his three sons to come forward and help his father in his work."
(Naguib Mahfouz, *Zuqāq al-Midaqq*, p. 63)

٥ كان لمصر أربعة أبواب فدخلوها من أبوابها الأربعة متفرقين

5 "Egypt had four gates, and they entered it separately via its four gates."
(Ṭabarsi, *Majmaʿ al-Bayān*, 5/331 on 12:68)

٦ وطلق نوح الغراب زوجاته الأربع

6 "Nūḥ al-Ghurāb divorced his four wives."
(Naguib Mahfouz, *al-Ḥarāfīsh*, p. 368)

٧ الرسائل السبع لاحتجاجات تونس

7 "The Seven Messages of the Tunis Protests"
(*al-Ḥayāt*, Jan. 14, 2011)

٨ ولم تفقد فرنسا الأمل في التوصل إلى جمع الأصوات التسعة الضرورية

8 "France has not lost hope that it will be able to gather the nine necessary votes."
(*al-Sharq al-Awsaṭ*, June 11, 2011)

٩ الفرقان: وهو الوصايا العشر . . . وهو الأخلاق المشتركة بين الديانات السماوية الثلاث

9 "The *furqān*: It is the ten commandments . . . and it is the morals shared by the three celestial religions."
(Muḥammad Shaḥrūr, *al-Kitāb wa-l-Qur'ān*, p. 214)

Hundreds, Thousands Before Counted Noun

One hundred and its multiples and 1000, contrary to what traditional grammars prescribe (see p. 117), are often placed before the counted noun and have the definite article الـ attached. The counted noun is in the singular.

المائة دولار "the hundred dollars"

'Abbās Ḥasan points out that this structure has always been frequently used. It is attested to in modern and classical texts and is even found in some Prophetic Hadiths. He also says that because it has been so commonly seen throughout the history of Arabic writing, it should be considered acceptable but not preferred.[59]

EXAMPLES

١ الـ ٢٠٠ فكرة

1 "*The 200 Ideas*"
(title of book by Muṣṭafa Amīn)

٢ تم التعارف عن طريق المدام. وقد قدمتني كعادتها بالكامل، أي بالمائة فدان والمشروع

2 "The introduction was done by Madame. As usual, she presented me in my entirety, i.e., with the 100 feddans and the project."
(Naguib Mahfouz, *Mīrāmār*, p. 115)

---

59. Hasan, *al-Naḥw al-Wāfi*, 1/438.

٣ الذهب يبدأ رحلة صعود نحو اختراق حاجز الألف دولار

3 "Gold Begins an Upward Journey Towards Breaking the 1,000-Dollar Barrier"
(*al-Sharq al-Awsaṭ*, July 13, 2008)

٤ والغالبية العظمى من الأربعة آلاف نوع من الدعاسيق، تتغذى . . .
على حشرات أخرى ضارة

4 "The vast majority of the 4000 types of ladybugs feed . . . on other, harmful insects."
(*al-Aṭlas al-ʿIlmi*, p. 97)

Hundreds, Thousands After Counted Noun

Alternatively, as with 3–10, 100 and its multiples and 1000 may be placed after the counted noun and function as an adjective, in which case they agree with the counted noun in definiteness. They do not vary by gender.

الشبابيك المائة "the hundred windows"

EXAMPLES

١ قاموا بالإضافة إلى تنقيح وتطوير تلك المسائل المائتين بشكل كبير

1 "They greatly added to, revised, and developed those 200 questions."
(*al-Ru'ya*, Nov. 30, 2010)

٢ فها هم الطلاب الثلاثمائة في الجامعة الاميركية بموسكو يحلمون
بالانخراط في عالم المال والعولمة

2 "Here are the 300 students in the American University in Moscow dreaming of getting into the world of money and globalization."
(*al-Sharq al-Awsaṭ*, June 6, 2002)

٣ ومنذ اكثر من ثلاثة شهور تماطل اسرائيل في الافراج عن الاسرى
الاربعمائة

3 "For more than three months, Israel has been procrastinating in releasing the 400 prisoners."
(*al-Riyāḍ*, June 3, 2005)

٤ . . . لكن مصادر دبلوماسية أفغانية قالت لـ الأهرام العربي إن مهمة
الجنود الألف البريطانيين ستكون أساسا لتأمين إقامة الملك ظاهر شاه

4 ". . . but diplomatic sources told *al-Ahrām al-ʿArabi* that the mission of the 1000 British soldiers will be basically

to ensure the establishment of King Zaher Shah in power."
(*al-Ahrām al-'Arabi*, Dec. 22, 2001)

Definite Articles on Both Elements

Sometimes, the counted noun is placed after the number, but both elements, the number and the counted noun, take the definite article ال.

الأربعة الرجال "the four men"

This method was not considered acceptable by the Basran grammar school, but was approved of by the Kufans, who argued that a numerical إضافة was similar to the إضافة غير محضة, the first element of which may take ال; for example, الحسن الوجه. Therefore, they claim, its first element may similarly take ال.[60] al-Farrā', one of the founding fathers of the Kufan school, used this structure in his own writings.

EXAMPLES

١ . . . لأن الذبح إنما يكون في هذه الثلاثة الأيام

1 ". . . because the slaughter is only in these three days."
(Farrā', *Ma'āni al-Qur'ān*, 1/123 on 2:203)

٢ وهن الثلاث الآياتِ في الأنعام

2 "They are the three verses in *Sūrat al-An'ām*."
(Farrā', *Ma'āni al-Qur'ān*, 1/190 on 3:7)

٣ هذه الآية إنما كان حكمها مدة الأربعة الأشهر التي ضربت لهم أجلاً

3 "This verse was in effect only for the four months during which they were granted reprieve."
(Andalusi, *al-Baḥr al-Muḥīṭ*, 5/13 on 9:6)

٤ وأقبل يوسف على جمع الطعام فجمع في السبع السنين المخصبة

4 "Yūsuf devoted himself to gathering food and gathered during the seven productive years."
(Ṭabarsi, *Majma' al-Bayān*, 5/324–5 on 12:54–57)

٥ ثم جمعت الأربعة الأناجيل

5 "Then the four gospels were gathered."
(Bīrūni, *al-Qānūn al-Mas'ūdi*, 1/252)

---

60. See Hasan, *al-Naḥw al-Wāfi*, 1/438; Ibn Sīda, *Kitāb al-'Adad fi-l-Lugha*, pp. 64–65; Zamakhshari, *al-Mufaṣṣal*, pp. 265–266.

٦ لقد جعلت قريش في محمد مائةَ ناقةٍ لمن رده عليهم . . . وكنت أرجو أن أرده على قريش فآخذ المائة الناقة

6 "Quraysh has offered (a reward of) 100 camels for anyone who can deliver Muhammad to them. And I was hoping to take him to them and receive the 100 camels."
(Tawfiq al-Hakim, *Muḥammad*, p. 119)

٧ فيبقى من الألف السنة الأربعون

7 "Of the thousand years, 40 remain."
(Bīrūni, *al-Qānūn al-Masʿūdi*, 1/171)

Numbers for Which the Counted Noun Is a *tamyīz*: Eleven Through Ninety-Nine

Eleven Through Ninety-Nine Before Counted Noun

One way to make a counted noun تمييز definite, that is, a counted noun for which the number is 11–99, is to do what is dictated by traditional grammars: place the definite article الـ on the number but not on the counted noun, and place the counted noun after the number. The counted noun in this case remains a تمييز and is therefore indefinite and in the منصوب case.

When the number is a teen, 11–19, the definite article الـ is attached only to the first of the two elements of the number.

الأحد عشر رجلا "the eleven men"

When the number is a compound number (20–90 plus ones), the definite article الـ is placed on both elements of the number.[61]

الخمس والأربعون امرأة "the 45 women"

Gender agreement is the same as when the number and counted noun are indefinite.

EXAMPLES

١ . . . خلال الاثنتي عَشْرَةَ ساعةً القادمة . . .

1 ". . . during the next twelve hours . . ."
(broadcast on Kuwait radio news, Nov. 23, 2001)

61. See, for example, Jārim and Amīn, *al-Naḥw al-Wāḍiḥ*, 5/205–206; Niʿma, *Mulakhkhaṣ Qawāʿid al-Lugha al-ʿArabiyya*, 1/90; Zamakhshari, *al-Mufaṣṣal*, pp. 265–266.

٢ . . . 18 متشددا من حركة طالبان وجنديين قتلوا على مدى الأربع والعشرين ساعة الماضية

2 ". . . 18 extremists from the Taliban movement and two soldiers were killed over the last 24 hours."
(*al-Sharq al-Awsaṭ*, Oct. 20, 2009)

٣ . . . بل انه لم يكد يتغير في مدى الثلاثين عامًا . . .

3 ". . . but he had hardly changed over the thirty years . . ."
(Naguib Mahfouz, *al-Ṭarīq*, p. 78)

٤ في غضون الأربعين سنة القادمة . . .

4 "During the next forty years . . ."
(*al-'Arabi*, June 1993)

٥ فإنّه يُبدَأُ بالخَمْسينَ دينارًا . . .

5 "One begins with the fifty dinars . . ."
(Mālik ibn Anas, *al-Muwaṭṭa'*, p. 817)

Eleven Through Ninety-Nine After Counted Noun

Alternatively, the number may be placed after the counted noun and function as an adjective to it. As such, it will agree in definiteness, and the counted noun will be plural.

الموظفون العشرون "the twenty employees"

Gender agreement is the same as when the numbers occur before the counted noun.

EXAMPLES

١ . . . والإفادة القصوى من الساعات الأربع والعشرين المقبلة . . .

1 ". . . the highest benefit from the coming twenty-four hours . . ."
('Ā'iḍ al-Qarni, *Lā Taḥzan*, p. 158)

٢ وبشّره بالنبوة ونبوة أولاده الاثنى عشر

2 "He gave him the good tidings of his prophethood and the prophethood of his twelve sons."
(*Mas'ūdi, Murūj al-Dhahab*, 1/47)

٣ وأقر الأعضاء ال18 في هذه الهيئة الاستشارية أن . . .

3 "The 18 members of this advisory board ruled that . . ."
(*al-Riyāḍ*, May 6, 2011)

٤ ... وانها ظلت تسعى حتى قبل ايام من الاعتداءات الى ادخال عناصر اخرى من التنظيم الى الولايات المتحدة للمشاركة في العمليات مع الخاطفين الـ19.

4 "... and up to a few days before the attacks, they were still trying to bring other elements from the organization into the United States to participate in the operations along with the 19 hijackers."
(*al-Sharq al-Awsaṭ*, Nov. 6, 2003)

٥ فإذا ضُرِبَت في حروفِ المُعجَمِ الثَّمانِيَةِ وَالعِشرينَ، خرج من ذلك ثلاثُمائةِ فصلٍ وثَمانِيَةُ فُصولٍ

5 "If you multiply that by the 28 letters of the alphabet, you end up with 308 chapters."
(Yāqūt, *Muʿjam al-Udabāʾ*, 1/419, #100 on Abu-l-ʿAlāʾ al-Maʿarri)

٦ هذه الأحرف الثلاثة من الأحرف التسعة والعشرين، دارت بها الألسن

6 "These three letters, out of the 28 letters, are frequently uttered."
(Suyūṭi, *al-Itqān fī ʿUlūm al-Qurʾān*, p. 512, *nawʿ* 43)

٧ والحروف الثمانية والعشرون على نحوين: معتلّ وصحيح

7 "The 28 letters are of two types: vowels and consonants."
(Azhari, *Tahdhīb al-Lugha*, 1/41, Bāb Aḥyāz al-Ḥurūf)

٨ على أن يُساعدهم أدومُ بنُ يَديثونَ مع أنسبائِهِ الثمانيةِ والستّينَ

8 "Edom son of Jeduthun and his 68 kinsmen were (designated) to help them."
(*al-Kitāb al-Muqaddas*, Akhbār al-Ayyām al-Awwal [1 Chronicles], 16:38)

Compound Numbers and Multiples of 1000

Similar rules apply to compound numbers greater than 100 and multiples of 1000.

The counted noun may be before or after the number.

All elements of compound numbers that are connected to the previous elements by وَ take the definite article الـ (see example 1).

The عشر or عشرة in the teens does not take الـ (see example 2).

Multiples of 1000 which are إضافة may occasionally take the definite article الـ on both elements of the إضافة (see example 4).

EXAMPLES

١ فرأيت امرأة ولدت في المائة والأربع والثمانين ليلة

1 "You will see a woman give birth in (the) 184 days (lit., nights)."[62]
(Rāzi, *Mafātīḥ al-Ghayb*, 28/15 on Qur'an 46:15)

٢ ذكران الآباء الثلاثمائة والثمانية عشر

2 "The Feast of the 318 Fathers"
(Bīrūni, *al-Qānūn al-Mas'ūdi*, 1/239)

٣ إنها بلد الثلاثة آلاف وادٍ

3 "It is the land of the 3000 valleys."
(*al-Ḥawādith*, Nov. 2–8, 2001, p. 5)

٤ وقد أدرك أنها تقتضيه قدرا من المال لا يقل عن الخمسة الآلاف جينه

4 "He realized it would require of him an amount of money no less than 5000 pounds."
(Naguib Mahfouz, *Zuqāq al-Midaqq*, p. 66)

٥ كان الأحمرُ يحفظُ الأربَعينَ ألفَ بَيتٍ شاهِدٍ

5 "Aḥmar had memorized the 40,000 poetical citations."
(Yāqūt, *Mu'jam al-Udabā'*, 4/6, #552 on 'Ali ibn Ḥasan al-Aḥmar)

٦ وذهب بالصبيان السبعين الألف حتى أقدمهم بابل

6 "He removed the 70,000 youths and took them to Babel."
(Ṭabari, *Tārīkh*, 1/553)

٧ وستبدأ الولايات المتحدة في انسحاب تدريجي لجنودها الـ١٠٠ ألف بدءاً من الصيف المقبل

7 "The United States will begin a gradual withdrawal of its 100,000 troops beginning this coming summer."
(*al-Ḥayāt*, Jan. 14, 2011)

٨ . . . فيما تم تحويل الـ25 مليار دولار المتبقية في سبتمبر (أيلول) إلى أسهم عادية

8 ". . . while the remaining 25 billion dollars were converted in September to ordinary shares."
(*al-Sharq al-Awsaṭ*, Mar. 28, 2010)

62. For the use of "nights" to count days, see p. 133.

"The Three/Four/Five of Them/Us"

A possessive pronoun may be attached to a number, rendering it "the three of us," "the four of them," etc.

It may stand alone or may serve as a حال or توكيد for a plural noun.

When functioning as a حال, it is in the منصوب case (حضر الطلابُ ثلاثَتهم), and when توكيد, it is in the same case as the noun it gives emphasis to (حضر الطلابُ ثلاثتُهم).[63]

EXAMPLES

١ وكانوا ثلاثتهم يمشون

1 "The three of them were walking."
(Taha Husain, *al-Ayyām*, 1/32)

٢ وثلاثتهم يشكلون فرقة واحدة اسمها (الأرض).

2 "The three of them constitute one group called 'Al-Arḍ.'"
(Usama Fawzi, "al-Ughniya al-Siyāsiyya," 1977)[64]

٣ فلما رأوا (أن) في غير هذين تكون للماضي والمستقبل استوثقوا لمعنى الاستقبال بكي وباللام التي في معنى كي. وربما جمعوا بين ثلاثهن

3 "When they saw that *an* in other contexts was used to refer to the past or the present, they emphasized that the future was intended by using *kay* or the *lām* which means 'in order to'. Sometimes they might use all three of them together."
(Farrā', *Ma'āni al-Qur'ān*, 1/261–2 on 4:26)

٤ وجلس ثلاثتهم يتبادلون طيب المجاملات

4 "The three of them sat exchanging pleasantries."
(Naguib Mahfouz, *Zuqāq al-Midaqq*, p. 103)

٥ و((النفس)) و((العين)) مختصان بهذه التفصلة بين الضمير المرفوع وصاحبيه، وفيما سواهما لا فصل في الجواز بين ثلاثتها

5 "*Nafs* and *'ayn* are subject to the same rules regarding the distinctions between the *marfū'* pronoun and a pronoun in the other two cases. For anything other than those two, there is no distinction in what is permitted between (any of) the three of them (i.e., the three grammatical cases)."
(Zamakhshari, *al-Mufaṣṣal*, 146–7)

63. See Ḥasan, *al-Naḥw al-Wāfi*, 4/529.
64. Republished at arabtimes.com

Number with No Counted Noun

A number may occur with no counted noun directly after it because it is separated from the counted noun by مِن, because the identity of the counted noun was stated previous to the number, or because it is understood without being stated.

If this happens, the gender of the number is the same as it would be if the number were stated. Thus, polar agreement (see p. 14) applies if the number is 3–10: if the implied counted noun is masculine, then the feminine form of the number (i.e., the form with a *tāʾ marbūṭa* at the end) is used. If the implied counted noun is feminine, then the masculine of the number is used (i.e., the form with no *tāʾ marbūṭa* at the end).

Note also that the feminine "two" اثنتان/اثنتين, when used alone, is sometimes rendered ثِنْتَانِ/ثِنْتَيْنِ in classical texts.

Min

A number may occur in the indefinite with no counted noun directly following, but be followed by مِن "of" and the counted noun in the plural.

أربع من الطالبات "four of the female students"

EXAMPLES

١ ذهب واحدٌ منهم إلى الأزهر

1 "One of them went to al-Azhar."
(Taha Hussein, *al-Ayyām*, 1/33–4)

٢ . . . رغم الشهادة المرفقة بالمسوغات والتي يقر فيها اثنان من الموظفين أنه حسن السير والسلوك . . .

2 ". . . despite the certificate accompanied by supporting material in which two of the employees certify that he is of good conduct and behavior . . ."
(Yūsuf Idrīs, *al-'Askari al-Aswad*, p. 33)

٣ وفجأة قامت معركة كلامية بين اثنين من النزلاء

3 "Suddenly an argument broke out between two of the guests."
(Naguib Mahfouz, *al-Ṭarīq*, p. 115)

٤ فهي ثنتان وعشرون فرقة، ثنتان منها ليستا من فرق الإسلام

4 "That makes twenty-three sects, two of which are not sects of Islam."
(Baghdādi, *al-Farq Bayn al-Firaq*, p. 38)

٥ فقام ثلاثة من بني عمها إلى بجرة

5 "Three of her cousins went to Bujra."
(*Qiṣaṣ al-ʿArab*, 1/19)

٦ وبالأمس قبضوا على أربعة من رفاقي

6 "Yesterday they arrested four of my companions."
(Naguib Mahfouz, *Zuqāq al-Midaqq*, p. 207)

٧ ألم يكن قد علّم قبل صاحبنا أربعةً من إخوته

7 "Before our friend, had he not taught four of his brothers?"
(Taha Hussein, *al-Ayyām*, 1/33)

٨ . . . وأن يسوق إليها مائة من الإبل . . .

8 ". . . and that he deliver to her 100 camels . . ."
(*Qiṣaṣ al-ʿArab*, 1/239)

٩ ولا سبيل الى الصبر او الطمأنينة لمن لم يعد يملك سوى مائتين من الجنيهات[65]

9 "It is not possible for a person who no longer has any more than 200 pounds to remain calm and feel secure."
(Naguib Mahfouz, *al-Ṭarīq*, p. 23)

١٠ ويذكر أن قسم الولادة بمستشفى جي ام سي استقبل العام الماضي 3 آلاف واثنين من المواليد

10 "It should be mentioned that the maternity ward in GMC Hospital last year welcomed 3,002 newborns."
(*al-Bayān*, Jan. 2, 2011)

١١ 250 ألف أسرة كويتية بحاجة إلى 750 ألفا من الخدم!!

11 "250,000 Kuwaiti families need 750,000 maids!!"
(*al-Waṭan* [Kuwait], Oct. 30, 2011)

65. Typo in original corrected: لم inserted.

Counted Noun Previously Stated

The number may also occur without a counted noun because the identity of the counted noun, having been stated previously in the sentence, is known.

EXAMPLES

١ فلما سار مرحلةً أو ثِنتَين . . .

1 "After he had walked a day's journey or two . . ."
(Ṭabari, *Tārīkh*, 6/431)

٢ قتل شرطيان باكستانيان وجرح خمسة آخرون

2 "Two Pakistani policemen were killed and five others were wounded."
(*al-Ḥayāt*, Jan. 14, 2011)

٣ يعنون السنة الثالثة ثم اثنتان بعدها

3 "They mean the third year then two after it."
(Bīrūni, *al-Qānūn al-Mas'ūdi*, 1/208)

٤ قتل مدني واصيب ثلاثة آخرون

4 "A civilian was killed and three others were wounded."
(*al-Ḥayāt*, Jan. 9, 2006)

٥ كان علماء المدينة ثلاثةً أو أربعة

5 "The scholars of the city were three or four (in number)."
(Taha Hussein, *al-Ayyām*, 1/80)

٦ ومات بعد ذلك بسنتين أو ثلاث

6 "He died two or three years after that."
(Yāqūt, *Mu'jam al-Buldān*, 4/296, #9181 on Fazz)

٧ وقد اغتسلت أرض الزقاق التي لا تستحم إلا مرتين أو ثلاثا في العام

7 "The ground of the alley, which doesn't get a bath but two or three times a year, was washed."
(Naguib Mahfouz, *Zuqāq al-Midaqq*, p. 79)

٨ فقوّم ما كان يساوي عشرةَ دنانير ثلاثةً

8 "He priced that which was worth ten dinars at three (dinars)."
(Yāqūt, *Mu'jam al-Udabā'*, 2/68, #206 on Tha'lab)

٩ والعين: مطر أيام لا يُقلع، خمسةٍ أو ستة أو نحو ذلك

9 "ʿAyn is rain (that falls) for days without letting up: five or six (days) or so."
(Anbāri, *Sharḥ al-Qaṣāʾid al-Sabʿ*, p. 312)

١٠ والبركة عشر بركات، تسع بمصر والواحدة في جميع الأرض

10 "Blessing consists of ten blessings: nine in Egypt and one in the rest of the earth."
(Jāhiẓ, *Kitāb al-Buldān*, p. 491)

١١ فإذا سمعت من شخص كلمة نابية، فلا تردَّها فتصبح عشراً

11 "If you hear an unkind word from someone, don't return the unkind word and let it turn into ten (unkind words)."
(ʿĀʾiḍ al-Qarni, *Lā Taḥzan*, p. 504)

١٢ العرب تقول للغلام إذا بلغ عشر سنين: رمى، أي قويت يده؛ فإذا بلغ عشرين قالوا: لَوَى، أي لوى يد غيره

12 "The Arabs say, of a boy who has reached ten years of age 'he shoots,' i.e., his arm has become strong. When he reaches 20 (years), they say 'he twists,' that is, he can twist the arm of another."
(Thaʿlab, *Majālis*, 1/78)

Counted Noun Understood

The identity of the counted noun is sometimes not stated when it is assumed that the reader will know its identity. The implied counted noun in these cases will often be مرات "times," or it may be the مصدر of the main verb of the sentence.

EXAMPLES

١ قتلت اثنين مع سبق الاصرار، واعترفت

1 "I killed two (people) with premeditation. And I confessed."
(Naguib Mahfouz, *al-Ṭarīq*, p. 208)

٢ لكن التعذيب في أمن الدولة عموما يتم بإشراف اثنين: العقيد صالح رشوان والعميد فتحي الوكيل

2 "But torture under the security police generally occurs under the supervision of two (people): Colonel Saleh Rashwan and Brigadier General Fathy al-Wakil."
(ʿAlāʾ al-Aswāni, *ʿImārat Yaʿqūbiyān*, p. 267)

٣ سألت ربي ثلاثا فأعطاني ثنتين ومنعني واحدة

3 "I asked of my Lord three (things), and he granted two and refused one."[66]
(*Ṣaḥīḥ Muslim*, 2/552 [*Bāb Halāk Hādhihi-l-Umma Baʿḍuhum bi-Baʿḍ*])

٤ وهكذا حان موعد القصاص من الثلاثة الذين قتلوا أسرة من ثلاثة أشخاص

4 "Now the time has come for retribution against the three (criminals) who killed a family of three."
(Fāṭima al-Sayyid, *Mudhakkirāt Ṣaḥafiyya fī Ghurfat al-Iʿdām*, pp. 57–58)

٥ أم تظنّ أني في سبيل ما تدفع إليّ أستحلُّ الحرام وأعيش مع امرأةٍ طلقتها ثلاثا بين يديك

5 "Or do you think that just because of what you pay me I will do something forbidden and live with a woman on whom I have pronounced the divorce declaration three (times) right in front of you?"
(Taha Hussein, *al-Ayyām*, 1/61)

٦ قدم علينا من دمشق ثلاثةٌ ما رأينا مثلهم

6 "Three (men) the likes of whom we had never seen before came to us from Damascus."
(Yāqūt, *Muʿjam al-Udabāʾ*, 4/45, #565 on Ibn ʿAsākir)

٧ نوح الغراب على العين والرأس ولكنه متزوج من أربع!

7 "Nuh al-Ghurab, fine, but he is married to four (women)!"
(Naguib Mahfouz, *al-Ḥarāfīsh*, p. 368)

٨ وكثيرًا ما خلا الصبى إلى نفسه وقرأ سورة يس أربعًا أو سبعًا أو إحدى وأربعين

8 "Frequently the boy would be alone and recite *sūra Yāsīn* four, seven, or 41 (times).
(Taha Hussein, *al-Ayyām*, 1/107)

٩ كنت أزحف على أربع حتى أبلغ حافة الطوار المطلة على الطريق

9 "I would crawl on (all) four (limbs) until I reached the edge of the sidewalk overlooking the road."
(Naguib Mahfouz, *Zuqāq al-Midaqq*, p. 130)

---

66. Here ثلاثا is masculine and ثنتين is feminine, indicating that the implied noun is feminine (see p. 14). Thus, it may be interpreted as مسألة, the *maṣdar* of سأل.

١٠ فكان يصلي الخمس لأوقاتها

10 "He was praying the five (prayers) at their proper times."
(Taha Hussein, *al-Ayyām*, 1/26)

١١ العصر ثلاث . . . الفاتحة: الجمهور سبع . . . البقرة: مائتان وثمانون وخمس، وقيل ستّ، وقيل سبع . . . المائدة: مائة وعشرون، وقيل واثنتان وقيل وثلاث

11 "(The *sūra*) *al-ʿAṣr* is three (verses) . . . *al-Fāthiḥa*: All agree that it consists of seven (verses) . . . *al-Baqara* is 285, some say 286, some 287 (verses) . . . *al-Māʾida* is 120, some say 122 or 123 (verses)."
(Suyūṭi, *al-Itqān fī ʿUlūm al-Qurʾān*, pp. 158–159, *nawʿ* 19)

١٢ وَيَحْمِلُ عَرْشَ رَبِّكَ فَوْقَهُمْ يَوْمَئِذٍ ثَمَانِيَةٌ

12 "Eight carry the throne of your Lord above them."[67]
(Qurʾan 69:17)

١٣ نزلت في خمسة عشر هموا بقتله

13 "(The verse) was revealed concerning 15 (people) who were planning to kill him."
(Andalusi, *al-Baḥr al-Muḥīṭ*, 5/73 on 9:74)

١٤ معناه انه خرج بثلثمائة وثلاثة عشر يقاتلون ألف رجل

14 "It means that he went out with 313 (men) to fight 1000 men."
(Rāzi, *Mafātīḥ al-Ghayb*, 15/182–3 on Qurʾan 8:49)

١٥ فيقول الله عز وجل من كل ألف تسعمائة وتسعة وتسعون إلى النار وواحد إلى الجنة

15 "God will say, 'out of every 1000 (people), 999 will go to hell, and one to heaven.'"
(Rāzi, *Mafātīḥ al-Ghayb*, 23/4 on Qurʾan 22:1)

١٦ يقول إنه أنفق في حب السيدة زينب مائة ألف، فهل يبخل بعشرة آلاف؟!

16 "He says he has spent 100,000 (pounds) out of love for Lady Zainab, so will he be too cheap to give 10,000 (pounds)?!"
(Naguib Mahfouz, *Zuqāq al-Midaqq*, p. 30)

---

67. Commentators have differed regarding exactly what the "eight" in this passage refers to. They agree it refers to angels, but some say it is eight angels, and others say eight rows of angels. See Ṭabari, *Tafsīr*, 12/215–16 on this passage; and Ṭabarsi, *Majmaʿ al-Bayān*, 10/85 on this passage.

١٧ ١٨ مليوناً تنهي أزمة إدارة الاتحاد

17 "18 million (riyals) ends the management crisis of the Ittihad club."
(*al-Ḥayāt*, Apr. 18, 2011)

Layālin

In classical texts, when a period of time is described as being a certain number of days in length (e.g., such-and-such an event took ten days), the unit used for counting is nights, not days. This recalls the way dates are sometimes given: with reference to the number of nights which have passed, not days (see p. 150). Thus, if the counted noun is not stated in these cases, it should be assumed to be ليلة or ليالٍ. Hence, if the number of nights is 3–10, polar agreement (see p. 14) will apply, and the number will be masculine and have no *tāʾ marbūṭa* since ليلة is feminine.

EXAMPLES

Note: In the translations of the following examples, "days" has been used as the (implied) unit of time. This has been done for the purposes of creating a more idiomatic English translation. However, the implied counted noun in the Arabic should be understood to be ليالٍ.

١ فلما ساروا ثلاثاً جمعهم أبو سفيان

1 "After they had walked for three (days), Abu Sufyān gathered them together."
(*Qiṣaṣ al-ʿArab*, 1/16)

٢ فمكثت سبعاً لا أطعم إلا ما ينال منه بعيري

2 "I stayed for seven (days) not eating anything other than what my camel ate."
(*Qiṣaṣ al-ʿArab*, 1/22)

٣ وكان يختِم في رمضان والعَشْرِ كل يوم ختمةً

3 "During Ramadan and the ten (first days of Dhu-l-Ḥijja) he used to complete a recitation of the entire Qurʾan every day."
(Yāqūt, *Muʿjam al-Udabāʾ*, 4/44–5, #565 on Ibn ʿAsākir)

٤ فما لبثنا إلا عشرًا حتى رأيتها روضةً تندى

4 "Not more than ten (days) had passed before I saw them turn into a well-watered garden."
(Tha'lab, *Majālis*, p. 295)

٥ يعني أنّه تُرك في الكلأ شهرين وعشرًا

5 "That is, he was left in the pasture for two months and ten (days)."
(Anbāri, *Sharḥ al-Qaṣāi'd al-Sab'*, p. 545)

Dozens, Hundreds, Millions, etc.

Large round numbers may be used in the plural and placed in an إضافة relationship with a definite plural noun, or followed by مِن and then a plural noun, to describe a very large amount of something, similar to "dozens," "hundreds," "thousands," and "millions" in English, as in "thousands of people."

عَشَرات is literally "tens," but should be translated as "dozens" or "scores."

مِئات hundreds

آلاف thousands (sometimes أُلوف)

عشرات الآلاف tens of thousands

مئات الآلاف hundreds of thousands

مَلايين millions

EXAMPLES

١ تستطيع أن تحكي عشرات القصص

1 "You are able to relate dozens of stories."
(Naguib Mahfouz, *al-Ṭarīq*, p. 95)

٢ لا بعد ليلة وانما بعد مئات الليالى

2 "Not after one night but after hundreds of nights."
(Yūsuf Idrīs, *al-'Askari al-Aswad*, p. 39)

٣ مئات الأطباء يتطوعون لتقديم الخدمات ((لثوار يناير))

3 "Hundreds of physicians volunteer to provide services to the 'January Revolutionaries.'"
(*al-Ahrām al-Dawli*, Feb. 12, 2011)

٤ وبتحليل الآلاف من نتاج الذبابات بتلك الطريقة . . .

4 "By analyzing thousands of the offspring of flies in this way . . ."
(*al-I'jāz al-'Ilmi*, Muḥarram 1421)

٥ خرج الآلاف من أنصار النظام للتظاهر في العاصمة

5 "Thousands of supporters of the regime went out to demonstrate in the capital."
(*al-Sharq al-Awsaṭ*, June 11, 2011)

٦ عشرات آلاف اليمنيين يفرون من العنف في الجنوب

6 "Tens of Thousands of Yemenis Flee the Violence in the South"
(*al-Sharq al-Awsaṭ*, July 5, 2011)

٧ خرج مئات الآلاف في دمشق وحلب واللاذقية ودرعا وحماه

7 "Hundreds of Thousands Went Out in Damascus, Aleppo, Latakia, Daraa, and Hama."
(*al-Sharq al-Awsaṭ*, June 11, 2011)

٨ . . . سياسات وصفقات وقوانين تركت تأثيرها على حياة ملايين المصريين . . .

8 ". . . policies, deals, and laws that left their mark on the lives of millions of Egyptians . . ."
('Alā' al-Aswāni, *'Imārat Ya'qūbiyān*, p. 203)

٩ يعتقد أكثر من خبير أن حجمها يزيد عن مئات ملايين الدولارات

9 "More than one expert believes it to be more than hundreds of millions of dollars in size."
(*al-Ḥayāt*, Jan. 14, 2011)

١٠ عرفتُ خبر تاجر كبير، وثري شهير عنده آلاف الملايين وعشرات القصور والدور

10 "I heard the story of a major merchant, who was rich and famous and had billions (money), and dozens of palaces and houses."
('Ā'iḍ al-Qarni, *Lā Taḥzan*, p. 275)

Dates

Writing Dates

Dates, when written with digits, are written with the day on the right, then the month to its left, followed by the year on the far left. Each element is separated by a slash. For example, February 24, 2007:

٢٠٠٧/٢/٢٤

EXAMPLES

١ نشرت ((الحياة)) مشكورة تحقيقاً طويلاً (في ٢٠١٠/١٢/٢٦) في صفحة ((منوعات))

1 "*al-Ḥayāt*, thankfully, published a long report (on 12/26/2010) on the 'miscellaneous' page."
(*al-Ḥayāt*, Jan. 14, 2011)

٢ إبراهيم أحمد إسماعيل مناع مواليد الغربية ١٩٤٦/١/٤

2 "Ibrahim Ahmad Ismail Mannāʿ was born in Gharbia on 1/4/1946."
(*al-Ahrām al-Dawli*, Feb. 1, 2011)

٣ . . . ثم عين محافظا لمحافظة الشرقية في ٢٠٠٤/٤/١٧.

3 ". . . then he was appointed governor of the Sharqia governate on 4/17/2004."
(*al-Ahrām al-Dawli*, Feb. 1, 2011)

٤ يعلن رئيس مصلحة كتابة الضبط بالمحكمة الابتدائية بالدار البيضاء
إنه بتاريخ 2010/01/26 على الساعة الواحدة بعد الزوال . . .
سيقع بيع العقار المحفظ بالمحافظة العقارية بالبيضاء

4 "The Clerk of the Court of First Instance in Casablanca announces that on 1/26/2010, at 1 PM, there will be a sale of real estate registered in the land registry in Casablanca."
(*al-Ṣabāḥ* [Morocco], Jan. 21, 2010)

٥ وعلى المؤسسات المشاركة في معرض الكتاب العربي الخامس
والعشرين أن تبعث بنسختين من كل كتاب ترشحه لنيل الجائزة في
موعد غايته ٢٠٠١/١٠/٣١ على العنوان الآتي:

5 "Organizations participating in the 25th Arab Book Exhibition must send two copies of each book

nominated for the prize no later than 10/31/2001 to the following address:"
(*al-'Arabi*, June 2001)

٦ فاستلمت اللواء في ٢٧/١١/١٩٣٣، وبقيت فيه حتى ٤/١٠/١٩٣٨

6 "I received (the governorship of) the province on 11/27/1933 and remained in it until 10/4/1938."
(Taḥsīn 'Ali, *Mudhakkirāt Taḥsīn 'Ali*, p. 134)

Writing out the month

Dates, or parts thereof (i.e., the day and month or the month and year), may also be given with the month written out. The format is: day on the right, followed by the name of the month to its left, then the year to the left of the month. February 24, 2007:

٢٤ فبراير ٢٠٠٧

EXAMPLES

١ ١١ فبراير ٢٠١١ . . . سقوط نظام مبارك

1 "February 11, 2011: The Fall of the Mubarak Regime"
(*al-Ahrām al-Dawli*, Feb. 12, 2011)

٢ من مواليد ١٨ سبتمبر ١٩٤٥ القاهرة

2 "(He was) born on Sept. 18, 1945, in Cairo."
(*al-Ahrām al-Dawli*, Feb. 1, 2011)

٣ وتوصل الطرفان الى اتفاق في ١٧ رجب ١٣٣٧/١٨ نيسان ١٩١٩

3 "The two sides reached an agreement on 17 Rajab, 1337/April 18, 1919."
('Abd al-Karīm Gharayba, *Tārīkh al-'Arab al-Ḥadīth*, p. 202–3)

٤ . . . حسب منطوق المذكرة الوزارية رقم 155، بتاريخ 10 نوفمبر 2009 . . .

4 ". . . according to ministerial decree #155, dated Nov. 10, 2009 . . ."
(*al-Ṣabāḥ* [Morocco], Jan. 21, 2010)

٥ ولما أعلنت الحرب في بداية تشرين الثاني ١٩١٤ . . .

5 "When war was declared at the beginning of November 1914 . . ."
(Taḥsīn 'Ali, *Mudhakkirāt Taḥsīn 'Ali*, p. 42)

٦ وأنا أكتب ما حفظته ذاكرتي في أيلول ١٩٧٠

6 "I am writing what I am able to remember in September 1970."
(Taḥsīn ʿAli, *Mudhakkirāt Taḥsīn ʿAli*, p. 205)

٧ وصل شاكر إلى طرابلس جمادى الأولى ١٢٥٠/أيلول ١٨٣٤[68]

7 "Shakir arrived in Tripoli on Jumāda I, 1250/September 1834."
(ʿAbd al-Karīm Gharayba, *Tārīkh al-ʿArab al-Ḥadīth*, p. 148)

٨ الحركة التي ولدت قبيل انتخابات ١٢ حزيران (يونيو) الرئاسية بإيران . . .

8 "The movement, which was born just before the presidential elections of June 12 in Iran . . ."
(*al-Ḥayāt*, Aug. 12, 2009)

٩ والمؤتمر السنوي للحزب ٣٠ أكتوبر

9 "The party's yearly conference will be on October 30."
(*al-Ahrām*, Aug. 20, 2009)

Reading Dates

Stating the Year

The year, when read alone, is preceded by سنة or عام. The numbers which constitute the year are in an إضافة relationship with سنة or عام. Thus, each element of the year is a مضاف إليه (or معطوف على مضاف إليه), and therefore in the مجرور case.

عام ألفٍ وتسعِمائة وسبعةٍ وسبعين "the year 1977"

If the desired expression is "in the year such-and-such," for example, "in the year 1980," then سنة or عام may be preceded by في, or may be preceded by no preposition. In the latter case, سنة or عام is in the منصوب case due to it being a ظرف زمان.

مات عامَ ١٩٨٠

مات في عامِ ١٩٨٠

"He died in the year 1980."

The gender of each element which makes up the year is the same as it would be if عام or سنة were a counted noun following the number. That is, polar agreement applies (see p. 14) to

68. Typo corrected: جمادى for جمادي

those parts of the year which are between 3 and 10, inclusive. Therefore, when عام is used, a number from 3 to 10 within the year is feminine, that is, it will have a *tā' marbūṭa*. When سنة is used, 3–10 are masculine, i.e., they have no *tā' marbūṭa*.

سنة ألف وتسعمائة وخمس وسبعين

عام ألف وتسعمائة وخمسة وسبعين

"the year 1975"

Parts of the year which are not between 3–10 and which require gender agreement will agree in gender with سنة or عام.

عام ألف وتسعمائة واثنين وستين

سنة ألف وتسعمائة واثنتين وستين

"The year 1962"

However, 2001 and 2002 are frequently rendered ألفين وواحد and ألفين واثنين, even when سنة is used (see examples 11 and 12).

EXAMPLES

١ وقد زعم الواقديُّ أنها كانت في يوم السبت، النصف من شوال سنة ثِنْتين من الهجرة[69]

1 "al-Wāqidi claimed that it was on Saturday, the 15th of Shawwal in the year 2 A.H."
(Ibn Kathīr, *al-Bidāya wa-l-Nihāya*, 5/318)

٢ وقال ابو الحسن وابو عبيدة بصرت البصرة سنة اربع عشرة وكوفت الكوفة سنة سبع عشرة[70]

2 "Abu al-Ḥasan and Abu 'Ubayda said, 'I went to Basra in the year 14, and I went to Kufa in the year 17.'"
(Jāḥiẓ, *Kitāb al-Buldān*, p. 498)

٣ وسمع من الشيخ أبي بكر أحمد بن منصور بن خلفٍ المغربي سنةَ ثَمانٍ وخَمسينَ وأَرْبَعِمائةٍ

3 "He studied with Shaykh Abū Bakr Aḥmad ibn Manṣūr ibn Khalaf al-Maghribi in the year 458."
(Yāqūt, *Mu'jam al-Udabā'*, 4/551, #711 on al-Faḍl ibn Ismā'īl al-Tamīmi)

---

69. For ثنتين see p. 127.
70. Typo in the original corrected: سنة for ستة

٤ حدثنا أبو الفضل يعقوب بن يوسف بن معقل النيسابوري، سنةَ إحدى وسبعين ومائتين، قال: سمعت أبا عبد الله محمد بن الجَهْم بن هارون السِّمَّري، سنةَ ثمانٍ وستين ومائتين، قال:

4 "Abu al-Faḍl Ya'qūb ibn Yūsuf ibn Ma'qil al-Nīsābūri, related to us in the in the year 271, saying, 'I heard Abu 'Abd Allah Muḥammad ibn al-Jahm ibn Hārūn al-Simmari, in the year 268, saying . . ."
(Farrā', *Ma'āni al-Qur'ān*, 1/1)

٥ انني في سنة ثماني عشرة وثلاثمئة وألف هجرية، هجرت دياري سرحا في الشرق

5 "In the year 1318 A.H., I left my homeland to roam around in the east."
(*al-Ḥayāt*, Apr. 16, 2011, quoting Abd al-Raḥmān al-Kawākibi, *Ṭabā'i' al-Istibdād*)

٦ . . . الا ان غواصةً المانية اغرقت عدةَ سفنٍ اميركية عامَ الفٍ وتسعِمائة وخَمْسَةَ عَشر

6 ". . . but a German submarine sank several American ships in the year 1915."
(broadcast on RT Arabic, Apr. 6, 2010)

٧ . . . البرنامج الكوني المشترك "ابولو—سويوز" الذي نفذ في عامِ الفٍ وتسعِمائةٍ وخمسةٍ وسبعين

7 ". . . the Apollo-Soyuz joint space project, which was carried out in the year 1975."
(broadcast on RT Arabic, June 18, 2010)

٨ واستطاع وانغ البالغ من العمر ستين عاما ان ينتج ما يزيد على الفي منحوتة "للقائد" ماو منذ وفاته عام الف وتسعمائة وستة وسبعين

8 "Wang, 60, has been able to produce more than 2000 sculptures of Chairman Mao since the latter's death in the year 1976."
(alquds.com, July 9, 2011)

٩ وكان عضواً بارزاً فيما سمي في سنة ألف وتسعمائة واثنتين وتسعين "لجنة الدولة العليا"

9 "He was a prominent member in what in 1992 was called the High Council of State."
(*al-Riyāḍ*, July 5, 2002)

١٠ اتفاقيات ديتون التي وقعت في باريس عامَ الفٍ وتسعِمائة وخمسةٍ وتسعين حملت السلام الى البوسنة

10 "The Dayton Accords, which were signed in Paris in the year 1995, brought peace to Bosnia."
(broadcast on RT Arabic, Apr. 6, 2010)

١١ . . . كما حدث في العراق في التسعينات، وفي أفغانستان في سنة الفين وواحد

11 ". . . as happened in Iraq in the 90s, and in Afghanistan in 2001."
(*al-Sharq al-Awsaṭ*, Jan. 16, 2003)

١٢ وهي ظاهرة تحدث لأول مرة منذ سنة ألفين واثنين حسب تقرير أصدره معهد أدامز للدراسات

12 "It is a phenomenon occuring for the first time since 2002, according to a report issued by Adams Media Research."
(arabic.euronews.net, Jan. 5, 2010)

١٣ في عامِ ألفينِ وستةِ زلزالٌ بحريٌ آخر أطلق موجات التسونامي على جزيرة جاوة الأندونيسية وخلف ستمئة وخمسين قتيلا

13 "In the year 2006, another undersea earthquake generated tidal waves on the Indonesian island of Java, leaving 650 dead."
(broadcast on Euronews Arabic, Mar. 11, 2011)

١٤ منذ تأسيسها سنةَ ألفينِ وستٍ أخذت مؤسسة الإمارات للعلوم والتقنية المتقدمة على عاتقها مهمة استثمار طاقات شباب الإمارات

14 "Since its founding in the year 2006, the Emirates Institute for Advanced Science and Technology has taken upon its shoulders the mission of investing in the energies of the Emirates' youth."
(broadcast on Alaan TV, June 1, 2011)[71]

١٥ ويمكن أن أذكر ما جرى في عام ألفينِ وثمانية

15 "I might mention what happened in the year 2008."
(broadcast on RT Arabic, Dec. 6, 2010)

١٦ أوباما يطلق حملته لاعادة انتخابه لرئاسة الولايات المتحدة في عام الفين واثنى عشر[72]

16 "Obama launches his campaign for reelection to the U.S. presidency in the year 2012."
(alquds.com, Apr. 5, 2011)

Reading Full Dates

When reading out the full date or a part thereof (day plus month, or month plus year), the day is read first, followed by

71. Retrieved from www.youtube.com/watch?v=JBYiyCa1MTM
72. Typo corrected: حملته for حملة

the month, then the year. The elements are most commonly combined in the following ways:

Day Plus Month

1. Day and month: ordinal number plus من

The day may be expressed with اليوم followed by an ordinal number functioning as an adjective, e.g., اليوم الخامس (see examples 17 and 22).

Alternatively, اليوم may be omitted, leaving just the ordinal number. The ordinal number will be masculine and definite, as it is describing an implied اليوم, for example, السابع (see examples 1, 5, 6, 7, 8, 10, 11, 15, 16, 19, 21, 23).

The day may also be expressed with يوم followed by a definite ordinal number. In this case, the two are in an إضافة relationship with each other, "the day of the seventh," for example, يوم السابع (see examples 27, 28, 29).

In all of these cases, the month will follow, preceded by مِن, for example, اليوم السابع من يوليو. The name of the month may be preceded by شهر, which is in an إضافة relationship with the name of the month.

اليوم السابع من شهر يوليو "the seventh of July"

Or, شهر may be omitted

اليوم السابع من يوليو "the seventh of July"

2. Day and month: iḍāfa

Alternatively, the day and the name of the month may be combined in an إضافة construction:

سبعة أغسطس (see examples 12, 18, 20).

Or, the number may be expressed as an ordinal in an إضافة relationship with the name of month:

سابع أغسطس "The seventh of August"
(see examples 2, 3, 4, 14, 30).

3. Day and month: the case

To say "on such-and-such date," the date may be given with no preposition preceding. The first element (يوم or the day alone without يوم) here is in the منصوب case as it is a ظرف زمان (see examples 1, 3, 6, 14, 28, 30).

Alternatively, the date may be preceded by في (see examples 2, 4, 5, 7, 8, 10, 11, 12, 15, 16, 17, 23).

When giving the month alone and no day, the month is usually preceded by في (see examples 24, 26, 31).

في شهر اغسطس سنة ١٩٢٥

The Year

The year follows the month and is preceded by عام or سنة. The numbers that constitute the year are in an إضافة relationship with سنة or عام. Thus, each element of the year is a مضاف إليه (or معطوف على مضاف إليه), and therefore in the مجرور case.

عام ألفٍ وتسعِمائة وسبعةٍ وسبعين "the year 1977"

Sometimes the year is given without سنة or عام preceding (see examples 24, 25).

The word سنة or عام may be given with no preposition preceding. In this case it will be in the منصوب case, as it is a ظرف زمان (see examples 1–8, 12, 13, 15, 16, 26, 31).

سافرت يوم ٢٧ يوليو عامَ ألفين "I traveled on July 27, 2000."

If the year is given without سنة or عام, then the elements that make up the year will be in the منصوب case due to being ظرف زمان (see examples 24, 25).

Alternatively, the year may be preceded by لِـ (see examples 17, 19) or مِن (see examples 9, 32).

When the year is preceded by سنة or عام, the rules of number agreement apply as if عام or سنة were the counted noun for each element in the year. Polar agreement also applies (see p. 14), so that any element in the year from 3 to 10 will have a *tāʾ marbūṭa* if the word عام is used (as عام is masculine and thus requires a feminine number) and lack a *tāʾ marbūṭa* if سنة is used (since سنة is feminine and requires a masculine number). Hence,

سنة ألفين وأربع

عام ألفين وأربعة

سنة ألف وتسعمائة وسبع وسبعين

عام ألف وتسعمائة وسبعة وسبعين

See also "Stating the Year" (p. 138).

If سنة or عام are omitted, then it is assumed that the missing word is عام, and gender agreement is implemented accordingly: Elements which constitute the year are masculine, unless they are between 3 and 10 (inclusive), in which case polar agreement applies (see p. 14), making them feminine (i.e., they take a *tā' marbūṭa*) (see examples 24, 25).

EXAMPLES

١ فتُوُفِّيَ فجأة بأصفهان يومَ الخميسِ العِشرينَ من شَهْرِ رَبيعٍ الأولِ سنةَ سبعٍ وخمسِمائةٍ

1 "He died suddenly in Isfahan on Thursday, the 20th of Rabī' I, 507."
(Yāqūt, *Mu'jam al-Udabā'*, 5/160, #807 on Muḥammad ibn Aḥmad al-Abīwardi al-Kūfani)

٢ ورحل عن حلبَ قاصدًا للحج في ثالثِ شعبانَ سَنَةَ سِتَّ عَشْرَةَ وَخَمْسِمِائَةٍ

2 "He departed from Aleppo on his way to the Hajj on the 3rd of Sha'bān, 516."
(Yāqūt, *Mu'jam al-Udabā'*, 4/436, #681 on Ibn al-'Adīm)

٣ وتوفي القاضي بهاء الدين أبو الحسن علي بن القاسم الشهرزوري الرسول المذكور يوم السبت سادس عشر رمضان سنة اثنتين وثلاثين وخمسمائة بحلب

3 "The aforementioned emissary, Judge Bahā' al-Dīn Abu-l-Ḥasan 'Ali ibn al-Qāsim al-Shahrazūri, died on Saturday, the 16th of Ramadan, 532 in Aleppo."
(Ibn Khallikān, *Wafayāt al-A'yān*, 2/275, #245 on Abu-l-Jūd 'Imād al-Dīn Zanki)

٤ ماتَ فيما ذكره صَدَقَةُ بنُ الحسين الحَيّارُ في حادِيَ عَشَرَ جُمادى الآخِرَةِ، سنةَ اثْنَتَيْنِ وَخَمْسِينَ وَخَمْسِمِائَةٍ للهجرة[73]

4 "According to Ṣadaqa ibn al-Ḥusayn al-Ḥayyār, he died on the 11th of Jumāda II, 552 A.H."
(Yāqūt, *Mu'jam al-Udabā'*, 4/464-5, #684 on 'Umar ibn al-Ḥusayn al-Khaṭṭāṭ)

73. Typo corrected: صدقة for صدقه.

٥ وماتَ في الحاديَ عَشَرَ من رجبٍ سَنَةَ إحدى وسبعين وخمسِمائةٍ

5 "He died on the 11th of Rajab, 571."
(Yāqūt, *Mu'jam al-Udabā'*, 4/41, #565 on Ibn 'Asākir)

٦ ومات رحمه الله يومَ الأحدِ بعد صلاة العصر الثامِنَ والعِشْرينَ من جُمادى الآخرةِ سنةَ تِسعينَ وخَمْسِمِائَةٍ

6 "He died, God rest his soul, on Sunday, after the afternoon prayer, on the 28th of Jumāda II, 590."
(Yāqūt, *Mu'jam al-Udabā'*, 4/619, #727 on al-Qāsim ibn Fīra ibn Abi-l-Qāsim)

٧ قدم بغداد مع أبيه في صباه فأقام بها إلى أن مات في السادسَ عشرَ من شعبانَ سنةَ ٱثْنَتَيْ عَشْرَةَ وستِّمائةٍ

7 "He came to Baghdad with his father during his childhood and resided there until he died on the 16th of Sha'bān, 612."
(Yāqūt, *Mu'jam al-Udabā'*, 5/41, #752 on al-Mubārak ibn al-Mubārak ibn Sa'īd)

٨ وتوفي في الحادي والعشرين من ربيع الثاني سنة اثنتين وخمسين ومئتين وألف عن أربع وخمسين سنة

8 "He died on the 21st of Rabī' II, 1252 at the age of 54."
(Ḥātim Ṣāliḥ al-Ḍāmin, *Nuṣūs Muḥaqqaqa fi-l-Lugha wa-l-Naḥw*, p. 740)

٩ كان هذا اليومُ يومَ ٢١ أغسطس من سنة ١٩٠٢

9 "That day was August 21, 1902."
(Taha Hussein, *al-Ayyām*, 1/126)

١٠ فدخلتها في الأول من شهر تشرين الثاني ١٩٠٨

10 "I entered it on the first of November 1908."
(Taḥsīn 'Ali, *Mudhakkirāt Taḥsīn 'Ali*, p. 15)

١١ قررنا في جلستنا المنعقدة في الثاني من تموز ١٩١٩ ما يأتي:

11 "In our session which met on the 2nd of July, 1919, we decided the following:"
(Taḥsīn 'Ali, *Mudhakkirāt Taḥsīn 'Ali*, p. 86)

١٢ ولذلك صدر قانون العقوبات العام في خمسة اغسطس عام ١٩٣٧

12 "Thus the common penal code was issued on August 5 of 1937."
(*al-Ahrām*, Apr. 24, 1999)

١٣ وفي أواخر شهر آذار سنة ١٩٣٩ أكملت مديرية الري العامة إنشاء سدة على نهر دجلة عند مدخل الغرّاف

13 "At the end of March 1939, the Public Irrigation Authority completed the construction of a dam on the Tigris at the opening of the Gharraf (canal)."
(Taḥsīn 'Ali, *Mudhakkirāt Taḥsīn 'Ali*, p. 159)

١٤ ومات في بمباي مساء الاربعاء . . . أول ايار ١٩٤٠

14 "He died in Bombay on Wednesday evening, May 1, 1940."
('Abd al-Karīm Gharayba, *Tārīkh al-'Arab al-Ḥadīth*, p. 201)

١٥ وصدر قرار من مجلس الوزراء بذلك في الرابع من فبراير عام 1957

15 "A decision to that effect was issued by the cabinet on the 4th of February, 1957."
(*al-Qabas*, Jan. 19, 2011)

١٦ يقام يوم الأربعاء القادم احتفال كبير بمناسبة مرور ٥٠ سنة على إنشاء التليفزيون والذي بدء بثه في الحادي والعشرين من شهر يوليو عام ١٩٦٠

16 "A large celebration will be held next Wednesday celebrating fifty years since the establishment of (Egyptian) television which began broadcasting on the 21st of July, 1960."
(*Akhbār al-Yawm*, July 16, 2010)

١٧ . . . في الأيام التي سبقت وفاتها في اليوم الخامس من شهر أغسطس لعام 1962م عن عمر يناهز ستة وثلاثين عاماً

17 ". . . on the days before her death on the 5th of August, 1962 A.D. at almost 36 years of age."
(*al-Riyāḍ*, Sept. 25, 2005)

١٨ . . . في أعقاب أحداث أحد عشر سبتمبر

18 ". . . in the aftermath of the events of September 11."
(*al-Riyāḍ*, Nov. 19, 2006)

١٩ التاسعَ والعشرين من شعبان لعام ألف وأربعمائة وواحد وعشرين هجرية الموافق الرابع عشر من نوفمبر لعام الفين وواحد ميلادية

19 "The 29th of Sha'bān, 1421 A.H., which corresponds to the 14th of November, 2001 A.D."
(heard on Kuwait Radio News, Nov. 13, 2001)

٢٠ . . . سواء في الفترة من الآن إلى واحد يوليو عندما يُنتظر أن تُسلم السيادة إلى الجانب العراقي أو بعد ذلك . . .

20 ". . . whether it be during the period from now until July 1, when power is expected to be handed over to the Iraqis, or after that . . ."
(aljazeera.net, Jan. 10, 2005)

٢١ . . . في حال فوز حركة "النهضة" الإسلامية بانتخابات المجلس التأسيسي المقرر تنظيمها في الرابع والعشرين من يوليو المقبل:

21 ". . . in the case of a victory of the Islamist Nahda movement in the elections for the constituent assembly, which have been set for the 24th of the coming July."
(*al-Riyāḍ*, May 6, 2011)

٢٢ أعلنت الخرطوم . . . انها اعترفت رسميا أمس باستقلال الجنوب من اليوم التاسع من يوليو

22 "Khartoum announced . . . that it officially recognized yesterday the independence of the south beginning on the 9th of July."
(*al-Anbā'*, July 9, 2011)

٢٣ نحتفل بذكري مولده في التاسع من مارس في كل عام.

23 "We celebrate the anniversary of its birth on the 9th of March every year."
(*al-Ahrām*, March 14, 2011)

٢٤ في يناير كانون الثاني ألفينِ وخمسة هبط المسبار هيغنز على تيتان

24 "In January 2005, the Huygens probe landed on Titan."
(broadcast on Euronews Arabic, Nov. 11, 2010)

٢٥ . . . حين أعلن أنه لن يترشح للانتخابات المقبلة التي كانت مقررة في آذار مارس ألفين واثني عشر . . .

25 ". . . when he announced that he will not run in the upcoming elections which have been slated for March of 2012 . . ."
(broadcast on Euronews Arabic, July 29, 2011)

٢٦ قُتِلَ في محرّمٍ سنةَ إحدى وثلاثينَ وأربعِمائةٍ

26 "He was killed in Muḥarram of 431."
(Yāqūt, *Mu'jam al-Udabā'*, 2/367, #275 on Thābit ibn Muḥammad al-Jurjāni)

٢٧ هذه الملاحظة تتكرر عادة مع اقتراب حلول يوم الثاني عشر من شهر ذي الحجة من كل عام

27 "This observation is usually repeated as the 12th of Dhu-l-Ḥijja approaches every year."
(*al-Riyāḍ*, Jan. 6, 2006)

٢٨ الخدمة المدنية تعلن بدء إجازة العيد يوم التاسع من ذي الحجة

28 "Municipal Services Announces the 9th of Dhu-l-Ḥijja as the Beginning of the Eid Vacation"
(*al-Jumhūriyya* [Yemen], Dec. 24, 2006)

٢٩ في فجر يوم السادس من تشرين الثاني ١٩١٤ أنزل البريطانيون قواتهم في الفاو بعد قصفها بالمدافع

29 "At dawn on the 6th of November, 1914, the British landed their forces at Fao after shelling it with artillery."
(Taḥsīn ʿAli, *Mudhakkirāt Taḥsīn ʿAli*, p. 37)

٣٠ عندما عقدنا المؤتمر التأسيسي للاتحاد الوطني يوم الأحد سادس سبتمبر (ايلول) 1959 في قاعة سينما الكواكب بالدار البيضاء . . .

30 "When we held the founding conference of the National Union (of Popular Forces) on Sunday, the 6th of September, 1959 in the al-Kawākib Cinema in Casablanca . . ."
(*al-Sharq al-Awsaṭ*, Dec. 19, 2000)

٣١ عندما سقطت حلب بيد هولاكو في شهر محرم سنة ٦٥٨ هجرية بعد حصار دام سبعة أيام

31 "When Aleppo fell at the hands of Hulegu in Muḥarram, 658 A.H., after a 7-day seige . . ."
(*al-Ḥayāt*, Aug. 6, 2011)

٣٢ وكان توجهه إليها في شهر ربيع الأول من سنة اثنتين وستين

32 "He headed there in Rabīʿ I, 62."
(Ibn Khallikān, *Wafayāt al-Aʿyān*, 2/397, #298 on Abu al-Ḥārith Shīrkūh ibn Shādhi)

B.C.

B.C. is قَبْلَ الميلاد and is abbreviated ق.م

EXAMPLES

١ في القرن الرابع عشر قبل الميلاد كانت مصر الفرعونية تسود بلاد جوارها الآسيوية

1 "In the 14th century B.C., Pharaonic Egypt ruled over the Asian countries neigboring it."
(*al-ʿArabi*, June 2001)

٢ شيشتي، أم تيتي الاول أول ملوك الاسرة السادسة (٢٣١١–٢٣٠٠ قبل الميلاد) . . .

2 "Sesheshet, the mother Teti I, the first of the kings of the 6th dynasty (2311–2300 B.C.) . . ."
(*al-Ḥayāt*, Jan. 9, 2009)

٣ . . . وليس بفعل زلزال سنة ١٤٣ ق.م وحده كما يتفق معظم الباحثين.

3 ". . . and not due solely to the action of the 143 B.C. earthquake, as most researchers agree."
(*al-'Arabi*, June 2001)

٤ قيصر (يوليوس) . . . (١٠١–٤٤ ق.م)

4 "Caesar, Julius, 101–44 B.C."
(*al-Munjid fi-l-A'lām*, p. 560)

A.D., A.H.

A.D. is abbreviated م and is usually read ميلادي when عام is used for "year" in the date given.

It is usually read ميلادية if سنة is used for "year."

Hijri dates (A.H.) are marked with the abbreviation هـ, usually read هِجْرية when سنة is used for "year" in the date given, and هِجْري when عام is used.

EXAMPLES

١ وتسوء الأحوال أيضاً في الهند ومصر بعد عام ١٢٠ هـ

1 "The situation was getting worse in India and Egypt also after the year 120 A.H."
(Yūsuf al-'Ishsh, *al-Dawla al-Umawiyya*, p. 298)

٢ ضرار بن مالك الأزور (ت ١١ هـ/٦٣٣ م): شاعر

2 "Ḍirār ibn Mālik al-Azwar (died 11 A.H./633 A.D.): poet."
(*al-Munjid fi-l-A'lām*, p. 431)

٣ يعود بناؤه الى زمن الدولة الاسلامية عام 1300 هجري

3 "Its construction goes back to the Islamic state in the year 1300 A.H."
(*al-'Arab al-Yawm*, Oct. 5, 2007)

٤ الحسين بن الضحاك المتوفى في سنة 250 هجرية . . .

4 "al-Ḥusayn ibn al-Ḍaḥḥāk, who died in 250 A.H. . . ."
(*al-Riyāḍ*, Mar. 16, 2006)

٥ فلما توفي الشيخ تقي الدين الهلالي سنة 1986 ميلادية . . .

5 "When Shaikh Taqi-ud-Din al-Hilali died in 1986 A.D. . . ."
(*al-Tajdīd*, Aug. 18, 2011)

٦ توجه الثلاثة إلى ساحل الخليج العربي حوالي عام 1885 ميلادي

6 "The three headed to the Arabian Gulf coast around the year 1885 A.D."
(*al-Yawm*, Aug. 29, 2003)

Giving Dates in Lunar Months: Classical Texts

In classical texts, an alternative way of giving dates is often used. In this system, dates are given with reference to the number of nights that have passed in the month or to the number of nights remaining.[74]

When the dates are given in this way, the preposition used for "in" or "on" (i.e., "on the date of such-and-such) is لِـ.

The month is assumed to begin when the new moon is sighted. The first day of the month is the day that occurs after the night of the moon sighting has passed. Thus, the 1st of the month is expressed as لِلَيْلةٍ خَلَتْ (see examples 5, 6, 36), or لِلَيْلةٍ مَضَتْ (see example 7), that is, "one night has passed." (خَلَى/مَضَى = "passed") The first of the month can also be called the غُرّة of the month (see examples 1, 2) or the مُسْتَهَلّ of the month (see examples 3, 4).

The second of the month is expressed as لليلتين خلتا (see examples 8, 9, 37) or لليلتين مضتا (see example 10), as two nights have now passed.

The third through the 10th of the month are also expressed by giving the number of nights which have passed. The verbs خلى (see examples 11, 12, 23) and مضى (see example 13) are given here in the feminine plural conjugation (خَلَوْنَ or مَضَيْنَ), for example, ثلاث ليالٍ خلون. The word ليال may be omitted, but remains implied.

The 11th to the 14th are also given with reference to the number of nights that have passed. However, here the verb خلى (see examples 14, 15, 17) or مضى (see examples 16, 18) is conjugated for the singular feminine (خَلَتْ or مَضَتْ), for example, لأربع عشرة ليلة خلت.

74. For more on this system of dating, see Ḥasan, *al-Naḥw al-Wāfī*, 4/564–565, and *EI*², 'Tārīkh,' 1/iii.

The 15th of the month is (الشهر) النِصْف من (see examples 19, 20) or the مُنْتَصَف of the month (see examples 21, 22).

The 16th to the 29th of the month are expressed not with reference to the number of nights which have passed but to the number of nights remaining in the month. The verb used is بَقِيَ. As with the 3rd to the 10th, when the number of nights remaining is 3–10, the verb is conjugated for the feminine plural (بَقِينَ) (see examples 26, 27, 36). When the number of nights is 11–14, it is conjugated for the feminine singular (بَقِيَتْ) (see examples 23, 24, 37).

When the number of nights remaining is 3–10, ليال may be omitted, in which case it remains implied.

For these purposes, the month is assumed to have thirty nights. Of course, the number of days (and nights) in the Islamic month varies, as the month may have 29 or 30 days depending on when the sighting of the new moon of the following month occurs. And which number of days a month will have cannot be known until that moon is sighted. Nonetheless, convention calls for the giver of dates to assume that the month is 30 days long, so that the 16th of the month, for example, is the day on which 14 nights remain (لأربع عشرة ليلة بقيت). The 17th is لثلاث عشرة ليلة بقيت. The 20th is لعشر ليالٍ بقين, and the 27th is لثلاث ليالٍ بقين.[75]

The 28th is لليلتين بقيتا (see examples 29, 30, 36, 37), and the 29th is لليلة بقيت (see examples 31, 32).[76]

Alternatively, the 16th to the 29th are sometimes expressed with reference to the number of nights which have passed, similar to the 1st to the 14th (hence, سبع عشرة ليلة خلت instead of ثلاث عشرة ليلة بقيت) (examples 25, 28).

The 30th of the month, in a month which has reached 30 days, is called the آخِر يوم of the month (see example 33), or the سَلْخ of the month (see examples 34, 35). The terms سلخ or آخر يوم can be used only in a month which has reached 30 days.

75. See Ibn Sīda's discussion of this in *Kitāb al-ʿAdad*, pp. 68–69, where he says that it is illogical to give a date by referring to the number of nights remaining, since a month may have 29 days and not 30. He points out that people, nonetheless, do it anyway.

76. Occasionally the 29th of the month is called the سَرار or سِرار of the month. See Ḥasan, *al-Naḥw al-Wāfi*, 4/565. The dictionary definition of سرار is the last night or two of the month in which the moon is no longer visible. However, when used in dates, it is the 29th.

EXAMPLES

١ وُلد في وقت الغروب ليلةَ الثلاثاءِ غُرَّةِ ربيعٍ الآخِرِ سنةَ اثنَتَينِ وعِشرينَ وخَمسِمِائةٍ.

1 "He was born at sunset, the night of Tuesday, the 1st of Rabī' I, 522."[77]
(Yāqūt, *Mu'jam al-Udabā'*, 5/353, #879 on Muḥammad ibn 'Abd al-Raḥmān ibn Muḥammad ibn Mas'ūd)

٢ وقدم البصرة في آخر شهر ربيع الآخر—أو غرة جُمادَى الأولى— سنة خمس

2 "He came to Basra at the end of Rabī' I, or on the 1st of Jumāda I, year 5."
(Ṭabari, *Tārīkh*, 5/217)

٣ كان خروج زيد بن حارثة في هذه السرية مُسْتَهَلَّ جُمادى الأولى على رأس ثمانيةٍ وعشرين شهرًا من الهجرة

3 "Zayd ibn Ḥāritha's departure with this raiding party was on the 1st of Jumāda I, 28 months after the Hijra."
(Ibn Kathīr, *al-Bidāya wa-l-Nihāya*, 5/324)

٤ وانتقل من دمشق إلى حلب ودخل قلعتها يوم الجمعة مستهل المحرم سنة سبعين وخمسمائة

4 "He moved from Damascus to Aleppo and entered its citadel on Friday, the 1st of Muḥarram, 570."
(Ibn Khallikān, *Wafayāt al-A'yān*, 4/412, #715 on al-'Ādil Nūr al-Dīn)

٥ فذهب إلى إبراهيم فحبسه عنده ثلاثة أيام أو أربعة، ثم إنه خلى عنه ليلة الاثنين لليلة خلت من ذي الحجة

5 "He went to Ibrahim and arrested and detained him for three or four days, then released him on the night of Monday, the 1st of Dhu-l-Ḥijja."[78]
(Ṭabari, *Tārīkh*, 8/571)

---

77. *Laylat al-thulāthā'* means the night before Tuesday, that is, Monday night. For examples of texts in which only this reading makes sense, see Ibn al-Jawzi, *Manāqib*, 544–545, in which Ibn Ḥanbal gets worse on Friday night (*laylat al-Jum'a*), then dies on Friday day around noon.

Similarly, Ibn Kathīr, discussing the death of Ṣalāḥ al-Dīn, says that he got worse on Wednesday night (*laylat al-Arbi'ā'*), then died the following morning. Ibn Khallikān says he died on a Wednesday. Thus, Wednesday night must be the night before Wednesday. Ibn Kathīr, *al-Bidāya wa-l-Nihāya*, 16/652; Ibn Khallikān, *Wafayāt*, 5/553.

Also see Ibn Kathīr, *al-Bidāya wa-l-Nihāya*, 17/709 and 17/695.

78. See n. 77.

٦ وصُلب ثم أُحرق بالنار، وذلك في يوم الثلاثاء لليلة خلت من ذي القعدة من السنة المذكورة

6 "He was crucified then burned. That was on Tuesday, the 1st of Dhu-l-Qaʿda in the aforementioned year."
(Ibn Khallikān, *Wafayāt al-Aʿyān*, 2/133, #189 on al-Ḥallāj)

٧ وذكر في آخر الجزء الأول منه: أنه فرغ منه ليلة الأحد لليلة مضت من ذي الحجة، سنة تسع وثلاثين وثلثمائة، بسمرقند

7 "He mentioned at the end of part one that he finished it on Sunday night, the 1st of Dhu-l-Ḥijja, 339, in Samarqand."
(Subki, *Ṭabaqāt al-Shāfiʿiyya al-Kubra*, 2/185, on Abu Bakr al-Fārisi)

٨ وكتب يوم الأربعاء لليلتين خلتا من ذي القعدة سنة ٢١٠

8 "He wrote (that) on Wednesday, the 2nd of Dhu-l-Qaʿda, 210."
(Balādhuri, *Futūḥ al-Buldān*, pp. 46–47)

٩ في يوم السبت لليلتين خلتا من جمادى الأولى من سنة سبع وخمسين وثلثمائة، جرت حربٌ بين أبي فراس . . . وبين أبي المعالي بن سيف الدولة

9 "On Saturday, the 2nd of Jumāda I, 357, war broke out between Abu Firās . . . and Abu Maʿāli, the son of Sayf al-Dawla."
(Ibn Khallikān, *Wafayāt al-Aʿyān*, 2/49, #153 on Abu Firās al-Ḥamdāni)

١٠ في المحرم منها عسكر أبو أحمد وموسى بن بغا بسامرّا، وخرجا منها لليلَتَين مضتا من صفر

10 "In Muḥarram of that year, Abu Aḥmad and Mūsa ibn Bugha gathered in Samarra and departed from there on the 2nd of Ṣafar."
(Ibn Kathīr, *al-Bidāya wa-l-Nihāya*, 14/562)

١١ خُلِعَ على أبي الفرج محمد بن العبّاس للوزارة لثلاثٍ خَلَونَ من جُمادى الأولى سنةَ تَسعٍ وخمسين وثلاثِمِائةٍ

11 "The ministry was granted to Abu-l-Faraj Muḥammad ibn al-ʿAbbas on the 3rd of Jumāda I, 359."
(Yāqūt, *Muʿjam al-Udabāʾ*, 3/537, #533 on ʿAli ibn Ibrāhīm ibn Muhammad al-Dihaki)

١٢ وكانت وفاته سنة إحدى وخمسين، وقيل يوم الأربعاء لست خلون من شهر رمضان بعد الفجر سنة ست وخمسين

12 "His death was in the year 51, and some say on Wednesday, the 6th of Ramadan after dawn in the year 56."
(Ibn Khallikān, *Wafayāt al-Aʿyān*, 2/299, #256 on Abu-l-Ḥasan Sari ibn al-Mughallis al-Saqaṭi)

١٣ وفي يوم الأحدِ لثمانٍ مضَين من شَوَّالٍ منها—وهو سابعُ كانونَ الأولِ—سقط ببغداد ثلجٌ عظيمٌ جدًّا وحصل بسببِه بَرْدٌ شديدٌ

13 "On Sunday, the 8th of Shawwal of that year, the 7th of December, a huge amount of snow fell on Baghdad resulting in extreme cold."
(Ibn Kathīr, *al-Bidāya wa-l-Nihāya*, 15/21)

١٤ وكانت ولادة أبي بكر بن الأنباري يوم الأحد لإحدى عَشْرَةَ لَيلةً خَلَتْ من رَجَبٍ سنةَ إحدى وسَبعين وَمائةٍ

14 "Abu Bakr ibn al-Anbāri was born on Sunday, the 11th of Rajab, 171."
(Yāqūt, *Muʿjam al-Udabāʾ*, 5/414, #904 on Muḥammad ibn al-Qāsim Abu Bakr ibn al-Anbāri)

١٥ ومات رحمه الله يومَ الأربعاءِ، لاثنتَيْ عَشْرَةَ ليلةً خَلَتْ من شهر ربيعِ الأولِ، سنةَ ثلاثٍ وعِشرينَ وثلاثِمائةٍ. وحضرتُ جنازته عِشاءً

15 "He died, God rest his soul, on Wednesday, the 12th of Rabīʿ I, 323. I went to his funeral in the evening."
(Yāqūt, *Muʿjam al-Udabāʾ*, 1/161, #32 on Ibrāhīm ibn Muḥammad Nifṭawayh)

١٦ وتوفي رسول الله صلى الله عليه وسلم لاثنتي عشرة ليلة مضت من شهر ربيع الأول

16 "The Messenger of God, peace be upon him, died on the 12th of Rabīʿ I."
(Ṭabari, *Tārīkh*, 3/215)

١٧ فقُدم به عليه يوم الاثنين لأربع عشرة ليلة خلت من شهر ربيع الآخر

17 "He was brought to him on Monday, the 14th of Rabīʿ II."
(Ṭabari, *Tārīkh*, 9/7)

١٨ فلم يزالوا كذلك وفي ذلك حتى مات يزيدُ بنُ معاوية يومَ الخميس لأربع عشرة ليلة مضت من شهر ربيع الأول سنة أربع وستين

18 "They continued on in this way until Yazīd ibn Muʿāwiya died on Thursday, the 14th of Rabīʿ I, 64."
(Ṭabari, *Tārīkh*, 5/558)

١٩ ومولده يوم الثلاثاء النصف من ذي القعدة سنة ثلاث وأربعمائة بمدينة بَطَلْيَوْسَ

19 "He was born on Tuesday, the 15th of Dhu-l-Qaʿda, 403, in the city of Badajoz."
(Ibn Khallikān, *Wafayāt al-Aʿyān*, 2/341, #275 on Abu al-Walīd al-Bāji)

٢٠ وكانت هذه الغزوة في شوالٍ سنةَ ثلاثٍ . . . قال ابن إسحاق: للنصفِ من شوالٍ

20 "This raid was in Shawwal of the year 3 . . . Ibn Isḥāq said, it was on the 15th of Shawwal."
(Ibn Kathīr, *al-Bidāya wa-l-Nihāya*, 5/338)

٢١ تُوُفِّيَ في مُنتَصَفِ ربيعٍ الأوّلِ سَنَةَ أربَعٍ وَأربَعينَ وخَمْسِمِائةٍ

21 "He died on the 15th of Rabīʿ I, 544."
(Yāqūt, *Muʿjam al-Udabāʾ*, 5/446, #920 on Muḥammad ibn Masʿūd)

٢٢ فلما وصل إلى الربذة توفي بها يوم الجمعة منتصف ذي الحجة سنة اثنتين وأربعين ومائتين

22 "When he arrived in al-Rabadha, he died there on Friday, the 15th of Dhu-l-Ḥijja, 242."
(Ibn Khallikān, *Wafayāt al-Aʿyān*, 5/134, #793 on Abu Muḥammad Yaḥya ibn Aktham)

٢٣ وكانت خلافته ثلاثاً وعشرين سنة وشهرين وثمانية عشر يومًا، أوّلها ليلة الجمعة لأربع عشرة ليلة بقيت من شهر ربيع الأول سنة سبعين ومائة، وآخرها ليلة السبت لثلاث ليال خلون من جمادى الآخرة سنة ثلاث وتسعين ومائة

23 "His Caliphate lasted 23 years, 2 months, and 18 days. It began on the night of Friday, the 16th of Rabīʿ I, 170, and ended on the night of Saturday, the 3rd of Jumāda II, 193."[79]
(Ṭabari, *Tārīkh*, 8/345)

٢٤ وكان استخفاؤه ليلة الأربعاء لثلاث عشرة ليلة بقيت من ذي الحجة سنة ثلاث ومائتين

24 "He went into hiding on the night of Wednesday, the 17th of Dhu-l-Ḥijja, 203."[80]
(Ibn Khallikān, *Wafayāt al-Aʿyān*, 1/66, #9 on Abu Isḥāq Ibrahīm ibn al-Mahdi)

٢٥ كان ابتداء الوَحيِ إلى رسولِ الله صلى الله عليه وسلم، يوم الاثنين، لسَبْعَ عَشْرَةَ ليلةً خلت من رمضان

25 "The beginning of revelation to the Messenger of God (peace be upon him) was on Monday, the 17th of Ramadan."
(Ibn Kathīr, *al-Bidāya wa-l-Nihāya*, 4/16)

---

79. See n.77.
80. See n.77.

٢٦ ثنا أبو العباس أحمد بن يحيى ثعلب، في يوم الثلاثاء لعشر بقين من المحرّم . . .

26 "Abu-l-ʿAbbās Thaʿlab related to us on Tuesday, the 20th of Muḥarram . . ."
(Thaʿlab, *Majālis*, p. 47)

٢٧ ومات لثلاث بقين من المحرم سنة ٣١٣، وكان ثقة مأموناً

27 "He died on the 27th of Muḥarram, 313, and was reliable and trustworthy."
(Yāqūt, *Muʿjam al-Buldān*, 3/169, #6062 on Zamlakān)

٢٨ مات يوم الأربعاء لِسَبعٍ وعشرين ليلةً خلت من ربيعٍ الآخرِ سنةَ تسعٍ وأربعين وأربعِمائةٍ

28 "He died on Wednesday, the 27th of Rabīʿ II, 449."
(Yāqūt, *Muʿjam al-Udabā'*, 5/153, #802 on Muḥammad ibn Aḥmad ibn ʿAli ibn Muḥammad)

٢٩ تُوُفِّيَ فَجْأَةً يَوْمَ الثُّلاثاءِ لِلَيْلَتَيْنِ بَقِيتا مِن جُمادى الأُولى سَنَةَ ٱثْنَتَيْنِ وَخَمْسِمائةٍ

29 "He died suddenly on Tuesday, the 28th of Jumāda I, 502."
(Yāqūt, *Muʿjam al-Udabā'*, 5/629, #1037 on Yaḥya ibn ʿAli ibn Muḥammad)

٣٠ وفي يوم الثلاثاء لليلتين بقيتا من المحرم سنة اثنتين وثلاثين ومائة وثب أبو مسلم على علي بن جديع بن علي الكرماني بنيسابور، فقتله بعد أن قيّده وحبسه

30 "On Tuesday, the 28th of Muḥarram, 132, Abu Muslim jumped ʿAli ibn Jadīʿ ibn ʿAli al-Kirmāni in Nishapur and killed him after shackling him and imprisoning him."
(Ibn Khallikān, *Wafayāt al-Aʿyān*, 3/126, #372 on Abu Muslim al-Khurāsāni)

٣١ وفي يوم الأربعاء لليلة بقيت من رجب من هذه السنة، بويع محمد بن الواثق؛ فسُمّي بالمهتدي بالله

31 "On Wednesday, the 29th of Rajab of that year, allegiance was paid to Muḥammad ibn al-Wāthiq, and he was given the name al-Muhtadi bi-Llāh."
(Ṭabari, *Tārīkh*, 9/391)

٣٢ ولم يزل ملكاً مستقلاً إلى أن توفي ليلة الأحد لليلة بقيت من جمادى الأولى سنة ثلاث وثلاثين وأربعمائة

32 "He remained an independent king until he died on the night of Sunday, the 29th of Jumāda I, 433."[81]
(Ibn Khallikān, *Wafayāt al-Aʿyān*, 4/275, #686 on al-Muʿtamid ibn ʿAbbād)

---

81. See n.77.

٣٣ فذُكر أنّ بندار خرج في آخر يوم من شهر رمضان متصّيداً

33 "It was mentioned that Bandār went out to go hunting on the 30th of Ramadan."
(Ṭabari, *Tārīkh*, 9/374)

٣٤ حدثنا أبو بكر محمد بن الحسن ابن يعقوب بن مِقْسَم المقرئ في منزله بحضرة الشرقية بدرب النحّاسين، يومَ الجمعة صلاةَ الغداة، سَلْخَ جمادى الآخرة من سنة أربع وأربعين وثلاثمائة . . .

34 Abu Bakr Muḥammad ibn al-Ḥasan ibn Yaʿqūb ibn Miqsam al-Muqriʾ related to us in his house near Sharqiyya in the coppersmith's alley, on Friday at the morning prayers, on the 30th of Jumāda II, 344 . . ."
(Thaʿlab, *Majālis*, pp. 3–4)

٣٥ وفيها التقى موسى بن بُغا والكوكبي الطالبي على فرسخ من قَزْوين يوم الاثنين سَلْخ ذي القعدة منها، فهزم موسى الكوكبي[82]

35 "And in (that year) Musa ibn Bugha and al-Kawkabi al-Ṭālibi met in battle a parasang away from Qazwin on Monday, the 30th of Dhu-l-Qaʿda of that year. Musa defeated al-Kawkabi."
(Ṭabari, *Tārīkh*, 9/378)

٣٦ وكان فيها—فيما ذكر الواقدي—ريح وظلمة وحُمرة ليلة الأحد لأربع ليال بقين من المحرم، ثم كانت ظلمة ليلة الأربعاء، لليلتين بقيتا من المحرم من هذه السنة؛ ثم كانت ريح وظلمة شديدة يوم الجمعة لليلة خلت من صفر

36 "According to al-Wāqidi, there was in that year wind, darkness and redness (in the sky) on the night of Sunday, the 26th of Muḥarram, then there was darkness on the night of Wednesday, the 28th of Muḥarram in this year. There was also wind and severe darkness on Friday, the 1st of Ṣafar." [83]
(Ṭabari, *Tārīkh*, 8/255)

---

82. Typo corrected: ذي القعدة for ذي القعد.

83. The translation of this passage in the English translation of Tabari's History incorrectly refers to لليلة خلت as the 2nd of the month, though it should be the 1st. See Tabari, *The History of al-Tabari, vol. XXX: The ʿAbbāsid Caliphate in Equilibrium*, p. 140. Also see n. 77.

٣٧ وكانت وقعة أجنادين يوم الاثنين لاثنتي عشرة ليلة بقيت من جمادى الاولى سنة ١٣ ويقال لليلتين خلتا من جمادى الاخرة ويقال لليلتين بقيتا منه[84]

37 "The Battle of Ajnadayn was on Monday, the 18th of Jumāda I, in the year 13. Some say (it occurred) on the 2nd of Jumāda II, and others say on the 28th of Jumāda II."
(Balādhuri, *Futūḥ al-Buldān*, p. 157)

Time

Writing Times

As in English, times are written with the hour to the left, and the minutes to the right. The hour and minutes may be separated by a comma or by a colon:

3,20 3:20 ٣,٢٠ ٣:٢٠

Sometimes a dot is used instead of the colon or comma.

Reading Times

The ordinal numbers, shown in table 2.1, are used to give times. The only exception is 1:00, which is الواحِدة instead of الأولى:

Table 2.1 Hours

1:00	الواحِدة	7:00	السابِعة
2:00	الثانِية	8:00	الثامِنة
3:00	الثالِثة	9:00	التاسِعة
4:00	الرابِعة	10:00	العاشِرة
5:00	الخامِسة	11:00	الحادِيَةَ عَشْرَةَ
6:00	السادِسة	12:00	الثانِيَةَ عَشْرَةَ

84. Typo corrected: جمادى for جمادي

Note that the endings on both elements of the expressions for "11:00" and "12:00" are fixed. They are both *fatḥa* regardless of case (see pp. 23 and 27).

To say "such-and-such o'clock", for example, "5:00," these ordinals are used as adjectives for الساعة, and as such take the same case as الساعة. Or, الساعة may be omitted, but the feminine form of the ordinal is still used, as الساعة is implied.

"10:00" الساعة العاشرة

"5:00" الخامسة

To say "*at* such-and-such o'clock", في is used. For example,

"I returned at 5 o'clock." رجعت في الساعة الخامسة

عِند "at" is also sometimes used (see examples 6, 27, 37).

"He came at 10:00." جاء عند العاشرة

Alternatively, the hour may be given with no preposition, in which case the time would be in the منصوب case, as it is a ظرف زمان (see examples 24, 25, 28).

"He left at 5:00." انصرف الساعةَ الخامسةَ

To say, "It is such-and-such o'clock," for example, "It is seven o'clock," the same construction is used: الساعة plus the ordinal number (see examples 14, 18, 19, 23). In this case, though, the two elements form a sentence. الساعة is the مبتدأ, and the number (here, السادسة) is the خبر. Both, therefore, are in the مرفوع case.

"It is six o'clock." الساعةُ السادسةُ

Hour plus minutes

For a quarter after the hour, والرُّبْع, literally "and the quarter," is used (see example 39).

"5:15" الساعة الخامسة والربع

For 20 minutes after, والثُّلْث, literally "and the third" (see examples 24, 31, 39).

"4:20" الرابعة والثّلث

For half past, وَالنِّصْف, literally "and the half" (see examples 10, 11, 16, 17, 25, 39, 40).

"7:30" السابعة والنصف

For other numbers of minutes from :01–:39, the number of minutes may simply be given (see examples 5, 20, 37, 38).

"4:23" الساعة الرابة وثلاث وعشرين دقيقة

"5:07" الساعة الخامسة وسبع دقائق

For 40 minutes after the hour, the following hour is given, followed by إلاّ الثلثَ, 'except, minus one third' (see examples 21, 22.). Or, ثلث may by indefinite. In either case ثلث or الثلث will be in the منصوب case, as it is a مستثنى (إلا ثلثاً) (see examples 14, 18).

"9:40" العاشرة إلا الثلثَ

"10:40" الساعة الحادية عشرة إلا ثلثاً

For 45 minutes after, the following hour is given, followed by إلاّ الربع (see example 11) or إلا ربعاً (see examples 26, 27). As is the case with ثلث, ربع here is منصوب since it is a مستثنى.

"9:45" العاشرة إلا ربعاً

"6:45" السابعة إلا الربعَ

For any time after :40 that is not exactly :45, the following hour plus إلا followed by the exact number of minutes may be used (see examples 6, 9, 36, 37).

"11:57" الثانية عشرة إلا ثلاث دقائق

Occasionally for times from :41 to :59, instead of using إلا, the number of minutes after the hour is used (see example 37).

Sometimes, even when a time falls right on a quarter, third, or half part of the hour, the number of minutes is nonetheless given instead of ثلث or ربع or نصف being used (see examples 34, 35, 37).

"5:20" الساعة الخامسة وعشرين دقيقة

AM/PM

AM is صباحاً, which may be used for any time after midnight but before noon (see examples 7, 8, 12, 22, 30, 33, 34, 35, 39, 40).

Sometimes, for a time shortly after midnight, بعد منتصف الليل is used (see examples 8, 38).

There is no one, standard way to express 'PM.' مَساءً, though it means "in the evening," is sometimes used with any time after noon but before midnight (see examples 5, 32, 34, 38, 40).

Or, different words for PM may be used depending on the time of the day in question. There are no exact rules specifying which word is used for which times. Thus, the following are general guidelines:

For the very early part of the afternoon, ظُهْراً may be used for "PM" (see examples 10, 30, 39, 40).

For times later in the afternoon, عَصْراً is sometimes used (see examples 11, 39).

For any time from the very early afternoon to the early evening, بَعْد الظهر may be used also (see examples 9, 13, 15, 40).

For evening times, مَساءً is used (see examples 18, 28, 40).

For times later at night, لَيْلاً may be used (see example 36).

Noon, Midnight

Noon is الظُّهْر. Used in the منصوب case and indefinite (ظهراً), it means "at noon" (see example 4).

The expression عِنْد الظهر also can be used to mean "at noon" (see example 3).

ظهراً may also be used in conjunction with الساعة الثانية عشرة to distinguish 12 noon from 12 midnight (see example 2).

Midnight is مُنْتَصَف اللَيْل. It may be used alone (see example 33) or in conjunction with الساعة الثانية عشرة to distinguish 12 midnight from 12 noon (see example 40). "At midnight" is في منتصف الليل (see example 1).

Other Time Words

When an approximate hour is wanted, حَوالَي "around, approximately" is usually used (see examples 5, 29, 36).

"Sharp," (as in "3 o'clock sharp"), or "exactly" is تَمام, which precedes the hour and is in an إضافة relationship with it (see examples 9, 13, 16).

To specify that a time given belongs to a particular time zone ("3:00 Cairo time"), بِتَوْقيت is used before the name of the city (see examples 5, 25).

EXAMPLES

١ ألاسكا أرض الشمس في منتصف الليل

1 "Alaska, Land of the Midnight Sun (the sun at midnight)"
(*al-Qabas*, Aug. 5, 2009)

٢ الاستشارات النيابية ستبدأ الإثنين المقبل في الثانية عشرة ظهراً

2 "The parliamentary consultations will begin next Monday at 12 noon."
(*al-Ḥayāt*, Jan. 14, 2011)

٣ وبيّنت نتائج التصويت—الذي بدأ صباح أمس وانتهى عند الظهر—أن 126 شخصاً من أصل 183 (68.8) صوتوا لصالح تحول تجمع الوحدة الوطنية

3 "The results of the voting, which began yesterday morning and ended at noon, revealed that 126 persons out of 183 (68.8%) voted in favor of converting the National Unity Gathering."
(*al-Wasaṭ* [Bahrain], June 12, 2011)

٤ ينعقد هذا اللقاء الذي يفتتح يوم الرابع من يونيو، بجلسات تبدأ ظهرا في الجامعة الأنطونية

4 "This meeting, which opens on the 4th of June, convenes with sessions which begin at noon at Antonine University."
(*al-Sharq al-Awsaṭ*, May 30, 2010)

٥ إلا أن هذه العقود ارتفعت 1.25 دولار إلى 98.95 دولار في تعاملات اليوم قبل أن تقلل ارتفاعاتها إلى 98.94 دولاراً في حوالي الساعة الثانية عشرة وإحدى وثلاثين دقيقة مساء بتوقيت مكة المكرمة.

5 "But these contracts went up by $1.25 to $98.95 in today's trading before going back down to $98.94 at approximately 12:31 PM, Mecca time."
(*al-Riyāḍ*, May 25, 2011)

٦ . . . كما دعت المعارضة إلى وقوف خمس دقائق حداداً على الرئيس الشهيد عند الواحدة إلا خمس دقائق لحظة وقوع الجريمة

6 ". . . just as the opposition called for a five-minute stoppage in memory of the martyred president at 12:55, the time the crime occurred."
(broadcast on Ṣawt Lubnān, Mar. 6, 2005)

٧ غادرت الفندق في العاشرة ولم ارجع اليه قبل الواحدة صباحا

7 "I left the hotel at 10 and did not go back there until 1 AM."
(Naguib Mahfouz, *al-Ṭarīq*, p. 126)

٨ سيظل مركزا الاتحاد والخالدية للرعاية الطارئة مفتوحين خلال فترة العطلة حسب جدولهما المعتاد من الساعة 08:00 صباحاً إلى الساعة 01:00 بعد منتصف الليل

8 "The Ittiḥād and Khālidiyya centers for emergency care will remain open their usual hours during the holiday period: from 8 AM to 1 AM."
(*al-Ittihād* [UAE], Feb. 16, 2011)

٩ فقد أعلن اليابانيون اليوم الاثنين عن دقيقةِ صمتٍ حداداً على أرواحِ ضحايا هاتينِ الكارثتينِ المأساويتين في تمام الساعة الثانية إلا أربع عشرة دقيقة بعد ظهر اليوم وقت وقوع الزلزال المدمّر

9 "The Japanese have announced today, Monday, a moment of silence in memory of the lives lost in those two huge tragedies (and it will be) at exactly 1:46 PM today, the time the devastating earthquake occurred."
(broadcast on CNTV Arabic, Apr. 12, 2011)

١٠ شاهد عيان: مسلمون تجمعوا فى الثانية والنصف ظهراً وفتشوا مبنى تابعاً للكنيسة وبعدها بدأ إطلاق الرصاص

10 "Eyewitness: Muslims gathered at 2:30 PM and searched a building belonging to the Church, and then firing began."
(almasryalyoum.com, May 9, 2011)

١١ تبدأ اللقاءات في الثانية والنصف عصرا بلقاء الجونة مع طلائع الجيش, وفي الخامسة إلا الربع يلتقي المقاولون العرب مع الإتحاد

11 "The matches begin at 2:30 PM with El-Gouna vs. Tala'ea El Gaish; at 4:45 the Arab Contractors (Sporting Club) plays al-Ittihad."
(*al-Ahrām*, Jan. 20, 2011)

١٢ أتجول فى شوارع القاهرة حتى الثالثة صباحاً..ولم أتعرض للسرقة!

12 "I walk around the streets of Cairo until 3 AM, and I have not been mugged!"
(shabab.ahram.org.eg, May 27, 2011)

١٣ وفي تمام الساعة الثالثة من بعد ظهر يوم الثامن من آذار اجتمع المؤتمر السوري في دار بلدية دمشق

13 "At 3:00 sharp on the afternoon of March 8, the Syrian conference met at Damascus Town Hall."
(Taḥsīn ʿAli, *Mudhakkirāt Taḥsīn ʿAli*, p. 91)

١٤ وبعد كشف اولى , وكانت الساعة الرابعة الا ثلثا وجد الدكتور الصاوى أن الامر خطير

14 "After an initial examination—it was 3:40—Dr. Sawy found that the situation was serious."
(shabab.ahram.org.eg, Sept. 28, 2010)

١٥ وأضاف علام انه طلب من جاره محمد شمص تأمين نقل الساحلي، الذي اتصل به قرابة الساعة الرابعة بعد الظهر

15 "ʿAllām added that he asked his neighbor, Muḥammad Shamaṣ, to provide transport for al-Sāḥili, who called him at about 4 PM."
(*al-Mustaqbal*, Jan. 25, 2011)

١٦ فرغت من تبيضه للمرة الثالثة في تمام الرابعة والنصف من بعد عصر الثلاثاء

16 "I finished a fair copy of it for the third time at exactly 4:30 on Tuesday afternoon."
(Dāwūdi, *Muʿjam al-Arqām fi-l-Qurʾān al-Karīm*, p. 134)

١٧ كانت الساعة تقترب من الرابعة والنصف

17 "It was getting close to 4:30."
(Yūsuf Idrīs, *al-ʿAskari al-Aswad*, p. 9)

١٨ تقول إن موعد المظاهرة كان في الساعة السادسة مساء، وكانت الساعة السادسة إلا ثلثا حين احتدم «نقاشنا مع عناصر الأمن الذين خيرونا بين الاعتقال وفك التجمع»

18 "She says that the time set for the demonstration was 6 PM. It was 5:40 when 'our conversation with security forces, who gave us a choice between arrest and dispersing,' became heated."
(*al-Sharq al-Awsaṭ*, July 22, 2011)

١٩ على ألا أتأخر، الساعة الآن السادسة

19 "I must not be late. It's 6:00 now."
(Naguib Mahfouz, *Qaṣr al-Shawq*, p. 277)

٢٠ . . . أن غرفة العمليات في الدفاع المدني بالرياض تلقت بلاغاً عن نشوب حريق في برج "العبيكان" تحت الإنشاء في الساعة السادسة وتسع وثلاثين دقيقة.

20 ". . . that the operations room in Civil Defense in Riyadh received word that a fire broke out in the Abikan tower, which is under construction, at 6:39."
(*al-Waṭan* [Saudi Arabia], June 2, 2010)

٢١ ويبدأ الأستوديو في السابعة إلا الثلث حيث يستضيف الحمادي المحلل منذر عبدالله

21 "The studio begins its broadcast at 6:40 when Hamadi welcomes analyst Mundhir ʿAbdallah."
(*al-Ittiḥād* [UAE], Sept. 2, 2007)

٢٢ حيث يأتى قطار فى السابعة إلا الثلث صباحاً، ثم يليه آخر بعد نصف ساعة تقريبا.

22 ". . . where a train comes at 6:40 AM, then another follows it approximately a half hour later."
(almasryalyoum.com, Aug. 15, 2009)

٢٣ عندما يرن جرس المنبه للمرة الأولى فانني أتحرك في الفراش متململا وأنا أسمعه يعلن أن الساعة الآن السابعة

23 "When the alarm clock goes off for the first time, I toss and turn in bed as I hear it announce that the time is now 7:00."
(*al-Waṭan* [Kuwait], Nov. 24, 2010)

٢٤ صلاة الإستسقاء الساعة السابعة والثلث في جامع الأمير بعرعر

24 "A Prayer for Water at 7:20 in the Amir Mosque in Arar"
(ararnews.net, Dec. 12, 2010)

٢٥ وكان الانفجار قد وقع الساعة السابعة والنصف من صباح اليوم بتوقيت عمان

25 "The explosion occurred at 7:30 this morning Amman time."
(aljazeera.net, Feb. 28, 2002)

٢٦ الوقت في الثامنة إلا ربعاً من نفس الصباح

26 "The (scheduled) time was 7:45 the same morning."
(Fāṭima al-Sayyid, *Mudhakkirāt Ṣaḥafiyya fī Ghurfat al-I'dām*, p. 58)

٢٧ اخترقت ليلةَ أمس عند الساعة التاسعة إلا ربعاً الأجواء اللبنانية طائرة استطلاع إسرائيلية

27 "At 8:45 last night, an Israeli reconnassaince plane penetrated Lebanese airspace."
(broadcast on Ṣawt Lubnan, Mar. 6, 2005)

٢٨ . . . قسطرة لقلب "سوزان مبارك" التاسعة مساءً

28 ". . . a Cardiac Catheter for Suzanne Mubarak at 9 PM."
(gate.ahram.org.eg, May 15, 2011)

٢٩ واستيقظ حوالي التاسعة من صباح اليوم التالي بعد ليلة سهاد

29 "He woke up around 9 the following morning after a sleepless night."
(Naguib Mahfouz, *al-Ṭarīq*, p. 21)

٣٠ دوام رمضان من التاسعة صباحاً إلى الثانية ظهراً

30 "Ramadan Work Hours Will Be from 9 AM to 2 PM"
(*al-Imārāt al-Yawm*, July 27, 2011)

٣١ وكانت الساعة قد بلغت التاسعة والثلث وحان وقت الإعدام

31 "It was now 9:20. The time for the execution had arrived."
(Fāṭima al-Sayyid, *Mudhakkirāt Ṣaḥafiyya fī Ghurfat al-I'dām*, p. 98)

٣٢ سيقف عمرك عند العاشرة مساء

32 "Your life will end at 10 PM."
(Naguib Mahfouz, *al-Ṭarīq*, p. 125)

٣٣ وكيف أمضيت أمس من الساعة العاشرة صباحا حتى منتصف الليل؟

33 "What did you do yesterday from 10 AM until midnight?"
(Naguib Mahfouz, *al-Ṭarīq*, p. 162)

٣٤ أعلى مستوى المد في الساعة العاشرة وخمس وأربعين دقيقة مساءً، وأدنى مستوى الجزر في الساعة الخامسة صباح الغد

34 "High tide will be at 10:45 PM, and low tide will be tomorrow morning at 5 AM."
(heard on Kuwait Radio news, Nov. 13, 2001)

٣٥ بدأت التجربة في الساعة الحادية عشرة وثلاثين دقيقة صباحا بورود بلاغ إلى غرفة عمليات الدفاع المدني يفيد عن نشوب حريق في المطبخ الرئيسي الواقع في المستوى الأول من الفندق

35 "The ordeal began at 11:30 AM when word was received in the operations room of Civil Defense that a fire had broken out in the main kitchen on the first floor of the hotel."
(*al-Bayān*, Jan. 12, 2007)

٣٦ في حوالي الساعة الثانية عشرة الا تسع عشرة دقيقة ليلاً من مساء يوم الجمعة الموافق 1423/11/28ه تبلغت الدوريات الامنية من موظف الاستقبال بشقق النخيل المفروشة بحي الروضة عن حضور شخص قام باستئجار شقة

36 "At approximately 11:41 PM, the night of Friday, the 28th of Dhu-l-Qaʿda 1423 A.H., security patrols were informed by the reception employee at the Nakheel Furnished Apartments in the Rawda area about the arrival of a person who had rented an apartment."
(*al-Riyāḍ*, Feb. 4, 2003)

٣٧ . . . ففي مدينة استكهولم السويدية التي يُؤذن لأذان الفجر فيها عند الساعة الثانية وخمس وعشرين دقيقة وهو وقت الإمساك، بينما يؤذن أذان المغرب عند الساعة العاشرة إلا خمس دقائق. وفي مدينة كوبنهاجن الدنماركية يبدأ وقت الإمساك عند الساعة الثانية وست وأربعين دقيقة، ويحل وقت الإفطار عند التاسعة وعشرين دقيقة مساء، أما في برلين الألمانية فيؤذن لأذان الفجر عند الثانية وثمان وأربعين دقيقة، وتبدأ الشمس في الغروب بعد التاسعة مساء ببضع دقائق.

37 ". . . as in Stockholm, Sweden, in which Adhan al-Fajr is sounded at 2:25, when fasting begins, whereas Adhan al-Maghrib is heard at 9:55. In Copenhagen, Denmark, the fast begins at 2:46, and ends at 9:20 PM. In Berlin, Germany, Adhan al-Fajr is sounded at 2:48, and sunset begins a few minutes after 9."
(*al-Waṭan* [Kuwait], July 31, 2011)

٣٨ وستكون ذروة ذلك الخسوف في الساعة الحادية عشرة وثلاث عشرة دقيقة مساء . . . اذ سيبدأ بدخول القمر منطقة شبه ظل الأرض في الساعة الثامنة وخمس وعشرين دقيقة مساء . . . ويحصل ذلك بدخول القمر منطقة ظل الأرض عند الساعة التاسعة وثلاث وعشرين دقيقة . . . الظل سيغطي كامل قرص القمر في الساعة العاشرة واثنتين وعشرين دقيقة . . . الخسوف المقبل سيستمر على هذه الحال لمدة 100 دقيقة تقريبا أي حتى الساعة الثانية عشرة ودقيقتين بعد منتصف الليل . . . القمر سيبدأ حينها بالخروج من ظل الأرض إلى منطقة شبه الظل في الساعة الواحدة ودقيقتين

38 "This eclipse will peak at 11:13 PM . . . as it will begin when the moon enters the earth's penumbra at 8:25 PM. . . . That will occur when the moon enters the earth's shadow at 9:23. . . . The shadow will cover the entire lunar orb at 10:22. . . . The coming eclipse will continue in this way for approximately 100 minutes, that is, until 12:02 AM. . . . At that time the moon will begin moving out from the earth's umbra to the penumbra at 1:02."
(ar.radionawa.com, June 5, 2011)

٣٩ تبدأ الفترة الأولي من الواحدة ظهرا إلي الثالثة عصرا تتخللها في الثانية والربع إذاعة مسلسل "سمارة" . . . أما الفترة الثانية التي تبدأ من الثانية عشرة ظهرا حتي الواحدة والنصف صباحا فيتخللها ساعة تبثها بالتتابع إذاعة من إذاعات الشبكة الاقليمية . . . ثم يذاع في الواحدة صباحا مسلسل "ست الدنيا" . . . وتختتم الفترة برامجها في الواحدة والثلث ببرنامج "لآلئ رمضان" تقديم فاروق شوشة

39 "The first period begins at 1 PM and runs until 3 PM and includes a broadcast of the series 'Samāra' at 2:15. . . . The second period, which begins at 12 noon and goes until 1:30 AM, includes an hour in which one of the stations on the regional network will broadcast it in sequence. . . . Then, at 1:00 AM, the series 'Lady of the World' will be broadcast. . . . The programming of this period ends at 1:20 with the program 'Pearls of Ramadan,' hosted by Faruq Shusha."
(digital.ahram.org.eg, July 30, 2011,)

٤٠ ستعمل محطات الحافلات المغذية للمترو (ميدان الاتحاد) حتى الواحدة صباحاً . . . وأوضح محبوب أن التعديلات الجديدة على مواعيد العمل ستكون كالآتي: مراكز خدمة العملاء . . . من الثامنة صباحا حتى الثانية بعد الظهر، ومركز الصفا من الثامنة صباحا

حتى الساعة الخامسة والنصف مساءً، ومركز الكرامة من التاسعة صباحا حتى الثانية بعد الظهر . . . وسيتم تعديل أوقات رسوم المواقف العامة للفترة المسائية خلال شهر رمضان المبارك لتصبح من الثامنة صباحاً حتى الواحدة بعد الظهر، ومن السابعة مساءً حتى الـ12 منتصف الليل من السبت إلى الخميس، وستكون أوقات مواقف سوق السمك من الثامنة صباحاً حتى الواحدة ظهراً ومن الرابعة مساءً حتى الـ11 مساءً طوال أيام الأسبوع . . . . وستكون مواعيد عمل وسائل النقل البحري كما يلي: الباص المائي من الثامنة صباحا حتى الساعة الـ12 منتصف الليل، والتاكسي المائي من الـ10 صباحاً حتى الـ12 منتصف الليل . . . وستكون مواعيد عمل فحص وتسجيل المركبات من السبت إلى الخميس من الثامنة صباحًا حتى الثالثة مساءً، ومن التاسعة مساءً حتى الـ12 منتصف الليل

40 "Bus stations providing connecting service to the metro (Ittihad square) will operate until 1 AM. . . . Mahbub announced that the new changes to working hours will be as follows: customer service centers . . . from 8 AM to 2 PM; the Safa Center from 8 AM until 5:30 PM; the Karama Center from 9 AM to 2 PM. . . . Changes will occur during the blessed month of Ramadan to the hours during the evening period in which fees for public parking will be in effect; the times will be from 8 AM until 1 PM, then from 7 PM to 12 midnight, Saturday to Thursday. The hours of the parking facilities at the fish market will be from 8 AM to 1 PM and from 4 PM until 11 PM every day of the week. . . . Hours of operation for aquatic transportation will be as follows: the water bus from 8 AM until 12 midnight; the water taxi from 10 AM until 12 midnight; hours of operation for inspection and registration of vehicles will be from Saturday to Thursday from 8 AM until 3 PM, and from 9 PM until 12 midnight."
(*al-Imārāt al-Yawm*, July 30, 2011)

Decimals

The decimal point is called العَلامة العُشْرِية or الفاصلة العشرية.

A decimal number is called a كَسر عُشري (plural, كسور عشرية).

Writing Decimals

The decimal is written just as in English, with the whole number to the left of the decimal point and the fraction to the right of it.

A comma is used for the decimal point. When the "Arabic numerals" are used as opposed to the "Hindi numerals," a dot may also be used for the decimal point.

EXAMPLES

١ ستحقق نحو ١,٦٦ تريليون دولار نهاية هذه السنة

1 "It will achieve around 1.66 trillion dollars at the end of this year."
(*al-Ḥayāt*, Aug. 12, 2009)

٢ البورصة تهبط ١,٦% قبيل حلول شهر رمضان

2 "The Stock Market Goes Down 1.6% Just before the Start of Ramadan"
(*al-Ahrām*, Aug. 20, 2009)

٣ 7,5 مليون شاب مغربي يرغبون في إطلاق مشاريع خاصة

3 "7.5 Million Moroccan Youths Would Like to Start Private Businesses"
(*al-Sharq al-Awsaṭ*, June 11, 2011)

٤ بلغ صافي أرباح بنك "الإثمار" خلال النصف الأول من العام الجاري 8,2 مليون دولار

4 "Net profits of the Ithmar Bank during the first half of this year reached 8.2 million dollars."
(*al-Waṭan* [Bahrain], Aug. 14, 2011)

٥ . . . طويلة القامة (1.78 متر)، قوية البنية، ملامحها حادة وشعرها مجعد . . .

5 ". . . tall of stature (1.78 meters), with a powerful build, with sharp features and curly hair . . ."
(*al-Ṣabāḥ* [Morocco], Aug. 12, 2011)

٦ وقد أقفل مؤشر السوق الكويتي منخفضاً بواقع 3.6% ليغلق على 5.851 نقطة

6 "The Kuwaiti stock market index closed down by 3.6%, closing at 5.851 points."
(*al-Waṭan* [Kuwait], Aug. 14, 2011)

Reading Decimals

When reading out decimal numbers, the decimal point is called فاصِلة or فاصِل. These are equivalent to "point" in English.[85]

Read as Tenths/Fraction

If the decimal is only to one digit, then it may be read as a number of tenths.

EXAMPLES

١ فتحت على انخفاض بنسبة واحد فاصل خمسة اعشار في المئة . . . ووصلت بورصة باريس الى صفر فاصل خمسة اعشار في المئة بعدما فتحت اسواقها بانخفاض بسيط

1 "It opened down 1.5%, . . . the Paris stock market reached 0.5% after its markets opened slightly down."
(broadcast on Euronews Arabic, Aug. 8, 2011)

٢ نسبة البطالة ما انفكت تنخفض بدءا من ديسمبر كانون الثاني الماضي حيث كانت تقدر بتسعِ نقاط وأربعة أعشار نقطةٍ مئوية إلى أن وصلت في الشهر المنصرم إلى ثماني نقاط وثمانية أعشار نقطةٍ مئوية

2 "The rate of unemployment has continued to go down since last December, when it was estimated to be 9.4 percent, and last month went down to 8.8 percent."
(broadcast on Euronews Arabic, Apr. 1, 2011)

---

85. One may also hear فارِزة sometimes used for the decimal point.

Read as Number (More than One Digit)

If the decimal goes to two places, or sometimes even if it goes to three places, the entire two- or three-digit number may be read as one two- or three-digit number, as opposed to reading each digit individually.

EXAMPLES

١ عادت لترتفع الى صفر فاصل خمسة و ثلاثينَ في المئة

1 "It rallied, going up to 0.35%."
(broadcast on Euronews Arabic, Aug. 8, 2011)

٢ معدل الفائدة على السندات بأجل عشر سنوات بلغ خمسة فاصلة سبعة وأربعين بالمئة

2 "The interest rate on the 10-year bonds is 5.47%."
(broadcast on Euronews Arabic, Apr. 20, 2011)

٣ . . . الحاسب الفائق الذي يتمتع بقدرة اجراء ثمانية فاصل مائة واثنينِ وستين كوادريليون عملية حسابية في الثانية الواحدة . . .

3 ". . . the supercomputer, which enjoys the ability to run 8.162 quadrillion computations in one second . . ."
(video news clip on alquds.com, June 22, 2011)

Each Digit Read

It is also acceptable to read each digit after the decimal point individually. This is especially necessary when there are a large number of digits following it.

EXAMPLES

١ . . . برفع قوة زلزال يوم الجمعة من ثمانية فاصل ثمانية إلى تسعة فاصل صفر

1 ". . . raising the strength of Friday's earthquake from 8.8 to 9.0."
(broadcast on Arirang Arabic News, Mar. 14, 2011)

٢ وبلغت قوة الزلزال ستة فاصل ثمانية على مقياس ريختر

2 "The strength of the earthquake was 6.8 on the Richter scale."
(broadcast on Euronews Arabic, Mar. 25, 2011)

٣ وهو عبارة عن مجرة صغيرة على بعد حوالي ثلاثةَ عشر فاصلة اثنين بليون سنة ضوئية

3 "It is a small galaxy approximately 13.2 billion light years away."
(broadcast on Euronews Arabic, Jan. 27, 2011)

٤ وكل جنيه يدفع له يعطي مقابله فاصلة واحد خمسة وحدة

4 "For each pound he is paid, he gives in return .15 units."
(masress.com, Apr. 3, 2008)

٥ نحن نُعَدُّ ضمن نسبةٍ صغيرة من السكان بحدود صفر فاصلة صفر اثنين في المئة من مجموع السكان الذين لا يمكن لهم التمتع بخدمات التدفق العالي

5 "We are among the small percentage of the residents, about 0.02% of all residents, who are not able to enjoy high-speed internet services."
(broadcast on Euronews Arabic, Oct. 29, 2010)

٦ فقد إحتل العراق المرتبة الأخيرة في مؤشر السلام العالمي مسجلاً ثلاثة فاصلة ثلاثة أربعة واحد في المرتبة رقم مئة وأربعة وأربعين

6 "Iraq is in last place in the world peace index, registering 3.341, 144th place."
(iraqhurr.org, June 6, 2009)

٧ كالوري تساوي أربعة فاصلة واحد ثمانية ستة ثمانية (4.1868) جول.

7 "A calorie equals 4.1868 joules."
(Agreement between Syrian Petroleum Company and Lebanon for the sale of gas, article 2, section 1–12, Nov. 27, 2002)[86]

Agreement of Counted Nouns

No Agreement

If there is a counted noun following the number that is after the decimal, it is not necessary to follow the grammatical rules regarding counted nouns. That is, the counted noun need not be plural if the number containing the decimal is between 3 and 10. And the counted noun of a decimal-containing number from 11 to 99 need not be in the منصوب case.

86. Posted at www.syrleb.org

EXAMPLES

١ أرباح الطيران الصيني ٦,٦ بليون دولار

1 "China Airlines' Profits Are 6.6 Billion Dollars"
(*al-Ḥayāt*, Jan. 14, 2011)

٢ وزاد سعر برميل خام «برنت» في لندن ٣٤ سنتاً إلى ٧٣,٨٤ دولار.

2 "The price of Brent crude in London went up 34 cents to 73.84 dollars."
(*al-Ḥayāt*, Aug. 12, 2009)

٣ . . . أن حصيلة الصادرات السلعية حققت انخفاضا قدره ٤,٢ مليار دولار

3 ". . . that the revenues from commodity exports underwent a reduction of 4.2 billion dollars."
(*al-Ahrām*, Aug. 20, 2009)

٤ وصباح أمس بلغ سعر عقود البترول الخام الامريكي الخفيف لتسليم يناير—مارس ٨٧,٢٦ دولار للبرميل

4 "Yesterday morning, the price of American crude oil contracts for January to March delivery reached 87.26 dollars per barrel."
(*al-Ahrām al-Dawli*, Feb. 12, 2011)

Agreement

Alternatively, the rules regarding counted nouns may be followed. So if the counted noun follows 3–10, it becomes plural. If it follows 11–99, it is singular but in the منصوب case.

EXAMPLES

١ . . . نتيجة لتراجع التحويلات الخاصة (أهمها تحويلات المصريين العاملين بالخارج) بمعدل ٨,٩٪ لتبلغ ٧,٦ مليارات دولار

1 ". . . due to a decline in private money transfers (the most important which are transfers made by Egyptians working abroad) by 8.9% to 7.6 billion dollars."
(*al-Ahrām*, Aug. 20, 2009)

٢ هذا وتراجعت أونسة الذهب في أسواق المستقبل 2.10 دولار لتغلق على 34.94 دولاراً

2 "Furthermore, an ounce of gold in futures markets went down 2.1 dollars to close at 34.94 dollars."
(*al-Riyāḍ*, Jan. 25, 2004)

٣ وارتفع دخل الاستثمارات والارباح الاخرى 4.9 ملايين إلى 48 مليونا . . . وتم تجنيب مبلغ 6.5 ملايين إلى الاحتياطيات وتبقى مبلغ 565.1 مليونا كأرباح مدورة لعام 2003.

3 "Income from investments and other profits went up 4.9 million to 48 million. . . . An amount of 6.5 million has been put aside in reserves, and 565.1 million remain as retained earnings for the year 2003."
(*al-Bayān*, March 24, 2003)

Fractions

Writing Fractions

When written with a slash, fractions are written like those in English: the numerator to the left of the slash, and the denominator to the right. When a whole number is part of the number along with the fraction, the whole number is to the left of the fraction.

EXAMPLES

١ كل منها طوله (٠,٧ أنش ١,٨ سم) وسماكته ١/٣ سماكة الشعر الأنساني

1 "Each one of them is .7 inches (1.8 cm) in length, and its width is ⅓ the width of a human hair."
(Ḥaffār, *Makkuk al-Faḍā'*, p. 194)

٢ بذور خردل ١/٢ ملعقة صغيرة . . .
زيت نباتي ٢ ١/٢ أونصة سائلة

2 "mustard seed: ½ teaspoon
vegetable oil: 2½ fluid ounces"
(*Muwsū'at al-Ṭabkh al-Muṣawwar*, p. 110)

٣ قطّعي كل جزرة . . . طوليًّا إلى شرائح بسماكة ١ سم/١/٢ بوصة

3 "Chop each carrot . . . lengthwise into strips 1 cm/½ inch wide."
(*Mawsū'a al-Ṭabkh al-Muṣawwar*, p. 69)

Reading Fractions

One-half is نِصْف.

As seen in table 2.2, the fractions, from one-third to one-tenth, are formed by placing the root of the number in the فُعْل pattern. One-sixth is سُدْس.

Table 2.2 Fractions

	Singular	Plural
half	نِصْف	أَنْصاف
third	ثُلْث	أَثْلاث
fourth/quarter	رُبْع	أَرْباع
fifth	خُمْس	أَخْماس
sixth	سُدْس	أَسْداس
seventh	سُبْع	أَسْباع
eighth	ثُمْن	أَثْمان
ninth	تُسْع	أَتْساع
tenth	عُشْر	أَعْشار

For ⅓ to ⅒, sometimes the pattern فُعُل is used, with a *ḍamma* on the second letter instead of a *sukūn*.

Fractions may be placed in an إضافة construction with a following noun.

ربع دولار "a quarter of a dollar"

If a multiple of a fraction is needed, the fraction may become a counted noun and thus placed in the plural. That fraction is in turn placed in an إضافة relationship with the following counted noun. Or, if two of some fraction is needed, then the fraction may be placed in the dual. (For more on the dual, see p. 7.)

أربعة أخماس السكّان "Four-fifths of the population"

ثُلْثا السكّان "two-thirds of the population"

EXAMPLES

١ فَإِن كُنَّ نِسَاءً فَوْقَ ٱثْنَتَيْنِ فَلَهُنَّ ثُلُثَا مَا تَرَكَ وَإِن كَانَتْ وَاحِدَةً فَلَهَا
ٱلنِّصْفُ وَلِأَبَوَيْهِ لِكُلِّ وَاحِدٍ مِنْهُمَا ٱلسُّدُسُ مِمَّا تَرَكَ إِن كَانَ لَهُ وَلَدٌ

1 "If there be more than two girls, they shall have two-thirds of the inheritance; but if there be one only, she shall inherit the half. Parents shall inherit a sixth each, if the deceased have a child."[87]
(Qur'an, 4:11)

٢ وَلَكُمْ نِصْفُ مَا تَرَكَ أَزْوَاجُكُمْ إِن لَمْ يَكُن لَهُنَّ وَلَدٌ فَإِن كَانَ لَهُنَّ وَلَدٌ
فَلَكُمُ ٱلرُّبُعُ مِمَّا تَرَكْنَ . . . فَإِن كَانَ لَكُمْ وَلَدٌ فَلَهُنَّ ٱلثُّمُنُ مِمَّا تَرَكْتُمْ

2 "You shall inherit the half of your wives' estate if they die childless. If they leave children, a quarter of their estate shall be yours. . . . If you leave children, they shall inherit one-eighth."[88]
(Qur'an, 4:12)

٣ وجعل هذان الصوتان يوقظان الصبى كل يوم في أول الثلث الأخير من الليل

3 "These two sounds started waking the boy up every night during the beginning of the last third of the night."
(Taha Husayn, *al-Ayyām*, 2/42)

٤ نصف رجال أوروبا أقرباء توت عنخ آمون

4 "Half of the Men of Europe Are Related to King Tut"
(*al-Qabas*, Aug. 3, 2011)

٥ وعشر السنة خمسة وثلاثون يوما وخمسا يوم

5 "A tenth of a year is 35 and two-fifths days."
(Bīrūni, *al-Qānūn al-Mas'ūdi*, 1/231)

٦ سار ومعه ثلاثة آلاف وخمسمائة ثُلُثهم من غافق

6 "He marched and had 3500 (men) with him, a third of whom were from Ghāfiq."
(Yāqūt, *Mu'jam al-Buldān*, 4/297, #9187 on al-Fusṭāṭ)

٧ تحتل الغابات ربع مساحة كندا الشاسعة

7 "Forests occupy a quarter of the vast area of Canada."
(*al-'Arabi*, June 1993)

87. Translation is N.J. Dawood's.
88. Translation is N.J. Dawood's.

٨ ومخرجه من جبل شقورة حيث الطول خمس عشرة درجة والعرض ثمان وثلثون وثلثان

8 "Its origin is from Shaqūra Mountain, where the longitude is 15 degrees and the latitude is 38 and two-thirds."
(Abu-l-Fidā', *Taqwīm al-Buldān*, pp. 46–47)

٩ إذا لم يخفض الإنتاج النفطي بمقدار مليونٍ ونصف مليون برميلٍ يوميا . . .

9 "If petroleum production is not reduced by 1.5 million barrels daily . . ."
(broadcast on Kuwait Radio News, Nov. 27, 2001)

١٠ . . . ما أدى إلى اعتبار الحكومة الحالية مستقيلة لخروج أكثر من ثلث أعضائها منها . . .

10 ". . . which led to the government being considered resigned due to the departure of over one third of its members . . ."
(*al-Ḥayāt*, Jan. 14, 2011)

١١ وان صابر لو بذل في البحث عن الله عشر ما بذله في البحث عن أبيه . . .

11 "If Saber had spent one tenth of the energy searching for God that he spent searching for his father . . ."
(Naguib Mahfouz, *al-Ṭarīq*, p. 207)

١٢ فرآه هذا بعد أن عبر ثلثى الطريق

12 "The latter saw him after he had crossed two-thirds of the road."
(Naguib Mahfouz, *Zuqāq Midaqq*, p. 49)

١٣ وخبر إسماعيل بأننى إذا طلبت إليه ماء أن يهيئ لى قدحا نصفه ماء عادى والنصف الآخر ماء دافئ

13 "Let Ismail know that, if I ask him for water, to prepare for me a glass half of which is regular water and half of which is warm water."
(Naguib Mahfouz, *Zuqāq al-Midaqq*, p. 172)

١٤ فترك الوكيل وظيفته بعد خدمة طويلة استمرت ربع قرن من حياته

14 "The manager left his position after a long period of service that lasted for a quarter of a century of his life."
(Naguib Mahfouz, *Zuqāq al-Midaqq*, p. 239)

١٥ وهكذا امتدت الدقائق الى ربع ساعة

15 "Thus the minutes stretched out into a quarter of an hour."
(Yūsuf Idrīs, *al-'Askari al-Aswad*, p. 67)

١٦ وطول سميساط أربع وخمسون درجة وثلثان وعرضها ست وثلاثون درجة وثلث

16 "The longitude of Sumaysāṭ is 54 and two-thirds degrees, and its latitude is 36 and one-third degrees."
(Yāqūt, *Muʿjam al-Buldān*, 3/293, #6631 on Sumaysāṭ)

١٧ . . . أنه حسب حروف القرآن فوجد النصف الأول من القرآن ينتهي إلى خمسٍ وستّين آيةً من سورة الكهف . . . وهو الربع الثاني والسُّدس الثالث والثُّمن الرابع والعُشر الخامس

17 ". . . that he counted the letters of the Qurʾan and found that the first half ends with at the 65th verse of *Sūrat al-Kahf* . . . it is the second quarter, and the third sixth, and the fourth eighth, and the fifth tenth."
(Thaʿlab, *Majālis*, pp. 50–51)

١٨ ويكون أطول نهار هؤلاء في أول الإقليم، ثلاث عشرة ساعة وربعاً، وآخره ثلاث عشرة ساعة وثلاثة أرباع الساعة

18 "Their longest day in the first part of the region is 13 and a quarter hours, and in the last part of it 13 and three-quarters hours."
(Yāqūt, *Muʿjam al-Buldān*, 1/46, chap. 2 of introduction)

١٩ وقسّم أربعة أخماسِها على السريّة

19 "He divided four-fifths of it amongst the raiding party."
(Ibn Kathīr, *al-Bidāya wa-l-Nihāya*, 5/325)

٢٠ . . . وفي اليوم الثامن يأخذ خروفين صحيحين . . . وثلاثةَ أعشارِ القُفّة من الدقيق

20 ". . . and on the eighth day he should bring two healthy lambs . . . and 3/10ths of an ephah of flour."
(*al-Kitāb al-Muqaddas*, al-Lāwiyyīn [Leviticus] 14:10)

٢١ وعند الحصاد تعطون خُمْسَ غِلالكم لفرعون، والأربعةُ الأخماس الباقيةُ تكون لكم بذارًا للحقول

21 "At harvest time, you give one-fifth of your yield to Pharaoh and the remaining four-fifths will be seeds for your fields."
(*al-Kitāb al-Muqaddas*, al-Takwīn [Genesis] 47:24)

٢٢ ثلاثة أرباع الألمان تقريباً يستخدمون شبكة الإنترنت

22 "Approximately three-quarters of Germans use the internet."
(*al-Quds*, July 4, 2011)

٢٣ ثلاثة أخماس الآباء في بريطانيا لا يثقون في التعليم المدرسي

23 "Three-fifths of fathers in Britain don't trust school education."
(*al-Sharq al-Awsaṭ*, Jan. 3, 2003)

٢٤ كان خمسة أسداس عدد الذكور البالغين لايستطيعون الإدلاء بأصواتهم

24 "Five-sixths of adult males were not able to cast votes."
(digital.ahram.org.eg, Dec. 7, 2010)

٢٥ وكان أربعة آلاف من البريطانيين يمتلكون أربعة أسباع الأرض

25 "Four thousand Brits owned four-sevenths of the earth."
(*al-Wasaṭ* [Bahrain], June 13, 2011)

٢٦ يؤيد منح كرد ولاية الموصل استقلالهم لانهم يمثلون خمسة اثمان سكانها وسبعة اثمان في حالة اضيف إليه التركمان والايزيديون

26 "It supports granting independence to the Kurds of the state of Mosul because they represent five-eighths of its population, or seven-eighths if you count the Turkomen and Yazidis."
(*al-Ittiḥād* [Kurdistan], July 26, 2009)

٢٧ . . . توصية بتأجير سبعة أثمان مياه الليطاني لإسرائيل

27 ". . . a recommendation to lease seven-eighths of the waters of the Litani River to Israel."
(*al-Sharq al-Awsaṭ*, Aug. 12, 2006)

٢٨ للجراد القدرة على إهلاك رِزق نحو عُشر سكان العالم.

28 "Locusts have the capability of destroying the livelihood of about one-tenth of the world's population."
(*al-ʿArabi*, Dec. 2004)

Juz' min

For fractions smaller than a tenth,

جُزْء من (plural, أجزاء من)

is used, followed by the denominator. The denominator may be followed by جُزْء or أجزاء, whichever is required by the number given (usually جزء). Or, this second instance of جزء/أجزاء may be omitted:

جزء من مائة

جزء من مائة جزء

"1/100th"

EXAMPLES

١ يسمح ببناء شرفات/فرندات/لا تزيد مساحتها عن 1/50 "جزء من خمسين" من مساحة المقسم

1 "It is permissible to build balconies the area of which is no greater than 1/50th of the area of the lot."
(from the webpage of the Ministry of Local Administration, Damascus)[89]

٢ . . . وموظفا اخر بقطاع حكومي وعلى نفس المسمى الوظيفي ونفس المؤهل لا يتقاضي جزء من عشرين من هذا الراتب

2 ". . . and that another employee in the government sector, and with the same job title and the same qualifications does not make 1/20th of this salary."
(*al-Ahrām*, May 5, 2011)

٣ يجري حساب المكافأة التي لم تحدد في هذا القانون على اساس جزء من اثني عشر جزءاً من راتب الموظف الشهري الاخير

3 "Stipends not specified in this law are to be calculated at 1/12th of the employee's last monthly salary."
(Jordan civil retirement law, 1959, article 21)[90]

٤ من الممكن إكساء صفيح السيارات بطبقة لا يتعدى سمكها 5 إلى 10 أجزاء من الف جزء من المليمتر تكفي لحماية أجسام السيارات من الخدوش

4 "It is possible to coat the surfaces of automobiles with a layer no thicker than 5–10 thousandths of a millimeter, which would suffice to protect the bodies of the cars from scratches."
(*al-Sharq al-Awsaṭ*, June 18, 2002)

٥ قد يكون الفارق الذي تفوق به الإسباني فيرناندو ألونسو سائق رينو على منافسه العنيد الالماني مايكل شوماخر نجم فريق فيراري في سباق جائزة تركيا الكبرى نحو ثمانية أجزاء من مئة جزء من الثانية

5 "The difference that allowed the Spaniard Fernando Alonso, driver for Renault, to prevail over his stubborn rival Michael Schumacher, star of the Ferrari team in the Turkish Grand Prix, may be about 8/100ths of a second."
(*al-Ittiḥād* [UAE], Aug. 31, 2006)

89. damascus.gov.sy

90. Retrieved from www.lob.gov.jo/ui/laws/search_no.jsp?no=34&year=1959

٦ . . . وهو نبضات ضوء الليزر التي تدوم أجزاء من المليون من النانوثانية . . .

6 ". . . pulses of laser light lasting millionths of a nanosecond . . ."[91]
(*al-'Ulūm*, Sept. 2001)

٧ مِلّيمِتْرٌ ج ـات: جزء من ألف جزء من المِتْرِ

7 "Millimeter: 1/1000th of a meter."
(*al-Mu'jam al-'Arabi al-Asāsi*, p. 1152)

٨ مِلّيغرام: جزء من ألف من الغرام

8 "Milligram: 1/1000th of a gram."
(*al-Munjid fi-l-Lugha al-'Arabiyya al-Mu'āṣira*, p. 1359)

Smaller Fractions in Classical Texts

In classical texts, a fraction smaller than 1/10 was expressed as a fraction of a fraction. Thus, any fraction of any size could be formed by adding and/or multiplying fractions from one-half to one-tenth.

EXAMPLES

١ ولا اعلم بين احد من اصحابنا خلافا انّ في المعدن الزكاة ربع العشر

1 "As far as I know none of our companions disagree that the zakat owed on mines is 1/40th (a quarter of a tenth)."
(Balādhuri, *Futūḥ al-Buldān*, p. 22)

٢ العمران من الأرض نصف سُدْسها، والباقي ليس فيه عمارة ولا نباتٌ ولا حيوان

2 "The populated part of the earth is 1/12th of it (half of sixth of it). The rest has no buildings, no plants, no animals."
(Yāqūt, *Mu'jam al-Buldān*, 1/33, chap. 1 of introduction)

---

91. English rendition from the article "Big Payoffs in a Flash," *Scientific American*, Sept. 2000. The Arabic passage is taken from a translation of this article which appeared in the magazine cited.

٣ أوله حيث يكون الظلّ نصف النهار إذا استوى الليل والنهار ثلاثة أقدام ونصفاً وعُشراً وسدس عشر قدم

3 "It starts where the shadow, at the midpoint of the day when day and night are equal, is three and 37⁄60ths feet (3 feet and a half and a tenth and a sixth of a tenth)"
(Yāqūt, *Muʿjam al-Buldān*, 1/46, chap. 2 of introduction)

Volume: Square/Cubic Units of Measurement

As in English, squared units of measurement (e.g. square feet) are represented with a superscript 2 immediately after (that is, to the left of) the unit of measure. Cubic units are represented with a superscript 3 immediately after (that is, to the left of) the unit of measure.

When reading the square units, مُرَبَّع is used for "square."

When reading the cubic units, مُكَعَّب is used for "cubic."

Each of these follows the word referring to the unit of measurement and functions as an adjective for it, and it therefore agrees with it in gender, case, and number.

EXAMPLES

١ تبلغ مساحة فرنسة (٥٥١,٥٠٠) كلم٢.

1 "The area of France is 551,500 km^2 (square kilometers)."
(*Aṭlas al-ʿĀlam al-Ṣaḥīḥ*, p. 94)

٢ ليس هناك أقوى من الفولاذ، الذي يتحمل قوة شد تساوي ١٠٠ كجم/مم٢

2 "There is nothing stronger than steel, which can withstand a pull equal to 100 kg/mm^2 (square millimeters)."
(Perelman, Yakov, *al-Fīziyāʾ al-Musalliya*, p. 83)

٣ . . . المساحات الشاسعة للغاية (١٦–٣٠ مليون كيلومتر مربع) التي يمكن أن يوجد بها.

3 ". . . the extremely vast area (16–30 million square kilometers) over which they may be found."
(*al-'Arabi*, Dec. 2004)

٤ يقوم أيكران بنقل البرامج التلفزيونية الملونة أو غير الملونة إلى مساحة تصل حتى ٣٥٠٠,٠٠٠ ميل مربع تقريباً أي ما يعادل ٩ ملايين كيلو متر مربع

4 "Ekran transmits television programs both in color and black and white to an area of up to approximately 3,500,000 square miles, i.e., the equivalent of 9 million square kilometers."
(Ḥaffār, *Makkūk al-Faḍā'*, p. 98)

٥ الفدان ٤٤٩٢ متراً مربعاً

5 "A feddan is 4492 square meters."
(*al-Ḥayāt*, Aug. 12, 2009)

٦ يساوي وزن ٢٠ م٣ من الماء

6 "That equals the weight of 20 m^3 (cubic meters) of water."
(Perelman, Yakov, *al-Fīziyā' al-Musalliya*, p. 123)

٧ وهكذا فإنّ كثافتَهُ قَليلةٌ جدًّا (حوالي ٠,٠١٢ غم للسم٣)

7 "Thus its density is very low (about 0.012 grams per cm^3 [cubic centimeter])."
(*al-Mawsū'a al-'Ilmiyya al-Muyassara*, p. 66)

٨ تستوعب الحاوية الواحدة 20 متراً مكعباً من المخلفات المنزلية

8 "One container holds 20 cubic meters of household garbage."
(*al-Ittiḥād* [UAE], Apr. 17, 2011)

٩ وقال ان الاسعار لم ترتفع وانها تحتسب بـ 23 قرشا لاول 10 أمتار مكعبة للمياه

9 "He said that the prices have not gone up, and that for water they are calculated at 23 piastres for the first 10 cubic meters."
(digital.ahram.org.eg, May 27, 2011)

١٠ وتوقعوا أن تؤمّن المحطة بعد الوصول إلى طاقتها القصوى مع نهاية السنة الجارية ٧٧٥ مليون قدم مكعبة يومياً (٨ بلايين متر مكعب سنوياً)

10 "They expect that the plant, after it reaches full capacity at the end of the current year, will provide 775 million cubic feet daily (8 billion cubic meters per year)."
(*al-Ḥayāt*, Aug. 12, 2009)

Percentages

Percentages are written with the percentage sign most often to the left of the number, and occasionally to its right.

They can be read out as the number followed by

بالمائة or في المائة

EXAMPLES

١ فإنه تمكن من جمع معلومات عن ٩٥% من محيطات العالم كل ست وثلاثين ساعة

1 "It was able to gather information about 95% of the world's oceans every 36 hours."
(Ḥaffār, *Makkūk al-Faḍā'*, p. 59)

٢ خسائر "أديكو" ترغمها على تسريح ١٢% من موظفيها

2 "Adecco's losses force it to let 12% of its employees go."
(*al-Ḥayāt*, Aug. 12, 2009)

٣ أظهرت ارتفاع شعبية الحزب الديمقراطي الياباني لتصل إلى ٢٤%، بينما بلغت نسبة التأييد الشعبي للحزب الليبرالي الديمقراطي نسبة ١٣% فقط

3 "They showed a rise in the popularity of the Japanese Democratic party to 24%, while the percentage of support for the Liberal Democratic party reached just 13%.
(*al-Ahrām*, Aug. 20, 2009)

٤ ويكفي أن نشير هنا إلى أن نسبة مساهمة الولايات المتحدة في انبعاثات غازات الدفيئة تربو على ٣٦% في حين أن عدد سكانها لا يزيد على أربعة في المائة من مجموع سكان العالم.

4 "It suffices to point out here that the United States' share of greenhouse gas emissions is 36%, while its population is no more than 4% of the world's total."
(*al-'Arabi*, Dec. 2004)

٥ الولايات المتحدة التي تنتج حاليا ١٠ في المئة من النفط العالمي وتستهلك ٢٤ في المئة منه . . .

5 "The United States, which currently produces 10% of the world's oil, but consumes 24% of it . . ."
(*al-Ḥayāt*, Jan. 9, 2009)

٦ ففي روسيا الاتحادية لم تزد نسبة الذكور في سن الخامسة عشرة الذين يتعاطون الكحوليات على (٢١) بالمائة

6 "In Soviet Russia, the number of males over the age of 15 who drank alcohol was no more than 21%."
(*al-'Arabi*, June 2001)

٧ 81 بالمائة من يهود أميركا يرفضون العودة لحدود 1967

7 "81% of American Jews Reject the Idea of Returning to 1967 Borders"
(*al-Yawm*, July 15, 2011)

VOCABULARY FOR BASIC ARITHMETICAL OPERATIONS

عَدَد موجَب = positive number

عدد سالِب = negative number

ناقِص ثلاثة or سالِب ثلاثة = −٣

عدد زَوْجي = even number

عدد فَرْدي = odd number

يُساوي = 'equals'

Addition

الجَمْع = addition

أَضاف/يُضيف . . . إلى . . . = to add

زائِد = +

أضفتُ ثلاثة إلى خمسة = "I added three to five."

٢ + ٣ = ٥

(اثنان زائد ثلاثة يساوي خمسة)

Subtraction

الطَرْح = subtraction

طَرَحَ/يَطرَح . . . من . . .

نَقَصَ/يَنقُص . . . من . . .

ناقِص = −

طرحتُ اثنين من ثلاثة = نقصتُ اثنين من ثلاثة = "I subtracted two from three."

٣ − ٢ = ١

(ثلاثة ناقص اثنين يساوي واحد)

Multiplication

الضَرْب = multiplication

ضَرَبَ/يَضرِب . . . في . . . = to multiply . . . by . . .

ضَرْب = × (or, less formally في)

ضربتُ خمسة في ثلاثة = "I multiplied five by three."

٥ × ٣ = ١٥

(خمسة ضرب ثلاثة يساوي خمسة عشر)

Division

القِسْمة = division

قَسَّمَ/يُقَسِّم or قَسَمَ/يَقْسِم . . . على . . . = to divide

تَقسيم = ÷ (or, less formally, على)

قسمتُ اربعة على اثنين = "I divided four by two."

٤ ÷ ٢ = ٢

(أربعة تقسيم اثنين يساوي اثنين)

GLOSSARY—ENGLISH

Arabic numerals: The set of digits used in English (0123456789) (and often in Arabic as well).

Hindi numerals: The set of digits used in Arabic (٠١٢٣٤٥٦٧٨٩).

masculine sound plural (**جمع المذكر السالم**)**:** The category of plurals which is formed by adding ـونَ to the singular in the مرفوع case and ـينَ in the منصوب and مجرور cases. This type of pluralization is used for nouns referring to human males. When nouns other than those referring to human males are pluralized with these endings, they are not considered true جمع مذكر سالم but rather مُلحَق بجمع المذكر السالم.

nunation: The act of placing a *tanwīn* at the end of a word.

GLOSSARY—ARABIC

إضافة: The possessive construction consisting of two nouns, the مضاف (q.v.) and the مضاف إليه (q.v.).

إضافة غير مَحضة: A type of *iḍāfa* used not to indicate possession but to describe characteristics. It is unlike a regular *iḍāfa* in that its مضاف can take the definite article الـ.

الرجل الكثير العلم: "The man who is much of knowledge," i.e., "very knowledgeable."

تَمييز: "Specifier," a noun in the منصوب case which specifies, or gives further information about, a word appearing previously in the sentence. For example, in هو أكثرهم حبّاً للوطن "He is the most patriotic of them," lit. "He is the greatest of them in terms of love for country," حبّا is a تمييز since it gives further information about أكثر. It answers the questions, "Greater in terms of what? In what way?"

For the numbers 11–99, the counted noun, which is منصوب, is also considered a تمييز, as it specifies, or gives further information about, the number. In أحد عشر كوكباً, كوكبا is a تمييز, as it answers the question, "Eleven of what?"

تَوكيد: "Emphasis." A noun which follows another noun to restate or emphasize it in some way. It follows it in case.

غادر الضيوف كلهم: "The guests all left" (literally, "The guests left, all of them")

Here, كلّهم is a توكيد.

حال: "Accusative of condition." A noun in the منصوب case which gives information about the state or condition usually of the subject or object of the sentence, while the action described is taking place.

دخل الغرفة ضاحكاً: "He entered the room laughing."

Here, ضاحكا is a حال.

خَبَر: The predicate of a nominal sentence. Its case is مرفوع.

صيغة مُنْتَهى الجُموع: The plural noun pattern CaCāCiC or CaCāCīC, where C stands for any consonant. Nouns on this pattern are مَمنوع من الصَرف, also called "diptotes." For example:

أَماكِن مَدارِس مَشاريع دَكاكين رَسائِل فَوائِد

ظَرف زَمان: A word in a sentence in the منصوب case which states when or for how long an action takes place.

رجع الجمعةَ: "He came back Friday."

نمتُ ساعةً: "I slept for an hour."

In these sentences, الجمعة and ساعةً are ظرف زمان, as جمعة states when the action took place, and ساعة states for what length of time.

عِقْد/عَقْد pl. عُقود: A multiple of 10 less than 100, not including 10, that is, the numbers 20, 30, 40, 50, 60, 70, 80, and 90.

مُبتَدَأ: The subject of a nominal sentence. Its case is مرفوع.

مَجْرور: In some systems of teaching Arabic, this case is called "genitive."

مَرْفوع: In some systems of teaching Arabic, this case is called "nominative."

مُرَكَّب: Composed of parts. An عدد مركب is a number between 11 and 19 (inclusive), so called because it is formed by combining two elements.

مُسْتَثْنى: The word which occurs after إلاّ. It is usually in the منصوب case, and sometimes in the مرفوع case.

مُضاف: The first of the two terms in an إضافة construction. The مضاف is the item owned, and the second term, the مضاف إليه, is the owner of the item. The case of the مضاف will be determined by its position in the sentence. It could be مرفوع, منصوب, or مجرور. It may never have a definite article الـ.

مُضاف إليه: The second of the two terms in an إضافة construction. The first term, the مضاف, is the item owned, and the مضاف إليه is the owner. It is in the مجرور case. A possessive pronoun attached to a noun, for example ـكم in داركم "your (plural) house", is also considered a مضاف إليه.

مَعْطوف: Connected to a previous word by a conjunction. In the sentence جاء سامي ورامي Rāmi is the مَعْطوف and Sāmi is the معطوف عَلَيْهِ. In the terminology of numbers, the عدد معطوف

is one of the عقود followed by a *wāw* then a number 1–9, for example, 29, 71, 33, etc.

ملحق بجمع المذكر السالم: A word which, like masculine sound plurals, ends in ـونَ or ـينَ and therefore is subject to all the rules of masculine sound plurals, but is not actually a human masculine plural. The عقود fall into this category.

منصوب: In some systems of teaching Arabic, this case is called "accusative."

منقوص: A word which ends in a long *yā*ʾ. When indefinite, this *yā*ʾ drops in the مرفوع and مجرور cases and is replaced with a *tanwīn kasra*. In the منصوب case, it takes the *tanwīn fatḥa*. For example:

(مرفوع/مجرور) قاضٍ

(منصوب) قاضيًا

When definite or مضاف, it retains its *yā*ʾ, but can never take a final *ḍamma* or *kasra*. It does take a final *fatḥa* if منصوب.

BIBLIOGRAPHY

ʿAbla, ʿAbd al-Hādi. 1997. *Mawsūʿa al-Ṭabkh al-Muṣawwar: al-Khuḍr*. Beirut: Maktabat Lubnān.

Abu-l-Fidāʾ, ʿImād al-Dīn Ismāʿīl ibn Muḥammad ibn ʿUmar (d. 1331). 1840. *Taqwīm al-Buldān*. Paris: Dār al-Ṭibāʿa al-Sulṭāniyya.

ʿAli, Taḥsīn. 2004. *Mudhakkirāt Taḥsīn ʿAli*, edited Ṣāliḥ Muḥammad al-ʿĀbid. Beirut: al-Muʾassasa al-ʿArabiyya li-l-Dirāsāt wa-l-Nashr.

Amīn, Muṣṭafa. 1987. *al-Miʾatā Fikra*. Beirut: al-ʿAṣr al-Ḥadīth.

al-Anbāri, Abu Bakr Muḥammad ibn al-Qāsim (d. 940). 1963. *Sharḥ al-Qaṣāʾid al-Sabʿ al-Ṭiwāl al-Jāhiliyyāt*, edited by ʿAbd al-Salām Hārūn. Cairo: Dār al-Maʿārif.

———. 1987. *Kitāb al-Aḍdād*, edited by Muḥammad Abu-l-Faḍl Ibrāhīm. Beirut: al-Maktaba al-ʿAṣriyya.

———. 1992. *al-Zāhir fī Maʿāni Kalimāt al-Nās*, edited by Ḥātim Ṣāliḥ al-Ḍāmin. Beirut: Muʾassasat al-Risāla.

al-Anbāri, Abu-l-Barakāt. 1998. *al-Inṣāf fī Masāʾil al-Khilāf bayn al-Naḥwiyyīn al-Baṣriyyīn wa-l-Kūfiyyīn*, edited by Ḥasan Aḥmad. Beirut, Dar al-Kotob al-Ilmiyah.

al-Andalusi, Muḥammad ibn Yūsuf Abu Ḥayyān (d. 1344). 2001. *al-Baḥr al-Muḥīṭ*, edited by ʿAbd al-Mawjūd, ʿAli Muḥammad Muʿawwaḍ, Zakariyya ʿAbd al-Majīd al-Nūti, and Aḥmad al-Najūli al-Jamal. Beirut: Dar al-Kotob al-Ilmiyah.

al-Ashʿari, Abu-l-Ḥasan ʿAli ibn Ismāʿīl (d. 936). 2005. *Maqālāt al-Islamiyyīn wa-Khtilāf al-Muṣallīn*, edited by Naʿīm Zarzūr. Beirut: al-Maktaba al-ʿAṣriyya.

al-Aswāni, ʿAlāʾ. 2005. *ʿImārat Yaʿqūbiyān*. Cairo: Maktabat Madbūli.

Aṭlas al-ʿĀlam al-Ṣaḥīḥ, see Ḥāmid, Ḥassān.

al-Aṭlas al-ʿIlmi: ʿĀlam al-Ḥayawān, see al-Karami, Zuhair, and M. Sabārīni.

al-Azhari, Abu Manṣūr Muḥammad ibn Aḥmad (d. 980). 2001. *Tahdhīb al-Lugha*, edited by Muḥammad ʿAwaḍ Murʿab. Beirut: Dār Iḥyāʾ al-Turāth al-ʿArabi.

Baghdādi, Abū Manṣūr ʿAbd al-Qāhir (d. 1037). 1998. *al-Farq Bayn al-Firaq*, edited by Muḥammad ʿUthmān al-Khusht. Cairo: Maktabat Ibn Sīna.

al-Balādhuri, Abu-l-ʿAbbās Aḥmad ibn Yaḥya ibn Jābir (d. 892). 1987. *Futūḥ al-Buldān*, edited by al-Ṭabbāʿ and al-Ṭabbāʿ. Beirut: Muʾassasat al-Maʿārif.

Bīrīlmān, Yākūf, see Perelman, Yakov.

Bīrūni, Abu Rayḥān (d. 1048). 1954. *al-Qānūn al-Masʿūdi*. Hyderabad: The Dāiratuʾl-Maʿārif-il-Oṣmānia.

al-Ḍāmin, Ḥātim Ṣāliḥ, ed. *Nusūs muḥaqqaqa fi-l-Lugha wa-l-Naḥw*. Baghdad: Jāmiʿat Baghdad, 1991.

Dawood, N.J. 2006. *The Koran*. London: Penguin Books.

Dāwūdi, Muḥammad Sayyid. 2003. *Muʿjam al-Arqām fi-l-Qurʾān al-Karīm*, 2nd edition. Cairo: Dār al-Kitāb al-Miṣri.

Ḍayf, Shawqi. 1992. *al-Madāris al-Naḥwiyya*. Cairo: Dār al-Maʿārif.

*EI*², see Gibb, H.A.R.

al-Farrāʾ, Abu Zakariyya Yaḥya ibn Ziyād (d. 822). [n.d.]. *Maʿāni al-Qurʾān*, edited by Aḥmad Yūsuf Najāti and Muḥammad ʿAli Najjār. Beirut: Dār al-Surūr.

Fayyūmi, Aḥmad ibn Muḥammad ibn ʿAli al-Muqri. [n.d.]. *al-Miṣbāḥ al-Munīr*. Beirut: al-Maktaba al-ʿIlmiyya.

al-Fīrūzābādi, Muḥammad ibn Yaʿqūb (d. 1415), *al-Qāmūs al-Muḥīṭ*. Beirut: Muʾassasat al-Risāla, 1987.

al-Gharayba, ʿAbd al-Karīm. 1984. *Tārīkh al-ʿArab al-Ḥadīth*. Beirut: al-Ahliyya li-l-Nashr wa-l-Tawzīʿ.

Gibb, H.A.R. et al. 1960-. *EI*² (*Encyclopaedia of Islam*, 2nd edition). Leiden and London: Brill.

al-Ḥaffār, Muḥammad Bashshār. 1986. *Makkūk al-Faḍāʾ wa-l-Aqmār al-Ṣināʿiyya*. Beirut: Dār al-Rashīd.

al-Ḥakīm, Tawfīq. 1976. *Maṣīr Ṣurṣār*. Cairo: Maktabat al-Ādāb.

———. *Muḥammad*. [n.d.]. Cairo: Maktabat al-Ādāb.

Ḥamawi, Ṣubḥi. 2000. *al-Munjid fi-l-Lugha al-ʿArabiyya al-Muʿāṣira*. Beirut: Dār al-Mashriq.

Ḥāmid, Ḥassān, ed. [n.d.]. *Aṭlas al-ʿĀlam al-Ṣaḥīḥ*. Beirut: Dār Maktabat al-Ḥayāt.

al-Ḥarīri, Abu Muḥammad al-Qāsim ibn ʿAli ibn Muḥammad ibn ʿUthmān (d. 1122). 2003. *Maqāmāt al-Ḥarīri*. Beirut: Dar al-Kotob al-Ilmiyah.

Ḥasan, ʿAbbās. 1975. *al-Naḥw al-Wāfi*. Cairo: Dār al-Maʿārif.

Hussein, Taha (Ḥusayn, Ṭāha). 1986. *al-Ayyām*. Cairo: Dār al-Maʿārif.

Ibn Abi Uṣaybiʿa, Muwaffaq al-Dīn Abu-l-ʿAbbās Aḥmad (d. 1270). [1965]. *ʿUyūn al-Anbāʾ fī Ṭabaqāt al-Aṭibbāʾ*, edited by Nizār Riḍa. Beirut: Dār Maktabat al-Ḥayāt.

Ibn Ḥajjāj al-Naysabūri, Muslim (d. 875). [n.d.] *Ṣaḥīḥ Muslim*. Egypt: al-Mujallad al-ʿArabi.

Ibn al-Jarrāḥ, ʿAli ibn ʿĪsa. 2008. "Financial statement, 918–19 A.D." Published in *al-Majalla al-Urduniyya li-l-Tārīkh wa-l-Āthār* 2:2.
Ibn al-Jawzi, Abu-l-Faraj ʿAbd al-Raḥmān ibn ʿAli (d. 1200). 1988. *Manāqib al-Imām Aḥmad ibn Ḥanbal*, edited by ʿAbd Allāh al-Turki. Cairo: Hajr.
Ibn Kathīr, ʿImād al-Dīn Abu-l-Fidāʾ Ismāʿīl ibn ʿUmar (d. 1373). 1997. *al-Bidāya wa-l-Nihāya*, edited by ʿAbd Allāh ibn ʿAbd al-Ḥasan al-Turki. Cairo: Hajr.
Ibn Khallikān, Abu-l-ʿAbbās Aḥmad ibn Muḥammad ibn Ibrāhīm ibn Abi Bakr (d. 1282). 1998. *Wafayāt al-Aʿyān*, edited by Yūsuf ʿAli Ṭawīl and Maryam Qāsim Ṭawīl. Beirut: Dar al-Kotob al-Ilmiyah.
Ibn Muqaffaʿ, ʿAbd Allāh, trans. (d. 759). [n.d.]. *Kalīla wa-Dimna*. Cairo: Maktabat al-Mutanabbi.
Ibn Qutayba, ʿAbd Allāh ibn Muslim (d. 889). 1988. *Adab al-Kātib*, edited by ʿAli Fāʿūr. Beirut: Dar al-Kotob al-Ilmiyah.
Ibn Sīda, Abu Ḥasan ʿAli ibn Ismāʿīl (d. 1066). [1993]. *Kitāb al-ʿAdad fi-l-Lugha*, edited by ʿAbd Allāh ibn al-Ḥusayn Nāṣīr and ʿAdnān ibn Muḥammad al-Ẓāhir. Amman.
Idrīs, Yūsuf. [1982]. *al-ʿAskari al-Aswad*. Cairo: Maktabat Misr.
al-ʿIshsh, Yūsuf. 1985. *al-Dawla al-Umawiyya wa-l-Aḥdāth allati Sabaqatha wa-Mahhadat laha-Btidāʾan min Fitnati ʿUthmān*. Damascus: Dār al-Fikr.
Jād al-Mawla, Muḥammad Aḥmad, ʿAli Muḥammad al-Bajāwi, and Muḥammad Abu-l-Faḍl Ibrāhīm, comp. 2003. *Qiṣaṣ al-ʿArab*. Beirut: al-Maktaba al-ʿAṣriyya, 2003. (A collection of stories taken from various classical texts)
al-Jāḥiẓ, ʿAmr ibn Baḥr (d. 868). 1970. *Kitāb al-Buldān*, edited by Ṣāliḥ Aḥmad al-ʿAli. Baghdad: Maṭbaʿat al-Ḥukūma.
Jārim, ʿAli & Muṣṭafa Amīn. 1984. *al-Naḥw al-Wāḍiḥ fī Qawāʿid al-Lugha al-ʿArabiyya*. Cairo: Dār al-Maʿārif.
al-Karami, Zuhair, and M. Sabārīni. 1991. *al-Aṭlas al-ʿIlmi: ʿĀlam al-Ḥayawān*. Beirut: Dār al-Kitāb al-Lubnāni.
al-Khaṭīb, Aḥmad Shafīq, ed. 1985. *al-Mawsūʿa al-ʿIlmiyya al-Muyassara*. Beirut: Maktabat Lubnān.
al-Kitāb al-Muqaddas (the Bible), produced by The Bible Society in Lebanon. 1995. Beirut: Dār al-Kitāb al-Muqaddas fi-l-Sharq al-Awsaṭ.
Mahfouz, Naguib (Maḥfūẓ, Najīb). [1977]. *al-Ḥarāfīsh*. Cairo: Maktabat Miṣr.
———. [1967]. *Mirāmār*. Cairo: Maktabat Miṣr.
———. [n.d.]. *Qaṣr al-Shawq*. Cairo: Maktabat Miṣr.
———. 1972. *al-Ṭarīq*. Beirut: Dār al-Qalam.
———. 1947. *Zuqāq al-Midaqq*. Cairo: Maktabat Miṣr.
Mālik ibn Anas (d. 796). 1985. *al-Muwaṭṭaʾ*, edited by Muḥammad Fuʾād ʿAbd al-Bāqi. Beirut: Dār Iḥyāʾ al-Turāth al-ʿArabi.
al-Manfalūṭi, Muṣṭafa Luṭfi. 1987. *Silsilat al-Aʿmāl al-Majhūla*, edited by ʿAli Shalash. London: Riad El-Rayyes.
al-Masʿūdi, Abu-l-Ḥasan ʿAli ibn al-Ḥusayn ibn ʿAli (d. 956). 1973. *Murūj al-Dhahab wa-Maʿādin al-Jawhar*, edited by Muḥammad Muḥyi-l-Dīn ʿAbd al-Ḥamīd. Beirut: Dār al-Fikr.

al-Mawsūʿa al-ʿIlmiyya al-Muyassara, see al-Khaṭīb.
Mawsūʿa al-Ṭabkh al-Muṣawwar, see ʿAbla, ʿAbd al-Hādi.
al-Muʿjam al-ʿArabi al-Asāsi. 1989. al-Munaẓẓama al-ʿArabiyya lil-Tarbiya wa-l-Thaqāfa wa-l-ʿUlūm. Larousse: [Paris].
al-Munjid fi-l-Aʿlām. 1976. Beirut: Dār al-Mashreq.
al-Munjid fi-l-Lugha al-ʿArabiyya al-Muʿāṣira, see Ḥamawi, Ṣubḥi.
Mustajāb, Muḥammad. 1996. *Dayrūṭ al-Sharīf wa Nuʿmān Abd al-Ḥāfiẓ*. Kotobarabia.com.
Niʿma, Fuʾād. [n.d.]. *Mulakhkhaṣ Qawāʿid al-Lugha al-ʿArabiyya*. Cairo: Maṭbaʿat Nahḍat Miṣr.
Nöldeke, Theodor. 1982. *Beitrage und Neue Beitrage zur Semitischen Sprachwissenschaft*. Amsterdam: Academic Publishers Associated.
Perelman, Yakov (Bīrīlmān, Yākūf). Translated 1984. *al-Fīziyāʾ al-Musalliya: al-Kitāb al-Thāni* (*Physics for Entertainment, Book 2*). Baghdad: Maktabat Āfāq ʿArabiyya.
al-Qarni, ʿĀʾiḍ. 2003. *Lā Taḥzan*. Riyadh: al-ʿAbīkān.
Qiṣaṣ al-ʿArab, see Jād al-Mawla, Muḥammad Aḥmad.
al-Rāzi, Abu Ḥātim Aḥmad ibn Ḥamdān (d. 934). [n.d.]. *Kitāb al-Zīna*, manuscript.
al-Rāzi, Fakhr al-Dīn (d. 1210). 1991. *Tafsīr al-Fakhr al-Rāzi*, a.k.a. *al-Tafsīr al-Kabīr wa-Mafātīḥ al-Ghayb*. Beirut: Dār al-Fikr.
Ṣaḥīḥ Muslim, see Ibn Ḥajjāj al-Naysabūri, Muslim.
al-Sayyid, Fāṭima. 1986. *Mudhakkirāt Ṣaḥafiyya fī Ghurfat al-Iʿdām*. Cairo: Maktabat Madbūli.
Shaḥrūr, Muḥammad. 2000. *al-Kitāb wa-l-Qurʾān: Qirāʾa Muʿāṣira*. Damascus: al-Ahāli.
Shalash, ʿAli, see al-Manfalūṭi, Muṣṭafa Luṭfi.
al-Sijistāni, Abu Dāwūd Sulaymān ibn al-Ashʿath al-Azdi (d. 889). 2009. *Sunan Abi Dāwūd*, edited by Shuʿayb Arnaʾūṭ. Dār al-Risāla al-ʿĀlamiyya.
al-Subki, Tāj al-Dīn Abu-l-Naṣr ʿAbd al-Wahhāb ibn ʿAli (d. 1370). 1964–1976. *Ṭabaqāt al-Shāfiʿiyya al-Kubra*, edited by Maḥmūd Muḥammad al-Ṭanāḥi and ʿAbd al-Fattāḥ al-Ḥulw. Cairo: al-Bābi al-Ḥalabi.
Sunan Abi Dāwūd, see al-Sijistāni, Abu Dāwūd Sulaymān ibn al-Ashʿath.
Suyūṭi, Jalāl al-Dīn ʿAbd al-Rahmān (d. 1505). 2006. *al-Itqān fī ʿUlūm al-Qurʾān*, edited by Muḥammad Abu-l-Faḍl Ibrāhīm. Beirut: al-Maktaba al-ʿAṣriyya.
al-Ṭabari, Abu Jaʿfar Muḥammad ibn Jarīr (d. 923). 1989. *The History of al-Tabari, vol. XXX: The ʿAbbāsid Caliphate in equilibrium*, translated by C.E. Bosworth. Albany: State University of New York Press.
———. 1999.*Tafsīr al-Ṭabari*, a.k.a. *Jāmiʿ al-Bayān fī Taʾwīl al-Qurʾān*. Beirut: Dar al-Kotob al-Ilmiyah.
———. 1967-. *Tārīkh al-Ṭabari*, a.k.a. *Tārīkh al-Rusul wa-l-Mulūk*, 2nd edition, edited by Muḥammad Abu-l-Faḍl Ibrāhīm. Cairo: Dār al-Maʿārif.

al-Ṭabarsi, Abu ʿAli al-Faḍl ibn Ḥasan (d. 1154). 1997. *Majmaʿ al-Bayān fī Tafsīr al-Qurʾān*, edited by Ibrāhīm Shams al-Dīn. Beirut: Dar al-Kotob al-Ilmiyah.
Thaʿlab, Abu-l-ʿAbbās Aḥmad ibn Yaḥya (d. 904). 1960. *Majālis Thaʿlab*, edited by ʿAbd al-Salām Hārūn. Cairo: Dār al-Maʿārif.
ʿUshayri, Muḥammad Riyāḍ. 1985. *al-Tasawwur al-Lughawi ind al-Ismāʿiliyya*. Alexandria: Munshaʾāt al-Maʿārif.
Wehr, Hans. 1993. *Arabic-English Dictionary: The Hans Wehr Dictionary of Modern Written Arabic*, edited by J M.Cowan. Ithaca, NY: Spoken Language Services, Inc.
Wright, W. 1896. *A Grammar of the Arabic Language*, 3rd edition. Reprint, Beirut: Librairie du Liban, 1996.
Yāqūt, Shihāb al-Dīn Abu ʿAbd Allāh (d. 1229). [1990]. *Muʿjam al-Buldān*, edited by Farīd ʿAbd al-ʿAzīz al-Jundi. Beirut: Dar al-Kotob al-Ilmiyah.
———. 1991. *Muʿjam al-Udabāʾ*. Beirut: Dar al-Kotob al-Ilmiyah.
al-Zamakhshari, Abu-l-Qāsim Jār Allāh Maḥmūd ibn ʿUmar (d. 1144). 1971. *al-Fāʾiq fī Gharīb al-Ḥadīth*, edited by ʿAli Muḥammad al-Bijāwi and Muḥammad Abu-l-Faḍl Ibrāhīm. Cairo: al-Bābi al-Ḥalabi.
———. 1999. *al-Mufassal fī Ṣunʿat al-Iʿrāb*, edited by Amīl Badīʿ Yaʿqūb. Beirut: Dar al-Kotob al-Ilmiyah.